CONTENTS

Acknowledgements

Reviewing the 1985 St. Ives artists exhibition at the London Tate for the magazine 'Artscribe', the late and much revered critic Peter Fuller wrote that 'all these artists were, in a sense, united, for as Peter Davies had put it in a rare moment of perception, their work invariably involved them ...in 'a particular response to the distinctive, irresistible, local landscape'. It is a pity that Fuller, the great, if embattled proponent of English landscape painting, is not able to see this latest book - with, I believe its many moments of perception - on one of the most important modern movements of that landscape tradition. My study is intended to make up for deficiencies in both my own short study 'The St. Ives Years' (1984), and the various other books like Denys Val Baker's 'Art Colony By The Sea' (1959) and Tom Cross's 'Painting the Warmth of the Sun' (1984). I have aimed for a tight, coherent study, keeping close to visual themes and aesthetic judgements based on degrees of originality or derivation. In the final analysis this is how art stands or falls. It is particularly encouraging to have had the endorsement for my present project from one of Fuller's chief admirers, the leading American critic Hilton Kramer. To him, I am grateful for a meaningful foreword based on his memories and perceptions of a visit to the colony during its heyday.

In the difficult task of writing and publishing this book as an independent venture, I am particularly indebted to a group of well wishers, who became 'godparents' of the project, offering a whole range of support. Sponsorship was also a success, vindicating a belief in the richness of British art that I shared with those self-made men and women - the salt of the earth where British art is concerned - the art dealers, connoisseurs, collectors and enthusiasts who hoist art in the face of more general, though thankfully slowly thawing, public philistinism. Their grass roots pragmatism was also a refreshing antidote to the hidebound art establishment. I am grateful in the first instance to Michael and Margaret Snow for their help in many aspects of the book's preparation, particularly the proof reading, Keith and Charmian Leonard, George Dannatt and Michael Canney, all of whom, typically, took particular interest in the project. Sadly, Leonard died recently, but in his obituary for the 'Independent' I wrote that he 'was particularly supportive to me in the new book.' Bob Simm, of the Graham Gallery, Tunbridge Wells was once again of prime help and I am grateful to the following for generous sponsorship, making this book possible. K.P.M.G. Management Consulting, Fast Atlas (Gordon Hepworth Gallery), Julian Morgan on behalf of Alleward Ltd., Alfred Legner of D.G. Bank, London, the Bernard Jacobson Gallery, the Belgrave Gallery (Irving Grose), the Montpelier Studio (Robert Sandelson), Blond Fine Art (Jonathan Blond), Barbara Hayman, Paisnel Gallery (Stephen Paisnel), Crane Kalman Gallery (Andreas Kalman), the Redfern Gallery (Gordon Samuel), the Wills Lane Gallery (Cyril Gilbert), The Sims Gallery (Leon Suddaby), the Francis Graham Dixon Gallery and England and Co. (Jane England). I am grateful also to the print dealer Wakako Nishida, to Valerie Lowndes, Leon Suddaby, Morag Ballard, Ann Christopherson, Michael and Madeleine Canney, Rowan James, W. Barns-Graham, Clive Blackmore, Michael Strang, Yankel Feather and Edward and Jenny Lewis.

I would also like to thank all the artists who patiently answered my questions. William Gear, Roger Leigh, the late Denis Mitchell, Brian Wall, Trevor Bell, Jeff Harris, the late Elena Gaputyte, Alex Mackenzie, Paul Mount, June Miles, Bob Bourne, John Christopherson, Alan Wood, Jeremy le Grice, Pat and Roger Leigh, Margo Mackelberghe and Michael Dean were very helpful. Bob Crossley gave much moral and practical assistance. Richard Ayeling also helped. Mike Tooby, curator of the new St. Ives Tate and Leon Suddaby provided book publication launches. Laurie Stewart showed customary enthusiasm.

For photography, I am grateful to Dr. Roger Slack, and to a rising star of journalistic photography, Nicholas Turpin of the Independent, Anthony Benjamin, Miki Slingsby, Carol Tee of David Messum, René Gimpel of Gimpel Fils, Sheila Lanyon, the staff of the Crane Kalman Gallery, Bob Berry, Toni Carver, Alan Kingsbury and the various sponsors and galleries who also contributed photographic material.

I am grateful to John Windsor of the Independent, in whose private library I wrote most of this book, also to Muriel Benjamin for word processing and computer support, Ambrose Shere and John Warmingham. Bob Devereux and Bill Bolger for tea and comfort; Pat Evans for tea, comfort and other services. Gwilym Davies and his staff of the Old Bakehouse Publications were marvellous and at the end of the day, helped make it all possible.

ST. IVES REVISITED

-innovators and followers

by Peter Davies

Old Bakehouse Publications

© Peter Davies

First published in January 1994

ISBN 1 874538 05 0

To A Lady
from the Welsh Hills

Published by
Old Bakehouse Publications, Church Street,
Abertillery, Gwent. NP3 1EA
Telephone: 0495 212600   Fax: 0495 216222

Printed in U.K. by J.R. Davies (Printers) Limited,
The Old Bakehouse, Church Street,
Abertillery, Gwent. NP3 1EA
Telephone: 0495 212600   Fax: 0495 216222

2

Foreword

By Hilton Kramer,
Editor of 'The New Criterion' and former New York Times Critic

Nearly four decades have passed since I visited Cornwall and met the remarkable group of artists who were then living and working in and around St. Ives. That was in the fall of 1957. For several years I had been on the staff of the monthly Arts Magazine in New York as an editor and critic, and this was my first trip to England. My principal contact with the London art world was Patrick Heron, who had begun writing about the art of his British contemporaries for Arts a few years earlier. Patrick had been recommended to me as the best writer on art in Britain by Clement Greenberg. It was owing to this connection that many people in the New York art world first read about the work of Peter Lanyon, Roger Hilton, Terry Frost, Bryan Wynter, Alan Davie, and others of that generation, in the pages of Arts, for these artists were otherwise unknown on the American side of the Atlantic. Patrick was a very persuasive champion of these painters, and some of them had their first New York exhibitions as a result of his promotion of their work in my journal. I didn't meet any of them - or Patrick, either - until I came to England in 1957. Patrick had suggested that I include St. Ives on my European itinerary that fall and winter, and that was how I came to spend a few delightful days as his guest at Eagle's Nest in Zennor. Until then, my acquaintance with St. Ives had been limited to my reading of Virginia Woolf.

As I had been born and raised by the sea - in Gloucester, on Cape Ann in Massachusetts - I felt a great affinity for St. Ives from the moment I arrived. Its bracing air, its captivating light, and its dramatic coastlines shrouded in mist and fog, all gave me the feeling of having known this terrain in another life. So did the gossip, the rivalries and alliances of the artists I met on that memorable visit. Like St. Ives, Cape Ann had once been the scene of a thriving artists' colony - Fitz Hugh Lane had painted Gloucester harbour in the nineteenth century, and John Sloan, Marsden Hartley, Stuart Davis, and Milton Avery, among others, had produced fine work there in the early decades of the twentieth century. Hans Hofmann had once conducted a summer art school in East Gloucester, and in my day it was still going under the partner from whom he had split. The legend of these artists was part of the folklore of the place, and to become an artist or somehow attached to the life of art was an ambition that my friends and I had harbored from an early age.

On Cape Ann, however, the artists all cleared out at the first signs of autumn and did not return until the early days of summer. In St. Ives and its environs, the artists I met all seemed more permanently rooted, or at least more settled into a year-round pattern of life and work. In their work, too, the visual character of the place - especially its soft, milky light, which at times seemed to transform the topography into a dreamlike landscape in which the objects of nature were no longer clearly discernible - was often pervasive, however diverse the artists' individual styles. St. Ives's distance from London also struck me as an important element in the lives of these artists. It seemed to give them a freedom to be themselves, to pursue new directions and explore unpopular possibilities, that the more conventional and conformist atmosphere of the London art scene did not at that time do much to encourage.

The artists I speak of were all, in one way or another, in pursuit of a mode of painterly abstraction that was already well advanced in different ways in New York and Paris. Yet in London, painting of this persuasion still met with a good deal of resistance. Nicholas de Stael, only recently dead, was still considered the most important postwar painter, and the artists of the New York School were just beginning to be known. Many of the London critics were openly opposed to abstract painting. The sensation of the moment was the so-called Kitchen Sink school. Even a veteran champion of the modernist movement like Herbert Read tended to reserve his praise for abstractions of an earlier generation - particularly Naum Gabo, Ben Nicholson, and Barbara Hepworth. He might aid in advancing the career or one or another of the younger artists, but he clearly did not bring the same sense of mission to their artistic endeavors. The painters I met on that visit to St. Ives had plenty of reason to feel that theirs would be an uphill struggle for public recognition and reward. Their physical distance from the world of the London art establishment at that time was thus both a symbol of their break with received opinion and a defence against its inhibiting influence.

Even so, the artists' community in St. Ives was not without its own generational and factional differences. Gabo had departed for America years before I came to St. Ives, but Nicholson and Hepworth, though now separated, were still the reigning celebrities, and treated as such. Their work was already known to me, of course, and it was assumed that I should be taken to meet them. Yet, as I recall, a good deal of agitated and amused discussion preceded the actual visits, for it took a while before a decision could be made about the order in which these visits were to be made - about, that is, which of these proud artists might feel the more aggrieved upon learning that I had been taken to meet the other first. It made absolutely no difference to me, of course, but it was a subject that clearly required some delicate negotiation. In the event, it was decided that I should go first to Barbara Hepworth, and she received me with great courtesy and volubility. Nicholson, on the other hand, though he was perfectly polite, said little, and conversation proved difficult. Perhaps he understood that my interest in coming to St. Ives lay elsewhere. Or was it that he was already preparing for his own departure, which occurred soon after? Still, you couldn't spend a day in St. Ives without being made aware of the presence of these two artists, who, as honored veterans in the campaign for modernist art in Britain, were constant subjects of gossip, jokes, criticism, and fond reminiscence.

The painter who made the most emphatic impression on me at the time was Peter Lanyon. He spoke with confidence, even a certain hauteur, about what he was up to; it was not in his nature to be diffident or provisional about his intentions. He was after a big international career, and it was only his untimely death, I believe, that prevented him from achieving that ambition. The other painters were more diffident, both in the way they spoke about their work and in the way they went about creating it. Yet to me, they represented a fresh spirit in British painting, and I felt it was right that Arts Magazine was engaged in advancing their interests.

Soon after my return to New York, I was asked to write an article for Cosmopolitan, which was not then the kind of magazine it has since become, about the art capitals I had visited during my travels in Europe that winter. I had never written for a mass-circulation magazine before, and scarcely knew how to go about it. I asked a friend to collaborate in the preparation of the article, and some months later it was published under the title, as I recall - my own copy of the article disappeared long ago - of 'Artists Around the World'. I had decided to include St. Ives in the article, and I was somewhat awestruck when the Hearst organisation, the publishers of Cosmopolitan, dispatched a team of photographers to travel from London to St. Ives to photograph some of the artists I had written about. The only one of these pictures I now recall was a fine shot of Terry Frost with several of his young children on the oceanfront in St. Ives. Cosmopolitan then had a circulation of about a million copies a month, but I never met a single person who ever saw the article. It was Patrick Heron's articles in Arts that spread the word.

The artists I met in St. Ives in the fall of 1957 were part of a larger history that was unknown to me at the time. Except for talk of Alfred Wallis, the primitive whose work all the artists venerated, not much was said about St. Ives's artistic past. Yet there is a sense in which all art history is local history before it enters history on a larger scale, and this is true whether the locale is Sienna or Montmartre or downtown Manhattan - or St. Ives. The artists of St. Ives, from the nineteenth century down to the present day, have had to wait a long time for a writer to tell their story, and Peter Davies has now written their story in exemplary fashion. This is history that conveys a vivid sense of time and place while also giving each of the many artists it encompasses the requisite individual attention. It is judicious in its judgements of the art, utterly absorbing in its biographical detail, and wonderfully comprehensive in its account of the successive generations of artists that have made St. Ives a place of historical significance to connoisseurs of modern art. About the part of this history that I once observed at first hand, it rings utterly true.

CHAPTER 1

Introduction: The traditional, the new and the nearly new

When the name St. Ives crops up in any artistic discussion it is taken to mean the whole West Penwith peninsula. The scores of artists who have been active in the region spread themselves as much in the outlying areas as in St. Ives itself. An artists' colony grew up simultaneously in both Newlyn and St. Ives. The strong quality of light, the clear sandy bays and picturesque harbours attracted artists in increasingly greater numbers from the 1870's onwards. Cheap accommodation, large studios made available through the decline of the fishing industry and improving rail links between St. Ives and the large cities helped draw artists down to Cornwall. Newlyn became the most important art colony in the late nineteenth century, while St. Ives slowly grew in eminence during the 1930's and finally burst into prominence as a modern art centre during the 1940's and 1950's. Some of the original Newlyn artists, exposed to the light and colour of sunnier climes, had studied in the ateliers of Paris and, more significantly, had practised plein air painting in Breton ports. Here they adopted as working subjects harbour or farmyard scenes.

In St. Ives a growing number of American and Scandinavian, as well as British painters, settled for varying lengths of time. The most distinguished of them was Whistler, who spent three months painting in St. Ives during the winter of 1883-84. Accompanied by two followers in the shape of Mortimer Menpes and a young Sickert, Whistler painted small pochade panels in outdoor locations. He delighted in a rapidly sketched and thinly painted style, highly alert through its use of tone to seasonal mood, climatic conditions and time of day. This use of tone to convey the atmosphere of time as well as of place was a common feature of the colourful works by the many Post Impressionist landscape painters during the inter-war years. Whistler chose as his subjects in St. Ives the windows and doors of shops, or marine views. The paint is thin and relayed in long streaky movements of the brush. Sickert adopted the alla prima manner of the rapid oil sketch in his 'Clodgy Point', one of the earliest known Sickert paintings. Whistler protégés like Sidney Starr followed the American master a year or two later and also painted pochade panels in the fishing port.

Yet it was Newlyn that hosted the first and most important congregation of artists. The 'plein air' naturalism they practised owed much to the square brush techniques of Bastien Lepage. The working harbour of Newlyn also provided them with subject matter close in kind to that which had absorbed them in Brittany. Indeed, the leader of this group, Stanhope Forbes, called Newlyn 'a sort of English Concarneau' when he discovered it for himself in 1884. The artists who followed his example and grouped around him in

Newlyn, painted in a sufficiently common style, one of naturalistic realism, to merit being called a 'school'. The contemporaneous Glasgow School found similar focus at Cockburnspath in Scotland, while others found Walderswick in Suffolk or Staithes on the North East coast of Yorkshire. The style they practised thus broke out in many places at once. Not being unique to one place, such an ubiquitous style was a response to the general state of art as it existed in the late years of the nineteenth century. The manner integrated Impressionism's interest in light into the still academic context of Realist painting. Realism can be a blanket phrase, having a variety of meanings in differing historical and cultural contexts. But the nature of Realism in the context of the Newlyn School's 'plein airism' was one focused sharply and unsentimentally on the social and economic conditions of the local fishing community - with attention to the community's traditional costume and everyday customs. The results were subject pictures that wedded figurative Realism to Impressionism's highly pitched sensitivity to behaviour of light. Light invested compositions with mood, giving the work an emotional charge in keeping with its human content.

James McNeill Whistler. Cliff and breakers. *Oil.*
Hunterian Art Gallery, Glasgow.

Prominent among this early Newlyn group, in addition to Forbes himself, were Walter Langley, T.C. Gotch, and the Falmouth-based painter of sunbathing youths and sparkling translucent seas, H.S. Tuke. Frank Bramley, famous for his poignant and anecdotal Newlyn interior 'A Hopeless Dawn' now in the Tate Gallery, and Norman Garstin, equally well known for his 'The Rain It Raineth', also distinguished the group. Forbes' 'Fish Sale on a Cornish Beach' (1886) is one of the early Newlyn School's prize paintings, integrating studies of figures, fish, boats and marine landscape in one large, composite, subject picture. The work of the pre-1900 Newlyn School was characterised by the use of a square brush, by a painterly relish used on top of disciplined and high quality academic drawing, and by a muted palette controlled by an extremely fine use of closely observed tone. This made the clear evocation of palpable daylight one of the most immediate and satisfying qualities of Newlyn painting, and the most telling outcome of its preoccupation with a 'plein air' ethos. The genre of the dark interior, recording the private and domestic aspects of traditional Newlyn life, also used light as a formal and psychological theme, this time in the form of shafts of strong light filtering through old windows into dark, often grubby, interiors.

By the turn of the century, big changes were occurring in the life of Newlyn and this was reflected in the nature of the art being produced there. Late in the century the harbour expanded and grew busier with the building of the new pier in 1894. The following year, the Passmore Edwards Gallery, (now the Newlyn Orion Gallery), was opened and became a public platform for these artists to display their work before being sent to the Academy. From the first generation only a few, like Forbes, Langley and Garstin stayed on. They became pivotal anchors against which younger artists could, within certain limits, twist and turn into new artistic directions. A Newlyn School of Painting, founded by Forbes in 1889, fostered high standards of craft while allowing for individual, expressive bent. The discipline of draughtsmanship and high finish remained. The years around 1900 are the turning point for the changing aspects of art and life in Newlyn. Forbes reflected the changing times in a number of notable canvases. His '22nd January 1901', depicts in typical Forbes manner, a family set around the breakfast table, reading about the death of Queen Victoria. This poignant narrative picture tells of an era's end and with it the ushering in of the new, symbolised by the morning light that streams in through the window. This 'conversation piece' does not have much conversation, in the sense that it is a study of the subservience of family members to the authoritative, paternal figure who sits centre stage. Similarly, the same artist's 'Saffron Cake' (1920) sees the man of the house assuming the central cake-cutting role. In spite of this, traditional Cornish family life had a strong matriarchal element. In Forbes' better known quayside compositions the moving of time is symbolised by the mingling of young and old against a tranquil backdrop of boats, rippled shadows and gently undulating waters.

The youngest artists later to distinguish themselves in Newlyn were Dod and Ernest Proctor, Eleanor and Robert Hughes and Frank Heath. In nearby Lamorna Cove a significant colony included Paris-trained and Cheshire-born S.J. 'Lamorna' Birch - he assumed the name of the cove in order to distinguish himself from another local painter Lionel Birch - Charles Simpson, Laura and Harold Knight, and A.J. Munnings. Indeed, in those years leading up to the

Great War, a new generation had emerged in Lamorna who dented the pre-eminence of earlier Newlyn-based art. They were attracted to the rocky and sunlit cove at Lamorna, situated at the bottom of a long, wooded valley of spectacular natural beauty. Laura Knight specialised in romantic cliff-top panoramas, animated with the windswept or sun-soaked figures of attractive young women. Her husband Harold's renowned ability at portraiture came to the fore and among many face studies was one depicting the one-legged 'supertramp' poet, W.H. Davies, who was a visitor to Lamorna. In these idyllic days before the Great War such artists had plenty of time to stand and stare. Friendships abounded during these years. Many of the stories about the extra-mural life and times of the Newlyn School's Edwardian era are conveyed in Laura Knight's 'Oil Paint and Grease Paint'. Charles Simpson, who later ran a painting school in St. Ives, also wrote books on wildlife and sporting subjects, that formed the thematic content of his work. 'Lamorna' Birch specialised in large and melodramatic paintings of quarries and tall cliffs or else concentrated on studies of running water, (he was an avid fisherman and had great knowledge of local rivers and streams). Although structure is important for Birch, the broad play of sunlight and shadows across the monumental aspects of Lamorna's cliffs and quarries is the real subject of his art, as it is in terms of the white froth or silvery tints that reflect across the surfaces of his streams. The grandeur of nature set Birch the artistic challenge he sought; his example later led to Lanyon's emotional identification with landscape, even though Lanyon's very different approach also owed much to early instruction received from another traditional artist, the academic seascape painter Borlase Smart.

In view of A.J. Munnings' later denunciation of modern art at a Royal Academy dinner speech, the presence of this conservative among Newlyn artists put into perspective the inherently traditionalist nature of Newlyn painting, particularly when compared to later developments in Cornish art. Indeed, many of the post-war St. Ives artists followed Nicholson's example in shunning the Royal Academy and refusing to exhibit with what was felt to be a reactionary and aesthetically uninteresting institution. Yet, Dod and Ernest Proctor responded positively to modern painting as early as the 1920's. Using the conventional genre of large figure groupings - Munnings and Laura Knight had each used populated fairgrounds, beaches or race meetings as suitable subjects for such themes - an artist like Ernest Proctor employed a stylised and colourful exuberance similar in feeling to the Vorticist crowd paintings of Gertler or William Roberts. Not unnaturally, such colourful scenes were accompanied by a markedly lighter and freer palette than had been the case in earlier Newlyn painting. His wife Dod's portraits of pensive or sleeping women garbed in white silvery drapery have a neo-classical, sculptural solidity that perhaps owes a distant debt to Picasso's own neo-classical pictures of the time. In 1926 Dod Proctor's 'Morning' was purchased by the 'Daily Mail' and presented to the Tate Gallery.

The contrast between Cornish-born Harold Harvey's pre- and post- 1900 work becomes a barometer for the changing features of earlier and later Newlyn painting. In earlier Newlyn harbour subjects, depicting boys rowing

10

out in small boats, Harvey introduced a pronounced painterly handling into plein air naturalism. Although based on tenacious drawing, these compositions have a tonal and painterly fluidity in which concrete forms are partly broken down by, and absorbed in, the play of light. Yet by the 1920's Harvey's smart Edwardian interiors were peopled with fashionable middle-class ladies. The cosmetic feeling is at variance with the rustic naturalism of harbour life; the handling of paint is also more controlled and the colour perfumed with the scent of leisurely domestic opulence. In humbler ways these pictures owe something to the post-Sargent fashion pieces of Orpen. Fashion of a less lofty kind characterises Harvey's twin portrait 'Girls Outside the Gaiety Cinema, Newlyn' (1925), their twenties hats, lipstick and eyelashes lighting up the picture. Forbes' own later works of the 1930's - Penzance street scenes or farming subjects - also carry a brighter palette and a looser handling. After the great war, a new bohemianism found its way into Newlyn, seen in the more direct, stylised and form-conscious modern work of Frank Dobson's

Augustus John. Fishermen.
Graham Gallery, Tunbridge Wells.

early carvings, Cedric Morris' bright and impastoed portraits or harbour scenes, and Augustus John's virtuoso drawing. Dobson's early paintings have a sculptor's feeling for volume and, significantly, he made his very first carvings in wood and stone while living in Newlyn. Cedric Morris encouraged Dobson's sister-in-law, Mary Jewels, to start painting. A home-grown talent who lived in Newlyn most of her life, Jewels painted with a freshness and a naivety that owed its quality to the fact of her being self-taught and therefore avoiding the kind of academic or classical training that the other artists had undergone and which Munnings prescribed as being of such importance. Augustus John, Kit Wood and later Ben Nicholson made frequent visits to the Jewels household. The cult of the untutored visionary, seen in the unaffected naivety of one in close touch with heart and eye, was therefore evident in Newlyn before Wallis had begun his second childhood over in St. Ives.

The modern artists who took up Wallis did so as part of a drive against the laboured academicism of the older generation. Sedentary Post Impressionists in the town, like Borlase Smart, John Park, Moffatt Lindner and Dorothea Sharpe had used the traditional motif of seascape, harbour, nocturne or beach

John Park. St. Ives Harbour. *Oil.*
Montpelier Studio.

12

scene. Julius Olsson had done much to lay the foundation of marine painting in Cornwall, while a turn-of-the-century contemporary, Louis Grier, had been a leading light at the old St. Ives Arts Club, which held meetings in a picturesque building on Westcott's Quay. Preston-born John Park had studied art in Paris and first hand knowledge of French Impressionist painting was a liberating factor in inter-war St. Ives painting. Park's work was a hot pot of rich colour applied in thick dabs over tenacious drawing. Park's customary harbour scenes were animated with bright colours that burst into life as a maze of reflections from moored vessels. He treated Smeaton's Pier as Monet did the road bridge at Argenteuil. As Sven Berlin, a younger contemporary from the 1940's scene remembers, he did to 'trees what Monet could do to cathedrals - fill them with light'. Park continued painting in St. Ives until the 1950's when he left for a short spell of living and painting in Brixham before finally returning, via Folkestone, to his native Preston, where he died in 1962. Among the older artists Park, along with Lamorna Birch and Borlase Smart, were most sympathetic to the moderns. The magnanimous Smart was very accommodating to the younger artists as he had been to his own generation. The author of a widely disseminated book, 'The Technique of Seascape Painting', Smart also shared the secrets of his craft with a young Peter Lanyon. In addition, he wrote art criticism for the 'Western Morning News' and helped acquire from the Church of England the large Mariners' Chapel, (most fishermen were Methodist), which became home for the traditional St. Ives Society of Artists. A corner near the font was given over to the modern artists like Hepworth and Nicholson. But it was through the generous loan of the Society's Crypt, enabling a younger generation of modern painters to exhibit their work as a group immediately after the war, that Smart's bridge-building reached auspicious dimensions. This accommodating role, which extended to the old and new, the traditional and modern, and the figurative and abstract, led to the new Penwith Society of Arts being founded as a tribute to Borlase Smart, who had died two years earlier in 1947.

The majority of older generation artists, however, viewed the influx of modern art with great suspicion. These stuffy traditionals had enjoyed 'carte blanche' during the years of false calm that marked the 1930's. These artists had formed the St. Ives Society of Artists in January 1927. The attendances peaked to over 4,000 visitors in 1936. The hotels and cafés were full of their colourful recordings of local life or coastal landscapes. They thought that the moderns were wrongheaded both in supporting the illiterate Wallis and in following Cézanne - generally dubbed 'The Father of Modern Art', an artist they felt could not draw and had had defective eyesight. Such attitudes were fairly widespread in Britain, however, and in addition to the Royal Academy, the regional academies in Manchester, Liverpool, as well as the Southport Spring Exhibition, The Bournemouth Arts Club and other organisations, upheld the conventional styles of floral still-life, domestic interior, picturesque idealised landscape or portrait painting. The popularity of pretty 1930's figurative painting - epitomised in Wilfred de Glehn's marine views, in Herbert Davis Richter's floral still-lifes or in Gerald Brockhurst's portraiture - was based on its accessibility. This accessibility was helped by social links between artist and society. Though class based in the sense that they were a middle-class bunch buffered from pressing social or economic obligations, the work of the pre-war artists did not have the élitist or mysterious aura of the modern movement. Modern works needed the kind of deciphering, even decoding within a broad, art historical perspective that a book like R.H. Wilenski's 'The Modern Movement in Art' provided. Wilenski's recipe for success was plainly spelt out on behalf of the modern artist. In pursuing the ideal of pure form, as advocated by Bell, Fry and later Wilenski, the modern artist needed to relinquish easy concessions to popular taste that a less elevated involvement with picture postcard imagery or with sentimental, derivative, clichéd subjects gave him. Moreover, the post-war moderns remained hidden from general view in St. Ives, privately engaged on what, to the general public, was an esoteric project into abstract formal relationships. They did not paint in outdoor locations around the harbour and were not as keen to exhibit their work locally. Equally, they did not perpetuate the March 6th Show Day, held religiously throughout the 1930's by the older generation as a public relations exercise as much as a commercial venture.

Many of the Cornish subjects put on display on Show Day, or else presented at the Royal Academy Summer Exhibition, or indeed included at the annual Manchester Academy Exhibition were essentially holiday pictures of an atmospheric kind. Buckets and spades on the beach, breezy evocations of sailing offshore, spectacular sunsets or moonlit seas were commonly featured. Sunny, idealised days on the beach in a picturesque port were painted with a Post Impressionist palette but were designed with the same simplified charm and vision that characterised many of the images created for railway holiday posters during this period. A number of the St. Ives painters produced commercial posters while Harry Rountree designed the label for the well known Cherry Blossom shoe polish tin. Herbert Truman, Bernard Ninnes, Fred Bottomley, Todd Brown, George Fagan Bradshaw, Leonard Richmond and Leonard Fuller were among those artists whose pursuit of accessible and popular subjects could also extend to the shamelessly commercial. Many of the artists' wives painted. In a post-suffragette age this was fully accepted, though before the radical feminist revolution of a few decades hence these women invariably found themselves in a secondary role to men. The best women painters included Misomé Peile, Billie Waters, Isobel Heath, Marcella Smith, Garlick Barnes, Agnes Drey, Inez Hoyton, Pauline Hewitt, Majorie Mostyn and Shearer Armstrong who was soon to come under the influence of Nicholson. Joan Manning Saunders, the so-called child prodigy from Sennen, had exhibited exceptionally accomplished landscapes at the R.A. when a mere fourteen years of age. Among the modern artists, two isolated, though highly distinguished women, Marlow Moss and Ithell Colquhoun, represented the international de Stijl and Surrealist movements respectively. Alice Moore, based in Lelant, applied modern design to the craft of tapestry and needlecraft.

A trend developed that saw many northern painters come down to Cornwall in order to paint. Early in the century a Manchester Academy artist, Byron Cooper, had one of his Cornish seascapes, 'Godrevy Light, Cornwall'

14

(1903) acquired by the City Art Gallery. Cooper followed the examples of Moffatt Lindner, Julius Olsson and Borlase Smart and concentrated on romantic seascape and evocative moonlit scenes. Other marine pictures by Cooper found their way into Manchester Academy Exhibitions during the inter-war years, apt reminders of what the Mancunian opined was the unrivalled, natural beauty of the English countryside. Indeed, another painter associated at differing times of her life with both Manchester and St. Ives, the New Zealand-born painter Frances Hodgkins, spoke of the English landscape as having the kind of pastoral, and in the case of Cornwall dramatic, beauty that could not be found to the same degree anywhere else in the world. A one time Manchester Academy President, Tom Mostyn, painted in Cornwall though the rosy romanticism of tall, silent woods, overgrown gardens or languishing mythological beauties was less expressive of the sharp profiles and bleached light of sub-classical Cornwall than symbolic of a nordic mood.

Shortly before the war, Mostyn's daughter, Marjorie, settled in St. Ives with her husband and fellow portraitist, Leonard Fuller. Together in 1938 they opened the still existing St. Ives School of Painting. John Park also contributed Cornish harbour subjects most years to the Manchester Academy. Coburn Witherop, whose more linear and stylised pictures of St. Ives were shown at the Liverpool Academy, visited Cornwall from the north on a regular basis though unlike Park, never settled there. Arnesby Brown, Algernon Talmadge and Frank Brangwyn were R.A's who made painting trips to Cornwall. Terrick Williams was perhaps the impressionist painter 'par excellence', who often showed Breton and Cornish harbour scenes at the Manchester Academy. Southport-born Arthur Hayward also much frequented St. Ives harbour with canvas and brush, and his more stylised and systematic impressions of Smeaton's Pier and the boats challenged Park's pre-eminence in this popular genre. Harry Rutherford was another Manchester painter who drifted down to paint in Cornwall while much later, Ian Grant made several painting excursions to Cornwall. Such was the popularity of the Cornish picture in these northern exhibitions that, on more than one occasion, notice was made in the Manchester press about happy 'holiday productions' of an escapist kind that had nothing to do with depicting urban realities closer to home. More recently, Fred Yates, a self-styled 'happy Lowry' came down to live in Cornwall. Lowry, on the other hand scored in Manchester exhibitions because he fulfilled the need for more locally relevant, industrial landscape imagery.

By the late 1940's the pre-eminence that these traditional artists had enjoyed during the inter-war years was being rapidly eroded by the new phenomenon of modern art. Although the younger artists responded to the local landscape, that response was as much cerebral as visual, a filtered range of memories and perceptions put to the service of an intellectual concern for the technical construction of a picture. Their interest in structure, in art as much as in life, led them to read the ideas of Jay Hambridge in the 'Dynamics of Symmetry' or of d'Arcy Thompson in 'On Growth and Form'. T.E. Hulme's distinction between geometric and vital art was also relevant. Ironically, by turning away from a faithful or literal recording of a landscape before their eyes, they produced equivalents of that landscape which were more effective in capturing both the residual look and the implicit feeling of the place - the elusive 'genius loci' - than was ever the case with tame academic reproductions. The post-war moderns were a very different species from the older artists. Though invariably well connected and middle-class to the extent even of sometimes having the aesthete aura of Bloomsbury, the younger artists were a tougher breed intellectually and were more adventurous in wanting to experience the landscape at first hand through vigorous physical activities. They used the Cornish ambience not for escape so much as for a contemplative aestheticism based on an irresistible, local landscape. For this reason the cult of craftsmanship, the ethos of the hand-made and an elevated formal preciousness took hold. The golden years of St. Ives art between 1939 and 1975 (the span used for the large St. Ives retrospective at the London Tate in 1985) were characterised by three main strands - the abstract constructivist artists who, with their hard-edge geometric forms responded to the looming presence of Barbara Hepworth and Ben Nicholson; the naive, primitive and romantic painters who worked alone and were innocent of the dialectics of art historical politics; and the painterly 'middle generation' artists like Paul Feiler, Terry Frost, Bryan Wynter and Patrick Heron who, in their use of exuberant colour and gestural handling, looked to a new international style, this time not based on the circle and the square but instead on the softer language of informal abstraction, Tachism, Abstract Expressionism and the like.

Many of the young artists who would later challenge the conventional status quo of the St. Ives Society of Artists, initially with the three annual Crypt exhibitions, then by breaking away entirely and forming the independent Penwith Society of Art, were engaged on active military or service duties during the war. They were unable to develop their art, though artists like Lanyon or Lowndes sketched in Italian or mid Eastern locations. Terry Frost made his first paintings as a P.O.W. in a Bavarian prison camp. Sven Berlin's wartime correspondence with Nicholson and Stokes - written from France while on active duty after a change of conscience - formed the basis of a later novel called 'Lazarus'. A wartime ban on outdoor sketching also curtailed the 'plein air' instincts of the older artists. Yet on the home front, significant artistic developments took place in Carbis Bay, where the Russian constructivist sculptor Naum Gabo, the art theorist and painter Adrian Stokes, Ben Nicholson and Barbara Hepworth lived. For the latter 'childcare was a dominant preoccupation when she first moved to the area'. This pressing responsibility reduced output of work. As a result she mostly produced drawings in the evenings, though these were significant linear explorations into the geometric world of crystal-like forms; they were plans for later sculptural ideas. The St. Ives Tate curator, Michael Tooby, wrote how these artists 'made predominantly small-scale work, due largely to lack of facilities, space and materials', during the war. The theoretical writings of Adrian Stokes were important for Hepworth, who was encouraged by Stokes's 'speculations on the relationship between the human body, solid forms and the surrounding space of the landscape'. In one of the sculptor's few wartime sculptures, 'Landscape Sculpture' (1944, though not cast into bronze until 1961), Hepworth put into practice an interest in the relationship of the human figure to the landscape in a way that betrayed subtle differences of approach from the more pure constructive art of Gabo. Not only for Peter Lanyon, who found Gabo's transparent perspex constructions such complete investigations into the dynamics of form in space that 'their very presence is paralysing', but also for Hepworth, the need was to invest extreme purism with some local reference, evocative naturalism, textural sensuality and even, in Lanyon's case, allusion to 'genius loci'. Gabo's pioneering use of strings therefore differed from Hepworth's, for the Russian wished to create autonomous, semi-transparent surfaces as part of the planar language of the piece and not just as points of visual reference between a figure and a vast enveloping landscape as Hepworth envisaged, in an evocative and pierced, concave piece like 'Landscape Sculpture'.

Gabo produced a number of stone carvings and small paintings in addition to the more familiar perspex and plastic constructions during the six years he spent as a war exile in Cornwall. He did much walking, enjoyed local geological and topographical features, and used local stones with which to pursue constructivist principles in a new context of carving opaque materials. Gabo was friendly with Bernard Leach, two very different artists who nonetheless shared a similar involvement with form as expressed in and through space. Leach suggested Gabo use clay for a model car that he made in response to the London-based Design Research Unit, a wartime organisation that sought to link artists with the world of commercial design. Gabo and Leach were also linked in the general philosophic sense that Clive Bell's concept of significant form espoused. Such a notion transcended the superficial boundaries of style, localised cultural sources, materials and the like. Indeed, Gabo was an innovator, not only in the provincial context of Cornish art, but also in international modernism as a whole. The 'Realist Manifesto' produced with his brother Antoine Pevsner in Russia in 1920, affirmed Space and Time as the 'only forms where life is built, the only forms, therefore, where art should be erected'. Their language of building, erecting and constructing not only carried with it the implications of new technical means and new materials, but also a utopian vision and democratic internationalism that became a salutary feature in the context of the 1930's descent into fascism and narrow nationalism. Gabo's affirmation of space is evident enough in the transparency and openness of his art, while time was an element best conveyed in kinetic works. The Tate have an electronically vibrating rod mobile called 'Kinetic Sculpture' (1920). Although Gabo looked for qualities of permanence, both technically and conceptually, in his work, the small perspex constructions made in Cornwall were hand-made entities made with great manual dexterity and visual precision. He used hands and only a basic range of tools. He used cellulose, acetate, perspex acquired from a contact at ICI, and nylon threads with which to bind together the intersecting planes or spiralling forms of his work.

As far as colour was concerned, Gabo followed the logic of the 'Realist Manifesto', viewing white as the truest representative of the value of pure undifferentiated light. As a result, his Carbis Bay studio was painted white and the virtues of unity, transparency and continuity were elevated as prime artistic, as well as scientific principles. He avoided accidental, incidental, or superficial colours that were considered fortuitous side-effects of the play of light across the surface of objects. He wanted colours to reflect the internal

Naum Gabo. Carbis Bay, 1941.

content of bodies in space, which would radiate their true nature from within themselves. The Constructivist notion of colour wedded scientific certainty with the mystery of the unknown. Moreover, Gabo's ideas in this direction corresponded with Adrian Stokes' own theories as conveyed in his contemporary book 'Colour and Form' (1937), about form being either carved or modelled - concrete or illusionistic. In the 'Realist Manifesto' Gabo and Pevsner repudiated superficial line as an arbitary or decorative graphic element. Line had no connection with 'the permanent structure of things', and space could therefore only be measured, in the plastic context of Constructivist art, through 'continuous depth'. The multi-directional lines crisscrossing in the geometric compositions of Hepworth, Nicholson, and followers like Barns-Graham and John Wells therefore sought to define the impossible - the limitless reality of ubiquitous space. In particular, the notion of continuous depth enabled Hepworth - probably aware that her post-war carvings were drifting into a more referential and associative realm than that advocated by Gabo - to state that in her work 'the colour in the concavities plunges me into depth of water, caves of shadows deeper than the concavities themselves'. Gabo was different from Hepworth in never wishing to localise

John Wells. Bastion, 1950. *Oil.*
The British Council.

his sculpture through colouring the transparent materials being used. Hepworth's sculpture in general witnessed a marked softening of form after the hard, geometric carvings produced in London during the 1930's. This softening led to a more organic and sensual morphology influenced by the sea, the cliffs and caves, and by the region's renowned light. Later, during the 1950's, she became involved with the theme of the figure in landscape and finally with the ancient, standing stone circles of Penwith.

The same softening of uncompromisingly abstract art attended Nicholson's wartime developments. For the first time his work saw the merging of still-life and landscape themes within the same composition. The still-life repertoire of the 1920's - the jugs, beakers and bottles adapted from his father's art - were silhouetted on windowsills against a Cornish landscape backdrop. The stark post 1933 white reliefs were for the moment left aside, although the stringent ordering of pictorial composition informed even the most referential of his

St. Ives landscape sketches and paintings. Thereafter Nicholson created a double play in his art, as formal abstractions with varying degrees of Post-Cubist geometricity were produced alongside more suggestively organic and naturalistic landscape drawings. Nicholson's natural demeanour was that of an artistic leader, a result of his elevated cultural background. He ordered the new Penwith Society with the same rigour that he had used when purging, and bringing into line with his own ideas, the 7+5 Society. His discovery of Wallis in 1928 was of seminal importance in the growth of modern art in Cornwall, and Nicholson's professional example of high seriousness rubbed off on many younger artists. The influence of Nicholson and Gabo long outlasted their Cornish years, (Gabo left for the United States in 1946 and Nicholson for Switzerland in 1958) and it runs through the work of Barns-Graham, John Wells, Michael Snow, George Dannatt, Alex Mackenzie right through to the gifted and much younger painter Morag Ballard. These artists were influenced by Nicholson's elegant and lyrical draughtsmanship and also by an astringent pictorial sensibility that demanded tonally disciplined but evocative use of colour, and the calculated divisions of modernist composition. The interrelationships between innovators and followers shows the closeness of the artistic community down the years, with a plethora of ideas and styles passed down as if from artistic father to son. It also shows how the meek and mighty have liberally mingled in what is surely one of the most painted towns in the world.

The importance of Wallis, who had died at the Madron Workhouse during the war, was disseminated widely. Wallis' work was collected by Adrian Stokes, as well as by Ben Nicholson, and it was through Stokes' collection that the far-reaching implications and importance of Wallis' childlike vision and direct painting of the sea, made itself felt on the younger generation. Among the younger generation was Sven Berlin, who worked as a gardener at Stokes' 'Little Park Owles' home. He wrote the first and most complete biography of the former mariner, published in 1948, and titled simply 'Alfred Wallis, Primitive'. The memory and perception of the sea, rendered in silvery greys and whites forms the heart and soul of Wallis' work. The greys and 'peculiarly pungent Cornish greens' that Nicholson spoke of in regard to Wallis' highly evocative and direct handling of colour (yacht paints) were used brilliantly in the more sophisticated context of Nicholson's own work. The same colours were used by David Haughton and Alex Mackenzie in their atmospheric renditions of Cornish hamlets positioned in a landscape of fields, hills and rocks. Berlin, in a more openly expressionistic vein, exploited Wallis' use of the 'ground' colour - predetermined by the nature of the support - which was left untouched and therefore made to play a role in the composition alongside more positive coloration. Barns-Graham's immediate post-war work, depicting the buildings of Downalong, also absorbed the simplicity of the older artist's view of the world, while his influence on Lanyon is all but obvious as will later be discussed.

The close social and artistic fraternity in Cornwall meant that personal and artistic interweaving was inevitable, and during the late 1940's more than at any time since, the artists worked, exhibited, and identified together as a loosely formed group. For three years between 1946-48 vanguard exhibitions were held by the new generation in the crypt of the old Mariners' Chapel. These three Crypt shows, held under the traditional Society's upstairs gallery,

The Crypt Group in the studio of W. Barns-Graham. 1946.

were like a gunpowder plot and led to the general rebellion, culminating in the 1949 breakaway by the younger artists from the old Society and the subsequent formation of the Penwith Society. Hepworth and Nicholson never exhibited with the Crypt group, though they kept a close watch on the new work produced by their juniors, as well they might. The original Crypt group was made up of Berlin, Lanyon, Wells and Wynter. The second exhibition included Barns-Graham in place of Wynter, while the third and final exhibition, in August 1948, included all previous exhibitors along with Patrick Heron, Adrian Ryan and David Haughton, each of whom had studied at the Slade. The catalogues for the Crypt exhibition were printed in Bembo by that

David Haughton. Carn Bosavern. *Oil 1955.*
Gordon Hepworth Gallery, Haynes Farm, Newton St. Cyres, Devon. (0392 851351)

modern classicist of typography, Guido Morris. Kit Barker, brother of the poet George, also participated.

In 1946 three Crypt artists, Lanyon, Wells and Berlin, drew down Geevor Mine. Barns-Graham visited the Scillies with Nicholson in the early 1950's; Barns-Graham produced a large oil 'Rock Forms St. Mary's, Scilly', in which she explored the spatial and textural aspects of huge configurations of rock. Similarly, Hepworth drew the standing stones, monolithic quoits and tors scattered across the moorlands of Cornwall and subsequently used them as thematic, if not formal, source material for her sculpture.

The spectacular phenomenon of art in South West Cornwall was caused in part by the influx, during the late 1940's, of more exotic, itinerant artists. They introduced a new international flavour that complemented the indigenous brand of 'Celtic' modernism that had been developing in response to a

Cornish 'genius loci'. Patrick Heron, prior to his taking up the status of a 'resident' in 1956, made frequent visits and painted sumptuous and colourful interiors incorporating views of St. Ives harbour. These views portrayed in these pictures were made possible by a rented flat on the harbour front. Influenced by Braque and Matisse, Heron introduced the shallow space of Cubist distortion into composite figure-and-interior settings. They are paradoxical pictures, for the density of visual information and richness of colour, is belied by a simplified Cubist structure of open and closed forms and spatial interval. The colours, which recall Braque with browns, purples and violets, later exploded into an optically vibrant range of hue owing more to Matisse. He later wrote that 'colour is both the subject and the means ...it is obvious that colour is now the only direction in which painting can travel'. But was it the only direction and for whom? In the context of such didactic remarks, it is hard to see Heron's programme as allowing a school of followers. Yet during the 1970's and 1980's colour conscious painters in London, like Alan Gouk and James Faure Walker, grouped around the influential contemporary magazine 'Artscribe', espoused the findings of Heron in ways that avoided deference to American influences. This was congenial to Heron, who in 1974 had hammered out in the 'Guardian' newspaper the harmful effects of American propaganda in promoting New York colour painting.

In 1951, Victor Pasmore, a recent and notorious 'convert' to Abstract art after relinquishing the measured Realism of atmospheric Thames-side subjects, visited St. Ives and made some spiral motif drawings of Porthmeor Beach. These were internalised compositions, using the same spiralling forms that had been a recent feature of Snowstorm paintings. The elements of sky, sea and rocky headland are still apparent through differing Camberwell colour schemes. At Camberwell Art School in the late 1940's Pasmore taught his student Terry Frost about the meaning of Abstraction; its relationship to the known world, and the plastic rigours of translating experiences and sensations to a flat surface. The results led to Frost integrating the recurring boat shapes and arc forms that Ben Nicholson told Frost would last a whole career, with the spiralling or eddying movements that Pasmore had been promulgating. William Scott also made visits to Cornwall in the early 1950's, producing some simplified compositions of Mousehole harbour. But more importantly, several of his animated and impastoed still-life compositions of pots, frying pans and knives created a kind of synthesis between the genre of still-life and harbour landscape with moored vessels. Scott ran the art department at Corsham near Bath and taught alongside key St. Ives contemporaries like Lanyon, Wynter and the Polish Expressionist who spent summers at Sancreed, Peter Potworowski. Scott and Alan Davie were the earliest British artists to experience the New American Painting at first hand. In Scott's case this led to an enlarged scale, though he identified strongly with a European heritage by looking to the traditions of still-life from Chardin onwards. A visiting Alan Davie introduced the colours and forms of the outdoors, experienced through the same gliding, diving or climbing pursuits that engaged the residents. Davie's fellow Scot, William Gear - a contemporary with Barns-Graham and Margaret Mellis at Edinburgh College of Art - also visited St. Ives in the late 1940's, when he made a series of gouache and watercolour studies loosely based on local harbour motifs. The line is however severely angularised, pointing to an artist who, by virtue of living in Paris, enjoyed first hand experience of contemporary French and Dutch Abstract art, to the extent of his becoming the only British member of the international Cobra group. Gear, Davie, Scott and Pasmore were but seasonal visitors, though each made notable contributions to the significant transitional styles of the period, their visits showing that the local environment could still exert an influence on the outcome of the supposedly autonomous Abstract art.

Lanyon, Heron and Wynter were among sixty artists commissioned to make large pictures for the Festival of Britain in 1951. Indicating the chief characteristic of advanced St. Ives art at the time, these artists created work where 'formal exploration of colour, space and line is combined with narrative or symbolic content'. The Penwith Society gave official voice to the many developing young artists of the 1950's, and became a springboard for promoting the careers of the most progressive artists in St. Ives. In addition to exhibiting at George Downing's bookshop, (an outlet that was later fulfilled by Elena Gaputyte's Sail Loft Gallery), the post-war St. Ives artists also enjoyed exhibitions at prestigious London locations. Berlin, Wells and later Lanyon held solo shows at Lefevre, while Wynter exhibited regularly with the Redfern after 1947. This was just as well because the new Penwith Society was racked with controversies and divisive art politics from the outset, and the history of the Society is littered with resignations. Indeed, Lanyon and Berlin soon resigned because a ruling that discriminated between abstract, traditional, and craft seemed to push the abstract category into a favoured position. Lanyon's awareness of art's traditions in Cornwall was important. This was the same Lanyon who could speak of 'sleazy researchers', artists in search of the 'emperor's clothes', whose work seemed without psychological or formal roots in their own experience. Lanyon resisted what he referred to as the pure alphabet searching of Abstract artists who timidly followed in the wake of Hepworth and Nicholson in St. Ives. Notwithstanding his own debt to Nicholson before the war, he turned his back and sought out an entirely personal, if formally rigorous, experience-based approach to the construction of painted or collaged landscape imagery. He knew Cornwall inside out, disliked cultural impositions of any kind that jarred with local customs, and took a stand against the Abstract-Constructivist orthodoxies of the Penwith 'house style' by forming an alternative avant-garde focus at the Newlyn Gallery, then run by his friend the painter, broadcaster and writer Michael Canney. Lanyon's small painting School 'The St. Peter's Loft' also fostered a local landscape style of breezy Expressionist vigour. Nancy Wynne-Jones, Jeremy Le Grice and Margo Maeckelberghe benefited from his definite experience-based teaching methods.

In the wake of these challenges to the hegemony of the 'hard edge school', a vein of Romantic, Expressionist and Primitive painting put colour on the sometime pallid cheeks of St. Ives art. In later years Albert Reuss, Yankel

Feather, George Lambourne, Patrick Hayman, Bob Bourne, Alan Lowndes and Karl Weschke brought variety to the traditions of figurative art in Cornwall. Their work often carried a poetic or symbolic intensity and so countered the extreme formalism of the artists who developed more in response to the modernism of Hepworth and Nicholson. Such is the variety of St. Ives art in a later, pluralistic climate that even the intellectually 'easy' category of naive painting carries with it, in the Cornish context, unexpected complexity. The latter day St. Ives primitive Bryan Pearce suffers from a rare brain disorder, so that his unbelievably simple and child-like compositions of a touchingly literal and perspectivally discordant St. Ives, look of very different kind to the raw painterliness of Wallis. Even within the 'middle generation', eccentric tones of individuality resulted in an unpredictable discord. Roger Hilton, who had brought with him to Cornwall deep knowledge of modern French painting, spent his final years of illness churning out gouaches in a self-conscious effort to shed sophistication and re-invent for himself the direct simplicity of the language of childhood. Bryan Wynter, whose post-war gouaches bathed in the eerie moonlit atmosphere of Neo-Romanticism, also contrived to strike a wayward note with the late mobiles - the IMOOS - unusual structures that dangled coloured forms in front of distorting searchlight mirrors. This series was leant unpredictability through surrealist chance effect. Surrealistic free association runs through Wynter's art. Surrealism had formed the alternative voice to Constructivist abstraction in pre-war avant-garde art. By moving the stylistic and conceptual

W. Barns-Graham with the author Wills Lane Gallery, Sept. 1982.

content of his art closer to the Surrealist polarity, Wynter created an authentically individual voice within the formalist orthodoxies of much St. Ives abstract art. Wynter and Paul Feiler both changed style, their painterly expressions eventually giving way to more coolly designed hard edge compositions, which responded to the patterns of meandering rivers or to subtle gradations of tone within tight colour bands.

By the mid 1970's some of the key actors on the stage of modern Cornish art had departed. Hepworth, the regal presence in St. Ives art during the 1960's, died in 1975, as did Hilton and Wynter. The Hepworth atelier, which in the 1950's fostered a group of apprentices who themselves later became reputable sculptors, no longer did so. Brian Wall, John Milne, Keith Leonard, Denis Mitchell, Breon O'Casey and Roger Leigh were among those who had profited from Trewyn studio's heyday. Some, like Mitchell, Milne and O'Casey stayed in Cornwall and developed their craft. Others, like Leigh, Leonard and Wall left in order to pursue teaching opportunities elsewhere. During the 1980's the Cornish art scene consolidated its previous achievements, mindful of better days, though the late work of Denis Mitchell, Tony O'Malley, Wilhelmina Barns-Graham, Patrick Heron and Bryan Pearce (among others), reached new levels of accomplishment. In 1982, as part of Robert Etherington's St. Ives September Festival, the Wills Lane Gallery put on an exhibition of recent work by an old St. Ives figure, the Dorset-based Sven Berlin. His return was greeted by former colleagues, who thronged to the opening in a way that proved the deep running durability of the extended

John Wells with Sven Berlin, Wills Lane Gallery, Sept. 1982.

26

family of St. Ives artists. Cyril Gilbert's Wills Lane Gallery, Bob Devereux's Salthouse Gallery and more recently Leon Suddaby's Sims Gallery have provided outlets for the best of recent art. Cornish-based artists, like Robert Floyd, Max Barratt, Tony Giles, Yankel Feather, Pauline Liu Devereux, Carole McDowall, Jeremy Annear, Michael Finn, Terry Wybrow and Noel Betowski have all exhibited at these prominent private and commercial venues. By the 1990's signs of a revitalised art scene have come in the wake of the spectacular new St. Ives Tate Gallery, an elegant and purpose-built modernist building designed by Shalev and Evans on the former gas works site, overlooking Porthmeor Beach. This will institutionalise and therefore give international stature to the remarkable achievement of Cornish art since the war, and in an unlikely, peripheral location on the edge of the Atlantic an international audience is now starting to appreciate that achievement.

In this context, it is important that a sense is also given of continuity between the high period of St. Ives Modernism and the more recent pluralistic Post-Modernism of the younger generation. This is where the role of smaller commercial galleries, in complementing the historical nature of the Tate displays, assumes such vital importance. The aforementioned younger artists have not built reputations beyond Cornwall, but this does not preclude potentially wider audiences within Cornwall. The watercolourist Richard Ayeling opened the Porthmeor Gallery where he shows local artists. Steve Dove and Kathy McNally excel in life drawings and both have taught at the St. Ives School of Painting. Michael Hocking, a notable young collector of St. Ives art, has benefited from part-time studies at this school. Robert Floyd's early 1980's paintings, in a style of almost photorealist clarity, depicted surfers, bikini-clad sunbathers or interiors behind light filtered venetian blinds. Tony Giles, based at St. Agnes, paints elaborate ink and watercolour compositions of coastal locations throughout the county. Blackburn-born and Liverpool-trained Pauline Liu Devereux, paints large still-lifes in a vibrant and rich colour key which hum with a full blown confidence and love of expressive paint surfaces. Porthleven-based Carole McDowell also enjoys a thick expressionist surface though her often large, chalky compositions are a lot more abstract. Jeremy Annear, Robert Culwick, Michael Finn and Liverpool trained Roger Large each compose abstract canvases with deep, rich colour and softened geometric shapes. John Clark constructs with 'found' materials. Bob Devereux's superbly-crafted watercolours of seascape subjects or oils of beachtents (he was once a deckchair attendant) have gradually been abstracted into purer shapes and interlocking rhythms. Anthony Frost's abstract compositions match the frontal immediacy of his father's forms with the colours of Howard Hodgkin. Roy Walker, a former car worker from Dagenham, uses the shapes of automobile componenets in flat Post-Cubist compositions. An accomplished etcher, he also occasionally makes memorable forays into watercolour with figure studies of underwater swimmers in pools. In the shadow of the new Tate younger artists are now beginning to appear.

CHAPTER 2

Ben Nicholson

Ben Nicholson's St. Ives years spanned nearly two decades, that of the 1940's and most of the 1950's. Yet this period represents less than a third of his prodigious sixty year career as a professional artist. Although the style for which he is internationally important - the white reliefs and their subsequent derivations using colour and texture in a more relaxed vein - had already formed by the time he moved to Carbis Bay in 1939, I resist the recent tendency to downplay the significance of the Cornish period in the context of his whole career. It is true that he purified his art, avoiding both personal romanticism and emotional association with extrinsic factors like landscape genius loci, but within its own concrete terms his work reflected something of a Cornish light, climate and atmosphere. Cornwall's remarkable landscape touched a raw nerve as much as Switzerland, Greece and Italy did, as we shall see in the course of this study. The influences that came to bear on his art were, however, directly perceived and personally felt ones. They were certainly not gleaned from glossy reproductions. Christopher Neve wrote that being 'a child in a family of artists, he listened and watched, forming strong ideas about what he did not want painting to do.'[1] One of the things he did not want his painting to do was to merely repeat or paraphrase the art of his parents.

The example of Sir William Nicholson's quintessential Edwardian tonal painting gave the young Ben a spur to react against glazed atmospheres and gleaming illusionism (though he was well capable of emulating his father in early pictures like 'The Red Necklace') and replace it with more absolute, hard headed pictorial objectives. He spoke of wanting to 'bust up' the stifling sophistication that surrounded him as a youth. Yet he was no iconoclast and retained in all but the starkest of later reliefs, a link with the same still-life motifs favoured by William. Oblique references to the profiles, handles, rims or 'lips' of jugs, plates and glasses soften the impact of a language of 'hard' planes, squares and circles. The influence of his father is therefore fundamental for both positive and negative reasons. The inter-war years, referred to by Jeremy Lewison as the 'Years of Experiment'[2], witnessed a wilful reaction against post Whistlerian mannerism. The reaction took the form of continental travels, to Switzerland, Italy and Paris, where he absorbed the art of the Italian Primitives and met some of the leading avant-garde artists who would inspire his own dialogue with modernism.

Ben Nicholson was born too late to have been a pioneer of Cubism and its immediate variants. International success came to him relatively late in life, too late according to his third wife, the German photographer Felicitas

Vogler.*3 Yet in his own inimitable way he made a late contribution to Cubism - the only English artist to do so - in terms of the windowsill and the kitchen table. 'Considering how close he felt to French thought,' Neve wrote, 'it seems extraordinary that, until the Tate retrospective goes to St. Etienne in 1994, there has never been a major exhibition devoted to Ben Nicholson in France.'*4 It is not really so surprising, for as René Gimpel remarked*5, Nicholson enjoys a largely Anglo Saxon following and, furthermore, the French can be very chauvinistic in their preferences. His work is perhaps not as obviously sensual as the French tend to like. The purist strain, the obsession with cleanness,

Ben Nicholson. Silver Relief 1968.
Private Collection.

order and precision, probably fits in better with Swiss Calvinism; the neutrality of countries like Switzerland and Sweden also matches Nicholson's moral detachment from political and social issues.

Standards of high finish and coherent perspective, fostered by William's suave painting, are attained in Ben's early work. Too much art, and with it good taste, in his background, render the Slade period a somewhat

29

perfunctory one. But his marriage to Winifred Dacre, more than studies or travels to Europe and California, proved to be the catalyst for a wholesale break with the past. The young couple positively luxuriated in the advanced painting culture of the day; they made frequent visits to Paris and Switzerland where work was seen by, among others, Miro, Calder and Picasso. The effect of Winifred's soft light and poetic colour, often using a pastel range, imprinted a new lyricism on his painting. The change from the dingy light of the Edwardian parlour to the clear, sparkling light of the outdoors was immediate, seen as early as 1921 in continental pictures like 'Pink House in the Snow' or in English subjects like 'Landscape from Bankshead Studio'. Also significant here is the emergence of a naive or nursery style using thin nonchalant dabs of paint across an airy and diffuse composition. Tightness has momentarily gone. During the 1920's he used loose handling in a pastel-hued key to articulate head studies of Winifred and the children, Cumbrian or Cornish landscapes as well as still-life configurations. Hints of the all out, autonomous abstraction that was to come could be evidenced in a couple of beautifully simple and relaxed still-lifes of the mid 1920's that portrayed goblets, bottles and pears. For the first time line and colour began to disassociate themselves from superficial descriptive objectives. 'Trout', a well-nigh abstract picture of the period, was composed with pastel colours and an emollient geometry of rectangles and squares.

By the early 1930's Nicholson's career, and with it his private life, enters a new phase. The association with Winifred and with Kit Wood, the original rush of blood at discovering Wallis, seemed things of the past. He had met Barbara Hepworth, whom he would marry in 1938, and the partnership led to a consolidation of their growing allegiance, through both painting and sculpture, to a fully non-representational mode of abstract art. Christopher Wood's untimely death in 1930 symbolised the end of the relaxed faux naive manner as the favoured form of painting. Nicholson's ambition saw him take effective leadership of the Seven and Five Society, a liberal and loose grouping of artists that lasted from 1920 to 1935. Nicholson was a member for the last decade of its existence. The earlier poetic still-life and landscape subjects, at one with Seven and Five liberalism and ethos of romantic individual expression, gave away to pursuit of an uncompromising international abstraction in the new decade. This does not mean that Nicholson would never return to the poetics of faux naive, but upon becoming chairman in 1932, he effectively purged the Society of its formerly loose and eclectic membership, and brought in his own people. In the words of Mark Glazebrook it led to 'a sort of aesthetic dictatorship with avant-garde aspirations'*6 The not inconsiderable names of Bawden, Aldridge, Hodgkins and Jowett disconsolately appear on the resignation sheet; they are echoed fifteen years later by those of Lanyon, Berlin and other Penwith Society members who similarly found fault with Nicholson's 'aesthetic dictatorship', geared to set abstract ends, in post-war Cornwall.

The effect of Arp and Miro can be seen in Nicholson's free form works of the early 1930's such as 'Milk and plain chocolate', where a skating curvilinear incision darts across a dark ground of coagulated paint. Nicholson appears to have mixed dust particles into the paint giving it a coarse texture. He then etched or scraped the surface to expose gesso. On other occasions, as in the Cornish Pill Creek and Cumbrian Walton Wood landscape pictures in the late 1920's, he used paint thinly, scrubbed on in a manner that allowed the textural idiosyncrasies of a gesso ground to show through. In drawings, too, he aimed for the effect of worn, old surfaces, and used ochre watercolour stains to promote a feeling of aged paper. The artist's habit of scraping and rubbing frequently resulted in bleached surfaces, creating an antique mood. Ucello was an influence of singular significance. Fresco painting generally inspired Nicholson's attention to surface, where flatness of design and integrity of mark retained the upper hand over illusionistic depth. The tilting up of the table top subject so that it became one with the picture surface allowed jugs to 'float' in a purely flat and integral space. The relationship of domestic objects to each other, sometimes overlapping, and the relationship of the still-life unit to a landscape beyond, form the content of these pictures. Images become intertwined in increasingly complex ways as positive and negative spaces are ambiguously played against one another. A jug may be formed as a negative image, the result of removing paint to expose gesso. The artist uses pattern, lettering or other incidents to add decorative gaiety and visual interest to the composition. The stripes of cloth or dots on ceramics are exploited and even become independent abstract designs, shorn of previous decorative function. Referring to the lettering in his famous 1932 painting 'Au Chat Botté' (Manchester City Art Gallery), Nicholson commented that 'being in French, and my French being a little mysterious, the words themselves had also an abstract quality.'

Nicholson was a pragmatic painter who entered dialogue with advanced avant-garde art on his own eclectic terms. He was no theorist, though his artistic statements are terse and to the point. The logic of cubist abbreviation (the numerous letters he was fond of scribbling to friends and colleagues were also short and note-like) ensured an uncompromisingly visual approach to the business of form construction. There was something of the craftsman, in particular the carpenter, about him, for as Neve again observes, 'Planning and rubbing boards down were pleasures to him, and it would be difficult to distinguish between the preparation of a surface and the beginning of a picture'*7. He disliked explaining his pictures, which he tried to imbue with clarity, order and simplicity. He retained links with the natural world, befitting an English artist, and never went as far as Mondrian's neo-plastic conclusions, though in the white reliefs and the compositions of coloured squares and rectangles like 'Painting 1937' he reached a high level of purism. Nicholson never shared a coherent philosophy such as Mondrian found in theosophic beliefs. In 1941, Nicholson remembered that as far as visiting Mondrian's studio was concerned, 'it was his silences and the feeling of his thought in the studio which moved me.' If anything Nicholson, a shy man who disliked the romantic cult of artistic personality, (he studiously avoided being filmed and is not buried in a known grave), used sport as a way of relating his art. He was fond of ball games, played tennis very well, and watched the great Arsenal teams of the 1930's while he was living in

31

Hampstead among what Herbert Read dubbed as a 'gentle nest of artists'. He saw qualities of linear precision in ball games that he felt were relevant to the activities of being a painter.

The Hampstead years saw him work in collaboration with sculptors, architects, writers and fellow painters. Among his colleagues were Barbara Hepworth, whose sculpture certainly influenced Nicholson in the adoption of uniform white surfaces, Gabo, Wells Coates, Herbert Read, Moholy-Nagy and Mondrian. Nicholson found in the group Unit One the commitment to the language of advanced abstraction that he attempted to achieve in the Seven and Five Society. Yet, in the co-operative endeavour of Unit One Nicholson introduced modesty to take the place of 'aesthetic dictatorship'. As the group's title suggests, part of Unit One's appeal lay in allowing individual voices to emerge out of a common international language of architectural form and abstract constructivist modes. It is easy to forget that Mondrian was of an older generation. To be fair, Nicholson probably desired to emulate this unity within diversity when influencing the Penwith Society in St. Ives during the early 1950's by introducing rules to distinguish between abstract and representational styles. He realised what a backwater English art could be, and in a justified ambition to transcend the provincial and square up to the international, was determined to marshal those groupings under his control - first the Seven and Five and later the Penwith - into a tough lean army, capable of competing on an international stage, with an abstract and constructive style which he did not see as élitist but as fostering 'a powerful, unlimited and universal language'. This lesson was lost on conventional taste in a major northern city like Manchester. When a Nicholson still-life picture of 1950 was wanted by the City Art Gallery, the Manchester Guardian ran a headline 'Councillors Attack Modern Art: Product of Disordered Minds'. It is no surprise, therefore, that eight years later he wrote that 'the word 'Manchester' certainly conjures up somewhere pretty difficult.'*8

In the same way that Wallis saw his pictures as events rather than simply paintings, Nicholson thought of his reliefs as 'a mental experience'. Furthermore, the experience did not preclude the practice of softer figurative work. The way Nicholson wandered freely between the stark purity of the reliefs and the softer, more referential works makes neat classification of his work fruitless. Andreas Kalman wrote in 1974 how Nicholson 'astounds us with a gentle drawing from nature after finishing a vigorous, hard fought out abstract relief.' During the war, resident in Carbis Bay, and alternating duties as a night firewatcher with the domestic practice of art, Nicholson produced soft landscape drawings, paintings of windowsills that incorporate jugs and domestic bric-a-brac with an outdoor scene, small geometric compositions of overlapping lines, circles and rectangles called the 'Project' series, and small compositions of coloured squares and rectangles. They were produced side by side as expressing differing aspects of Nicholson's artistic 'personality'. The abstract compositions benefit from intimate scale. Coloured rectangles are laid across one another - placed in relation to each other according to the dictates of the eye rather than according to precisely measured mathematical concepts - within the bounds of a larger rectangle. Nicholson also makes a lyrical play between the various colours of these rectangular components and counterpoises vertical elements against horizontally placed ones. The edge of tightly concealed colour defines the angular movement of line as the picture becomes an exercise in movement, check, and counter-movement.

These works have the clean precision and order of a game of chess. Primary colours, blacks and whites alternate with more naturalistic umber, olive or light blue colours. In 1941, during this eclectic period of eminent cross-fertilisation between stylistic alternatives, the artist stated that 'one of the main differences between a representational and an abstract painting is that the former can transport you to Greece by a representation of blue skies and seas, olive trees and marble columns... whereas the abstract version by its free use of form and colour will give you the actual quality of Greece itself, and will become a part of the light and space and life in the room.' Nicholson thus eschews the mimetic and theatrical role of painting unless paraphrased through irony and self-conscious adaptations. He is also aware of painting's role as domestic object, a quintessential piece of décor.

The critic John Russell, author of the first major monograph on the artist, described Nicholson's colour as 'used sparingly, but with a most complex and eloquent derivation'. Eloquence was a natural attribute for an artist of cultivated heritage, but the 'complex derivation' was in part due to eclecticism and in part to the use of memory as a factor in the expressive quality of Nicholson's art. An essential ingredient of Wallis' art, after all, had been the memory of the sea encountered during voyages earlier in life, and it is certainly the case that for Nicholson too, colour possessed the evocative aura to recall past experiences of time and place. Artistic influences may have also played a secondary role - Mondrian's primaries in the rectangle compositions, 'the peculiarly pungent Cornish greens' of Wallis that were used in his own landscapes, and Moholy-Nagy's use of overlapping secondary hues in Nicholson's semi-abstract derivations of still-life. Moholy-Nagy, a Hungarian contributor to 'Circle' and a cohabitant of the Hampstead 'nest', used what Lynton referred to as 'interference'[*9] colour, an opaque hue created when one colour traversed another in overlapping geometric compositions. Albers referred to this superimposing as film colour, but whatever the theory distinguishing the colour of natural light from that of opaque pigment or matter, there would invariably be, in Nicholson's adaptations, a degree of poetic licence and with it unpredictable distortions. In the post-war works Nicholson introduced subtle pinks, peaches, mustards, olives and magentas into his large scale overlapping linear compositions.

Ben Nicholson's post-war paintings became increasingly playful; they witness a new breadth and confidence in the expressive possibilities of a restricted language. He repeats motifs in new combinations, evokes humour through visual punning (exploiting correspondences between a steeple or spire and a glass decanter), pastiches or paraphrases passages from pre-war work, and, even in the same picture, continues to sway between the representational and the abstract. He uses both hardboard and canvas and continues to draw on paper from the landscape. Far from being a derivative pasticheur, who holds Cubism's passion at bay, Nicholson is a quintessential

English artist able to use the international language of constructivism and abstraction while maintaining an English link with nature. He differed here - to no disadvantage - from purist artists like Gabo and Mondrian. The canvases of the early 1950's are often large in scale and, in distinction to the smoothly painted wartime abstractions in gouache and oil, exploit the grain or weave of the ground support as part of the underlying texture, an intention made simpler through thinly applied paint, scraped or rubbed down to create characteristic analogies with natural phenomena. This reaches extreme proportions in large rectangular compositions such as 'Silver Relief' (1968) of the later period. Nicholson carves into the pre-cut hardboard components,

Ben Nicholson. Nov 1951 (Scilly Isles). *Oil.*
Courtesy: Crane Kalman Gallery.

creating a shallow planar relief. The board is either primed, sandpapered, left untouched, gouged into, or else painted with nebulous white, evocative of crisp Alpine snow. The link with nature is explained by Stephen Nash, who writes how, even in more smoothly painted works, 'Blue passages evoke the sea, whites suggest whitewashed Mediterrenean buildings or the marble of Greece'.*10 Pencil line continues to weave its magic above painted grounds. The planes and straight or curved lines intersect and truncate one another but the unmistakable reading is a still-life even when, as in 'November 1951 (Scilly Isles)' the title suggests landscape. Nicholson visited the Scillies with David Lewis and Wilhelmina Barns-Graham in 1951, where he sketched from the landscape and it is likely that the work derived its title from the recent experience. On the flat surface of canvas Nicholson delights in 'a finely controlled equilibrium between the given order of nature and the invented order of art',*11 and more particularly in the playful tension between the shallow, flattened space of Cubism and the evocative depth of landscape. The still life objects of this composition are embedded in a pronounced graphite chiaroscuro, throwing them into an illusory relief. 'Film' colour is also created where objects overlap or merge into one another, creating the metamorphosis of a third chromatic zone. The jostling rectilinearity of 'Nov. 1951' is offset by a curving pencil line that sweeps around the central conglomeration of jugs, handles, goblets and planes.

Nicholson was unusually adept with the fine point of a pencil, which he used to create a full tonal and graphic range. The result was an ability to strike at the heart of mood and atmosphere, though his topographical drawings are structural in character. Psychologically, if not visually, an effect of colour is created in fluent architectural drawings of chimneys, roof tops, middle-

Ben Nicholson. Penzance 1948. *Pencil.*
Private Collection.

35

distant harbours and outlying landscape. The artist's open-ended working methods frequently called into question the dividing line between drawing and painting. In a well-known painting, 'St. Ives harbour from Trezion' (1951) the artist uses the vantage point of his house overlooking St. Ives harbour. Oil, pencil and untouched gesso are used in equal proportions; this 'painting' has the appearance of a drawing in that much of the surface is untouched and drained of colour. Small boats in the harbour are, however, highlighted by tiny but strong areas of Indian red colour that contradict normal rules of tonal recession. The same device is used in a similarly composed roof-top view, 'Penzance' (1948). In this pencil drawing, Nicholson uses heavy shades of graphite to draw attention to a large centrally placed fishing vessel in the middle distance of Mount's Bay. Typically for Nicholson, the foreground is made up from the irregular geometry of interlocking roofs, which are left untouched, without the versatile tonal treatment of the coastal landscape behind. Our eye is encouraged to focus on the distance rather than foreground. The dichotomy between heavy shading and untouched paper, between faint and heavy linear inscriptions, and between contradictory perspectival emphases, is an outcome of the artist's rigorous procedures.

The drawing of Penzance roof-tops is nevertheless a relatively straight and conventional piece of topographical reporting. Reference to what seems an

Ben Nicholson. Higher Carnstabba Farm 1944. *Oil.*
Private Collection.

obvious window view setting is entirely missing and no still objects are placed in the foreground such as we find in 'Higher Carnstabba Farm' (1944), a composite subject that merges the naive poetry of the Cumbrian period with the tough, flattened neo-cubism of the later period. When a ship at sea occurs, as in the Penzance drawing, it offsets the impersonal precision and architectural purity of jugs, decanters, roofs, domes, arches and the like. It is a reference to Wallis, and through him to the poetry of the naive. The Penzance drawing follows the example set by 'Higher Carnstabba Farm', which sees the artist working from motifs on offer beyond St. Ives. In 1948, the year that the Penzance drawing was executed, Nicholson wrote that 'the kind of painting which I find exciting is not necessarily representational or non-representational, but it is both musical and architectural, where the architectural construction is used to express a 'musical' relationship between form, tone and colour'. Thus we are not surprised to find linear rhythms, colour harmonies and spatial intervals in the visual language.

Nicholson's austerity, an attribute of linear precision and reluctance to use impasto and strident colour, is not to everyone's taste. He was nevertheless able to parallel the qualities of automatism and spontaneity of execution normally reserved for 'action painting' in the contrasting context of concrete formalism. 'His impulse was to banish the fatty highlight and to rub and scrape off excess pigment', Neve writes, and 'he began to see how pictures could be turned into physical events by treating them physically, by incising and scraping'.*12 Though not a juicy or painterly artist himself, he was open minded and enjoyed these values in others, providing, they were used in an authentic context. In Switzerland, he was friendly with Mark Tobey, whom he described in a letter to Michael Snow as being 'a lovely painter'.*13 Returning from the frequently visited Venice Biennale in 1962 he expresses a regret that the prize had not 'gone to Poliakoff, or failing Poliakoff to Riopelle'.*14 His reverence for Cézanne stayed with him, and as late as 1966 suspected that 'there's never been a better painter than Cézanne'. Although couched in his entirely different terms, Nicholson shares with the so-called father of modern art a similar awareness of the inherent two dimensionalism of pictorial art and a preoccupation with the shallow pictorial space whereby form is subjected to a plastic and illusionistic relationship to, and accord with, surface.

As far as removal from the St. Ives, and indeed English art scene is concerned, factors to do with career opportunities played a leading part. There were also cultural and psychological reasons; his marriage to Felicitas Vogler and disillusionment with the insular character of English culture when it came to the visual arts were clearly of importance in his leaving for Switzerland. By temperament he seemed suited to a country of clear white light, hygiene, affluence and orderliness. Not long after moving he wrote that 'we like very much the international character of Switzerland and particularly like Zurich. It strikes one as being very lively and prosperous'.*15 Nicholson enjoyed his privacy and felt increasingly at odds with the growing St. Ives bandwagon of the later 1950's. 'This place has become more and more of an art colony and hot-house', he wrote shortly before leaving St. Ives, 'so we've decided to go and live in Northern Italy or maybe Ticino…. After St. Ives one could scarcely live anywhere else in England'*16 In the 1920's he had been in Cumbria, and in the 1930's he and Hepworth were among a group who considered East Anglia. There was also Hampstead, to where he returned for the last period of his life. But the significance of St. Ives was that it offered the kind of spectacular scenery that only Switzerland could replace; furthermore, he left a big-mark on St. Ives, influencing many younger painters, most notably John Wells, Barns-Graham and Peter Lanyon.

The grandness of Yorkshire may also have become an option; Herbert Read returned there in later years, but the largest of English counties seemed a

Ben Nicholson. Jug and Sexagonal 1968. *Pencil and Ink.*
Bernard Jacobson Gallery.

recourse to the past in the sense that Nicholson's closest colleagues - Read, Moore and Hepworth - all originated from here. Nonetheless, while on honeymoon with Vogler in 1957 he stayed in Yorkshire with his collector friend Cyril Reddihough, visited Read, and made some notable drawings at Rievaulx Abbey, the spectacular Cistercian ruin. One of these, 'Rievaulx

Abbey' (1957), is an exercise in great graphic control, visual editing that brings to the fore stone pillars, arches, tracery and steps, and use of selected ink highlights to imply rather than illustrate mass. At the same time the pronounced black ridges balanced out the intervals of untouched paper. The Yorkshire trip was one of the last he made from St. Ives before moving to the Ticino. During the 1960's Nicholson, settled in Switzerland, continued to produce drawings, reliefs and paintings with fluctuating degrees of abstraction. In 'Jug and Sexagonal' (1968), a drawing made in the same year as

Ben Nicholson. Rievaulx Abbey 1957. *Pencil.*
Bernard Jacobson Gallery.

'Silver Relief', Nicholson rescues a prominent jug motif from a 'bottleneck' of intersecting lines and image fragments. Further, the work is drawn on an embossed sheet of etching paper, thereby creating a subtle relief-like surface. This drawing is a coup de force, emulating with a thin, exact pencil line, the same all-over treatment and immediacy usually associated with more sensual media and gestural modes of execution. The line dances about the entire sheet with an energy that prompts Neve to call Nicholson 'a classical artist with a lyrical method'.*17 Referring to this drawing in his large 1993 monograph, Norbert Lynton describes the line as 'clean, clear, classical. If there is emotion it is not in the line itself but in what it does'.*18 The enjoyment with line encouraged him to make etchings, and in the later period Nicholson leaves the architectural subjects behind and focuses on the sensation of pure shape provided by still-life objects. He delights in a fast, spontaneous bite into copper or zinc on which he enters a dialogue with empty space. Nicholson creates unity out of separateness. He also exploits the visual characteristics of one medium in the context of another. Lynton explains how 'The large reliefs project. Each etching is negative relief and Ben Nicholson's frequent use of odd shapes remind us of that'.*19 The odd shapes retain their significance to the very end, for even in the early 1980's, in a series of tiny faltering felt tip compositions on paper, Nicholson enjoys the given irregularity of scissored fragments as a means of echoing a preoccupation with pure shape. These small irregular sheets are not 'papier coupé' or 'object trouvé' in quality, but are rather instances of a perverse streak in a great craftsman's ethos of perfection. The device derives, of course, from Alfred Wallis's habit of painting on irregular pieces of cardboard.

NOTES

1.   Christopher Neve. *Intuition and Order*. p.5. Modern British Masters. Bernard Jacobson 1993.
2.   See *Ben Nicholson. The Years of Experiment*. Kettles Yard 1983.
3.   Conversations with the author. St. Ives. September 1982.
4.   *Neve*. p.6 Bernard Jacobson 1993.
5.   Conversation with the author. London 1983.
6.   Mark Glazebrook. Introduction to *The Seven and Five Society*. Michael Parkin 1970.
7.   Neve. p.8 Bernard Jacobson 1993.
8.   Ben Nicholson. Letter to Michael Snow. October 1958.
9.   Norbert Lynton. *Ben Nicholson*. Phaidon Press 1993.
10.   Stephen Nash. *Ben Nicholson, Fifty Years of his Art*. p.34 New York 1979.
11.   Stephen Nash. *Ben Nicholson, Fifty Years of his Art*. p.34 New York 1979.
12.   Christopher Neve. p.6 Bernard Jacobson 1993.
13.   Ben Nicholson. Letter to Michael Snow. 30 June 1961.
14.   Ben Nicholson. Letter to Michael Snow. 21 June 1962.
15.   Ben Nicholson. Letter to Michael Snow. October 1958.
16.   Ben Nicholson. Letter to Michael Snow. c.1957.
17.   Christopher Neve. p.5 Bernard Jacobson 1993.
18.   Norbert Lynton. p.361 Phaidon Press 1993.
19.   Norbert Lynton. p.362 Phaidon Press 1993.

CHAPTER 3

Barbara Hepworth

Barbara Hepworth, one of the greatest sculptors of the twentieth century, lived and worked in St. Ives from 1939 until her death in 1975. It is no coincidence that this time span was used for the large St. Ives retrospective at the London Tate in 1985. Hepworth's presence in St. Ives therefore coincided with, and was symptomatic of, the golden era of St. Ives art. Though the modern movement would have taken place in Cornwall without her, there is no doubt that she occupied centre stage during the best years, particularly after her former colleague and husband, Ben Nicholson, moved to Switzerland in 1958. The genuine international reputation she enjoys is symbolised by her large bronze 'Single Form' (1964), which stands outside the front of the U.N. building in New York City. During the 1960's and early 1970's she enjoyed a pre-eminent position though her later work, viewed by some as outlasting its avant-garde significance, became the butt for a younger generation who reacted against its precious formalism and outdated assumptions. Since the 1970's, prices for her work have risen steadily, however, and the time has come for fresh evaluations of her work. At the time of writing, a large retrospective is being organised for October 1994 at the Tate Gallery's Albert Dock location in Liverpool. It will provide this major artist, subject of much unfair rebuke from a number of jumped up contemporary critics, with a much needed reassessment.

Although this international reputation came to her during the late 1940's and 1950's, the artist's post-war achievement was based on a formal language developed in the 1930's. Furthermore, her distilled and perfectly crafted forms were produced in Hampstead as a response to a vein of international abstract and constructive art that had developed in the cosmopolitan milieu of London and Paris. Long before coming to Cornwall, therefore, Hepworth had found her feet as a young but fully mature sculptor. She had also shown remarkable dedication and commitment to her sculpture; not only was this a courageous feat for a woman on a male-dominated avant-garde stage but it also represented the steely grit and determination of a Yorkshire woman who brought to the physically demanding and emotionally draining activity of direct carving in wood, stone and marble, a northern 'work ethic'. In later years she invested all her emotional energy into work. Both Hepworth and Nicholson put work before other human considerations. Late in life Nicholson, displaying a greater degree of self-critical effacement than Hepworth was able to muster, admitted the regret that he had not been able to give as much time to people as he had to his art.

Hepworth felt through her materials. She expressed ideas through the actual physical processes of carving into blocks of stone. Though the beautifully crafted objects have a smoothed perfection and effortless rhythmic unity, they were the product of lengthy physical struggle. The nature of the material played a role in determining the outcome. She delighted in exploiting the natural veins in wood or marble as well as creating a famous interplay between outer surface and opened-up interiors. She also used paints, chemicals or other colouring agents to evoke lyrical and formal contrast

Barbara Hepworth at the Penwith Gallery 1970.
Photo: Roger Slack.

between differing planes. A visitor to the artist's Trewyn studio, now the Barbara Hepworth Museum, is struck by the workshop that has been left untouched since the day in May 1975 that she died. The small space is crammed with tools and implements that she used to make work. In later years, she was partly incapacitated and was suffering from throat cancer at the time of her death in an accidental fire at Trewyn. Her later works were, therefore, usually produced to her specifications by assistants, a practice moreover, that extended to all periods of her professional life as a famous sculptor, particularly since her 'breakthrough' to fame with successes at the Venice Biennale in 1950 and the Festival of Britain the following year.

Barbara Hepworth was therefore a mature artist when she moved down to St. Ives in 1939 to escape wartime London. In one sense, the move marked a decisive break with the past, though she used the new context of wartime to affirm the artistic but also moral convictions of the late 1930's. 'I do not think this preoccupation with abstract forms was escapism', she wrote, 'I see it as a logical way of expressing the instinctive 'will to live' as opposed to the extrinsic disaster of the world war'. She, therefore, found an enduring relevance for abstraction in the new decade, though her post-1939 work responded to Cornwall in terms of a softer, more personal geometry that was opened to the possibilities for full landscape association. The dark years of the early 1940's restricted her artistic output. In addition to common wartime privations she was also burdened with the responsibility of raising three young children. Her work took the form of numerous crystal drawings, in which intersecting lines of great complexity evoked a hidden, geometric order beyond defined appearances. These were produced during the evenings when she found a little time for herself after daytime responsibilities. As a result, the colours of night - blacks, dark blues and whites - dominated and gave distinctive mood to gouache paintings. These were composed with hard-edged blocks of colour - sub-divided squares and rectangles in an absolute visual symmetry. The paintings evoked the atmosphere of night and reflected, through the magical analogy of abstraction, the classical features of Cornwall - the gleaming light, unbounded ocean and ancient granite profiles. She created drawings, paintings and associated lithograph prints throughout her distinguished career. But seldom do the later works on a flat surface emulate the inventive magic of these wartime graphic investigations into pure spatial relationships. These early works were indeed indicative of the way that her art would proceed when she could once again commence with full scale sculpture.

Like the drawings, the small number of carvings executed in the first half of the 1940's are also harbingers of things to come. They open up the solid spheres and faceted forms of the Hampstead works in a manner that gives space a new role, equal to enclosed volume. Interior space assumes equal validity to the outer shell. In 'Oval Sculpture' (1943) the exterior and interior is merged in one spiralling curvilinear movement. In this work and in a small plaster maquette 'Sculpture With Colour' (1940), she introduces colour as a means of distinguishing the interior (colour) with the exterior (natural wood grain or white plaster). The practice continued after the war in notable sculptures based on turning wave forms like 'Pelagos' (1946). Significantly, the artist later stated that 'the colour in the concavities plunges me into the depth of water, caves of shadows deeper than the concavities themselves'. This remark is indicative of Hepworth's move away from the purism of the Paris-based 'Association - Abstraction - Creation' group and also away from Gabo, who would not wish to invest his dynamic transparent forms with any degree of naturalistic association. Hepworth was in fact softening the hard minimal geometry of the 1930's with that irresistible English pull towards landscape. The introduction of painted colour represented Hepworth investing form with a degree of association and meaning beyond its actual physical and plastic dimension; in other words, she was introducing a degree of illusionism into the abstraction of pure formal relationships. Accompanying this romantic development was a use of strings that also referred to landscape. Gabo's use of strings, therefore, differed from Hepworth's, for he integrated stringed surfaces with transparent perspex planes in a way that created compositional harmony and reduced any evocations of subjective landscape experience. Miriam Gabo made this clear when she wrote how 'Gabo's strings form semi-transparent surfaces. Barbara's are point to point; she never quite understood this. She used them to show a direction, not as a surface in themselves'[*1] In two subsequent sculptures, 'Wave' and 'Wood and Strings' Hepworth alluded to natural phenomena such as a wave and a human figure respectively.

It is in fact easy to see the influence of Gabo on the evolving sculpture of Barbara Hepworth during this period when they were living as near neighbours in Carbis Bay. The red and blue colours in 'Sculpture with Colour', for instance, echoed the rare use of coloured plastics in the contemporary constructions of Gabo. If the Russian could not find the desired coloured plastics he used powdered red or blue. These powders were mixed with a plastic medium in order to colour the shapes he was making. Similarly, Gabo's looping curvilinear forms worked out in the spheric theme, - the sculpture series that preoccupied him during the late 1930's, shortly before he moved from London to live in St. Ives, - had a marked correspondence with Hepworth's spiralling 'Oval Sculpture' (1943). Gabo considered that a true sculptural representation of space required 'one curved continuous surface', rather than the 'angular intersection of planes' that had previously engaged him on works derived from the stereometric cube.

Indeed, Hepworth appreciated Gabo's presence for reasons other than to do with artistic correspondence or influence. She wrote that Gabo's 'unusual powers of expression in discussion and the exceptional charm of his personality when talking of creative processes seemed to unleash a great energy in all who came near him.' Influences on Hepworth at this fertile time for the exchange of ideas extended beyond the studio into the area of social interaction. In spite of wartime privations there was considerable communication between an extended family of artists, friends, collectors, critics and well wishers. They included Solly Zuckerman, Margaret Gardiner, Herbert Read, J. Bernal and Michael Ventris. Yet, it was not all plain sailing for, not long after the war, rivalries between fiercely ambitious artists led to discord. Miriam Gabo later recalled that 'towards the end of the war, when Tambimuttu was running 'Poetry London ' he proposed to publish a book about Gabo's work which would of course have been terribly helpful but, after some months of negotiations and hopeful preparations, Ben suddenly announced that they were going to do one about him first. In the event, neither was ever published… but it did cause a real rift between Ben and Gabo which was not mended for many years… right into the 1970's, when they met again at the Leslie Martin's both old by then and in a more forgiving mood'*2

The war years were valuable for Hepworth in spite, or perhaps because of the restrictions on artistic output. It gave her much needed time to consolidate her position as a radical artist committed to abstraction. Just as importantly, it provided the opportunity for her to develop as a person; she evolved a personal philosophy concerning the role of the artist in society that was imparted in letters to others. The wartime letters written to Sven Berlin concerning Wallis, were paricularly clear statements along these lines. During this introspective period she also developed her graphic work in response to a developing fascination with the Penwith landscape, which she explored on foot with colleagues or friends like Nicholson and the Gabos. 'It was during this time that I discovered the remarkable pagan landscape which lies between St. Ives, Penzance and Land's End', she wrote before explaining that this area 'has a very deep effect on me, developing all my ideas about the relationship of the human figure in landscape-sculpture and landscape'*3 This new openness to landscape culminated in 'Landscape Sculpture' (1944), a low lying horizontal concave form pierced with two holes. In similar way, Hepworth's drawing delighted in exploring spatial dynamics, expressed in terms of a taut linear language of straight pencil lines creating sensations of unrestricted movement and direction.

The affirmation of art as a salutary force in society was espoused by Hepworth after the war. She wrote that after a period of 'universal suffering, people are much more aware that science and economy will not solve human life and happiness alone. Science must walk hand in hand with art'*4 'This comes close to investing art with the anti-materialistic significance of spiritual advancement. The association between art and science is, however, clear in her work, despite the fact that she never embraced the kind of new plastic materials and technological processes that Gabo favoured. Nowhere is the humanistic call for a higher and ennobling synthesis between art and science in greater evidence than in her post-war series of hospital drawings, which briefly represented a return to the kind of figuration that we saw in her early student carvings, but which had been entirely absent in her crystalline or hard geometrical forms during the war. She produced well over one hundred operating theatre drawings, an idea that started when her daughter underwent surgery in Exeter. The medical teams are formally linked creating a sculptural sensation of unity. This unity expressed what she felt was 'the extraordinary beauty of purpose and co-ordination between human beings all dedicated to the saving of human life'. The encircling figures, all eyes and hands, are in perfect synchrony with one another and elicit the same kind of Italianate drawing of flowing drapery and merging figure groups that characterise the shelter drawings produced a few years before by her former Leeds contemporary, Henry Moore. They also illustrated her enduring fascination with Masaccio and Piero. Hepworth's hospital series, though oils on board, are essentially coloured drawings, using the typical St. Ives idiom of scraped, pared down textural surfaces. A pronounced feeling for the linear and for the visual crispness of form is complemented by thin colour washes that create mood and evoke atmosphere. The imagery of a surgeon's hammer at work, as in 'Fenestration of the Ear' (1948) or of stitches being sewn to bind wounds clearly echo her life as a carving sculptor, in whose work cavities and strings provide spatial complexity to the opened-up monoliths of wood or stone.

The next important stage in her distinguished career was ushered in by the acquisition of Trewyn studios in 1949, by the separation and subsequent divorce from Ben Nicholson in 1951, and by a new decade that saw her begin to gain fame and fortune as a fully independent sculptor with the world as her oyster. The hospital drawings were not alone in representing a return to the figure; the slim, upright vertical carvings of the late 1940's also owe a debt, through analogy, to the motif of the standing figure. A horizontal landscape-evoking sculpture like 'Pendour' (1947) was an exception rather than rule amongst a body of post-war carvings that once again allude to the figure. These post-war sculptures were the ones used to establish an international reputation. The works included 'Two Figures' (1948), the Rosewood 'Rhythmic Form', the Blue limestone 'Bicentric Form', shown in the St. Ives Tate's inaugural installation, and 'Cosdon Head' (Birmingham City Art Gallery), all executed in 1949. The following year she won a prize at the Venice Biennale with 'Biolith'. However, the difficulty of merging abstraction with traditional figurative form led to some over-stylised works, like 'Bicentric Form' and 'Contrapuntal Forms' (1950), that are not among her finest works. Hammacher wrote that the latter work assigned 'to the human figure too important a role in abstract work.'[*5] Subsequent wood carvings produced in the 1952-54 period - tall, pierced monoliths - were more successful by virtue of subordinating figural overtones to the morphology of pure abstract form. The material of wood engaged her hand - or rather the hand of her assistants - after the acquisition of large quantities (17 tons) of African hardwoods (guarea) in the mid 1950's. The blocks played a hand in determining the formal outcome - the bulky 'Oval Sculpture' (Delos), (National Museum of Wales), for instance, effectively exploited the simple contrast between open space and enclosed volume, between smooth and hewn surfaces, and between wood grain and painted colour. A tall thin block resulted in the Brancusi-like 'Vertical Form', a minimal wood column with prominent serrated edges. These upright 'figure' carvings culminated in the huge, over life-size 'Figure (Requiem)' 1957 (Aberdeen Art Gallery), a tall column of walnut prised open, almost from top to bottom, with one long undulating vertical incision.

The introduction of Greek titles to accompany more usual Cornish ones originates in a visit made to Greece in 1954, where she was intrigued by the relationship of the figure to both architecture and the surrounding landscape. Wood carvings produced from large blocks after the Greek visit were

Barbara Hepworth. Requiem.
Aberdeen Art Gallery.

considered by Tom Cross not to be 'based on landscape or the figure, but on the rhythm of growth'*6 All the same, vertical sculptures always tend to have human significance in Hepworth's 'oeuvre' while the horizontal shapes inevitably allude to landscape. The year 1955, which the sculptor called 'a year of dedication', saw her hard at work on more large wood carvings. The death of her first son (from her marriage to John Skeaping) in a plane crash over Thailand in 1953 had followed her recent divorce from Ben Nicholson. For the first time in her life, Hepworth, now over 50 years of age, was on her own and she sought solace, even salvation in her work. The spirit of dedication she spoke of at this time, therefore, complemented both a contemplative approach to the construction of form and undiminished professional standards. As a result, the practice of sculpture assumed, in her able hands, a therapeutic significance of a kind, moreover, that had characterised Wallis's adoption of painting in the mid 1920's, after the death of his wife.

The final twenty years of her life witnessed a wider use of materials. In 1956, she used metal for the first time, in particular bronze, a material cast from plaster forms. Where the modelling of form with wet plaster was concerned, Hepworth still felt unable to jettison carving. She finished off the white surfaces of plaster with the action of the chisel and hammer. The forms, however, have a freer and more pronounced organic character than was possible in the more pre-determined context of wood and stone carving. Furthermore, the processes of modelling and casting, once considered anathema to a pre-war modernist generation, were re-introduced in a more relaxed, less hidebound, climate. Modern sculpture's reaction to nineteenth century academic naturalism was by now successfully secured, courtesy of direct carving's physical engagement and dialogue with the material at hand. A series of 'Torso' bronzes produced by Hepworth in the late 1950's - tall, free standing abstractions of anatomy - retain pock-marked surfaces and patinated textures. In so doing they trap and create an even distribution of light across the surface. This was clearly impossible with the later polished bronzes that are highly reflective according to the angle of vision. These patinated bronze forms are also evocative of landscape, in particular a marine landscape; notable works like 'Sea Form (Porthmeor)' (1958) take on a swaying biomorphism suggestive of submarine life, - a reading made all the more apparent through a vivid green verdigris, through a series of pebble-like cavities, and through an undulating shell-like outer form. Bronze also allowed her to relate the art of sculpture to outdoor architectural settings; two of her most accomplished and well-known works, 'Meridian' (1959) and 'Single Form' (1962) are sited in prominent locations outside State House in London and the United Nations building in New York.

The material of bronze enabled a new permanence and gave her the scope to undertake architectural commissions, fitting for an artist who, in the 1930's, had collaborated with architects like Wells Coates in Unit One and Gropius on the purist programmes of 'Circle' and 'Association Abstraction Creation'. The flat planar bronze forms that crop up in the late period are perhaps a response to the new involvement with architecture. In the same way that medieval figure sculpture adapted to architecture in the form of shallow bas relief, so a modern sculptor like Hepworth blended her art with pure and functional architecture through a faceted language of squares and rectangles. This is as apparent in the Rietveld Pavilion bronze (1965) as in the London and New York pieces. The development of an architectural dimension in her sculpture encouraged a return to the minimalism of pre-war marble forms - a more relevant spur to progress than that provided by operatic décor and costume designs. The versatility of metal also allowed the kind of drawing in space that steel welders like David Smith and his British follower Anthony Caro favoured. In 'Meridian' and 'Cantate Domino' (1958) Hepworth creates a spontaneous linear movement within a static conception. She was also able to

Barbara Hepworth. Disc with strings. *Bronze. Gimpel Fils.*

make more immediate play of gestural handling in terms of oil paint on the flat surfaces of board. The versatility of metal allowed her to bend, curve or shape the material in unpredictable ways and enabled a continuing use of strings denied her in the inert wood and stone sculptures. In 'Disc with strings (Sun)' (1969) Hepworth uses the abstract language of discs and intersecting string forms to allude to the movement and changing aspects of the sun across morning and afternoon skies. The strings not only harmonise a simple planar composition by replacing solid mass with centripetal movement across displaced open voids but also evoke associations with sunrays. Hepworth creates complexity out of a simple range of circular forms made possible by a sheet of bronze pierced, bent and drilled with strings.

During the 1960's, Hepworth produced many small marble carvings, bronzes and paintings. One exquisite example, the marble 'Pierced form

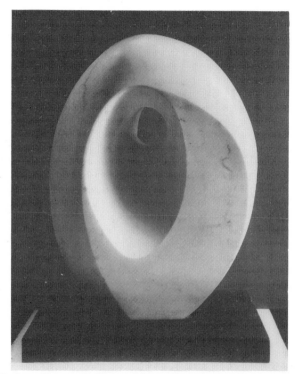

Barbara Hepworth. Pierced form (Santorin). *Marble, 1963.*
Courtesy: Gimpel Fils.

(Santorin)' (1963) continues to evoke classical feeling by using a title based on the name of the volcanic Greek island. The work prises lyricism from a solid mass of contrasting curved and flattened surfaces. The outer convex form finally gives way to a receding concavity which opens the sculpture to space

50

and links the front and back. As far as the paintings and lithographs are concerned she used a range of naturalistic colours, sometimes vivid and strong, other times scraped back to reveal the gesso ground. The gestural slashes of paint and splashes of colour, while responding in a general way to the automatic handling of the Abstract Expressionist period, never cut the umbilical cord with nature, the splashed and gestural marks evoking sea spray or wave movements respectively.

Scraped down surfaces were pictorial equivalents to the process of filing down and refining marble or wood. The use of line to connect deep space with surface or else to identify ideal formal relationships, assumes a visionary quality. The ground, on the other hand, is coloured and textured in a manner that evokes nature while softening the impact of pure geometric conceptions. Hepworth is not as versatile a draughtsman as Ben Nicholson; she lacks his linear athleticism and her line is more 'wooden'. Yet, its use alongside, or rather on top of colour is one that represents a search for sculptural form, a form conceived in the third dimension, though relayed in the flat pictorial context of pencil and paint on board. Pictorial illusionism is not an aim; rather she seeks out of a given abstract, even mathematically precise language of pure form a symbolic significance where, to quote Hammacher, 'the natural and the human have become metaphorical'*7 The same writer concludes that 'the harmony in her work is not a classical harmony, but a spiritual accord between the abstract and her feeling for nature'*8 Yet, this harmony is a quintessentially visual one. The absolute and static grouped forms in the small bronze and marble sculptures of the 1960's relate to one another through time and space… as the viewer walks around new aspects emerge and the shapes yield differing relationships to one another; a factor as much to do with the fluctuating play of light as with the relative positioning of forms to one another. The dual and triple forms on a single base thus create a unity through many related facets of visual explorations. They are not altogether inert sculptures but are ones that require an active response from the spectator.

The group forms, originating in marble carvings like 'Group (People waiting)' (1952), become more common in the late period. The groups perhaps became humanistic metaphors for the importance of the individual in the context of the larger crowd. The relationship of the single to the whole, seen in overlapping as well as in dispersed shapes, forms an important theme in her mature work. She is a master of oblique reference, association and metaphor. Even in the most geometric sculptures, Hepworth maintains an oblique link with nature in terms of the organic wood, marble or stone materials she uses. Paradoxically, more openly suggestive natural forms, such as we see in 'Sea Form, Porthmeor' (1958), require the industrial material and process of cast bronze. Two of Hepworth's largest works, 'Four-square (walk through)' (1966) and 'The Family of Man' (1970) take the idea of the group further, by introducing an unprecedented degree of stacking. Hepworth's late interest in stacking - seen also in white marbles like 'Three part vertical' (1971) - assumes the metaphorical significance of an ascension, a personal ascension in the face of an inevitable and approaching demise. The totemic drama of 'The family' bronzes perhaps emphasises continuity and the oneness of

51

humanity. These large environment-sized works also allude to the architectural, for they invite human entry in the form of a walk through. There is something of Brancusi in her stacked mode using minimal components; something, too, of Stonehenge and the architecture of neolithic man, inviting in visual terms a powerful meeting between the inner and outer cosmos, counterpoised in the concrete form of the present time and place.

NOTES

1.   Miriam Gabo. Letter to the author. Dec. 7, 1982.
2.   Miriam Gabo. Letter to the author. Dec. 7, 1982.
3.   Herbert Read. *Barbara Hepworth* (London: Lund Humphries) 1952.
4.   Barbara Hepworth. Letter to Sven Berlin. Feb. 21, 1944.
5.   A.M. Hammacher. *Barbara Hepworth* p.109. Thames and Hudson 1968.
6.   Tom Cross. *Painting the Warmth of the Sun* p.115. Alison Hodge 1984.
7.   A.M. Hammacher. *Barbara Hepworth* p.174. 1968.
8.   A.M. Hammacher. *Barbara Hepworth* p.186.

CHAPTER 4

In the shadow of a giant tree

In the early days before Barbara Hepworth, St. Ives was exclusively a painter's colony, attracting mainly middle class post-impressionist painters of the landscape. They were attracted, like most of us, by the physical geographical beauty, but the special light and atmosphere added an extra dimension for the plein-air artist seeking professional inspiration. During the 1920's the craft of creative pottery was established in St. Ives through Bernard Leach and his Japanese associate Shoji Hamada (1891-1978). Leach's preoccupation with reviving the ancient craft of creative pottery took it into the innovatory orbit of the modern movement, while his pusuit of three dimensional form through ceramics hoisted the aesthetic value of the object over its functional aspects and made it worthy of prime consideration. No sculptors worked in St. Ives before Hepworth but her abstract style, evolved in the sophisticated aesthetic atmosphere of Paris and London, echoed the pure shapes and stylised forms of modern pottery.

Hepworth was 36 years old when she alighted on St. Ives as a domestic refugee from what was soon to become war-torn London. During the course of the 1950's her presence in St. Ives led to the establishment of one of the most professional and internationally acknowledged of all creative studios in British sculpture. Her success also made possible the formation of a group of emerging sculptors who learnt their trade in her atelier and came to know her work inside out. Like Moore she did not encourage potential rivals to her own crown. On the other hand her working studio had the unwitting effect of launching the careers of several sculptors to a greater extent than ever happened at Much Hadham, the notable example of Anthony Caro notwithstanding. But Brancusi's famous remark, made in reference to the colossal presence of Rodin, that nothing grew in the shadow of giant trees is borne out in the case of the band of Trewyn assistants who had to leave her hegmonic presence before properly striking out on their own. Even then Hepworth's reputation continued to be a kind of eminence gris for these sculptors, most of whom found themselves in important public collections, notably the Tate, probably in advance of their time. In this chapter the half dozen sculptors who emerged from under her wing are looked at retrospectively as mature artists in their own right. The most important of them, Denis Mitchell, came to Cornwall from south Wales in 1930, aged only 18.

The sculptor who therefore most clearly emerges from under the shadow of Hepworth is Denis Mitchell (1912-1993). One of the greatest craftsmen in post-war British sculpture, his importance to Cornish, and therefore British art has yet to be fully appreciated. He was literally her right hand man during the years of ascendency in the 1950's. At a time when traditional craftsmanship is unfashionable and viewed as delaying the spontaneous urge of individual expression, Mitchell's painstakingly executed oeuvre of sparkling bronzes, refined woods and clean-cut slates reminds us of the classical virtues of poise,

Denis Mitchell.

strength, balance and formal perfection. These works were displayed by Angela Flowers at her Hackney gallery in the spring of 1993. The artist died during the show, turning a long overdue London celebration of his achievement into a memorial exhibition. The sculptures are generally slim, often frontal or relief-like, contrasting with Hepworth's rounder forms. The later slates have an emollient geometry. He titled the sculptures with Cornish names in a way that reminds us of the Cornishness of his entire oeuvre. Something of the unyielding character of Cornwall's granite landscape enters his work. Timelessness is not only a classic quality associated with the Latin world, for in sub Mediterranean Cornwall something of the same pervades the culture. Mitchell's spiralling corkscrew or fish-hook shapes clearly derive from the tools of his trade as a fisherman and miner.

Constantine Brancusi employed the shapes and techniques of traditional Romanian folk carving, identifying with functional everyday objects such as tables, chairs, gateways and so on. Similarly, Mitchell used uniquely Cornish

Denis Mitchell's studio.

materials such as Delabole slate, named the results after Cornish place names, and finally extracted from functional objects and tools of local mining and fishing industries shapes that would inform his abstract sculpture. But allowing the material an excessive role in shaping the final form - an essential part of the 'truth to materials' ethos of modernist practice - was too self-conscious an approach for Brancusi. Mitchell was also too much of an honest craftsman to depend on the ideology of others and any involvement in this aesthetic cult would only have come about through the Hepworth atelier, and then perhaps only as a semi-conscious mode. After visiting Columbia on a British Council tour, Mitchell collected tribal carvings whose shapes provided ideas in subsequent work.

Denis Mitchell was born in Middlesex but grew up in Swansea (a boyhood friend in south Wales was Dylan Thomas). His father left home early, leaving the mother to bring up both Denis and his brother Endell alone. The matriarchial influence in Denis's life was dominant and his long 11 year apprenticeship with Barbara Hepworth, his marriage to a local St. Ives girl Jane Stevens in 1939 and the birth of three daughters, continued an influence that is sometimes borne out in the sculpture, as we see in the figural duos and trios and in the mother and child carvings. In 1930 Denis and Endell impecuniously adopted Cornwall as their home. They renovated and later lived in an aunt's cottage. Although Mitchell was painting landscapes as a part-time recreational activity (he was self-taught) he worked on a market garden and generally relied on making a living from the land. This continued throughout the war, a period that saw him fish and work down Geevor mine near St. Just. An important early contact was Bernard Leach, like himself in the Home Guard, and manual skills led to Mitchell undertaking odd jobs not only at the Leach pottery, but also at Adrian Stokes's market garden and at Guido Morris's printing works. The artist wrote that his aim in painting 'is to be as uninfluenced as possible and to develop my outlook on Cornish landscape as felt and seen through my job of working on the land and under it in the mine, and around it on the sea, which gives me a much more intimate feeling towards it.'

His earliest paintings have a charming simplicity and directness and certainly convey the experience-based association with the landscape that is a quintessential feature of St. Ives art. Unintentionally, they subvert a thirties feeling of calm and elegance with an at times awkward, but nonetheless direct and forthright handling. The landscapes are lively with a limpid light - Stanhope Forbes once remarked that he liked Mitchell's animated skies - and an orchestration of greys, light blues and a muted, even chalky range of greens, gives to these landscape studies a breezy atmosphere perhaps suggesting that the outdoors was the artist's favoured location. A broad dichotomy seems to exist between the landscape-orientated plain airists, so popular around the pier during the pre-war days, and the post-war abstractionists who were altogether more secretive and closeted away in their professional studios out of the public gaze. Here they pursued explorations into the non-figurative sphere of pure geometric form with the same intensity as nuclear physicists engaged on some highly secret abstract project. (No wonder Nicholson and a number of his circle were interested in Christian Science). The point about Mitchell's early work, in both painting and sculpture, was that it belonged to the earlier period.

As we have already seen, the artist's earliest sculptures in wood, such as 'Ballet Dancer' (1949) in holly wood, and 'Maternal Form' (1950) in elm wood, show the early matriarchal influence. Tentative compared to later abstract wood carvings such as the superb 'Porthgwarra' (1961), these earliest carvings show a predilection for upward rhythm and for an active dialogue between interior and exterior form. The instistent upright rhythm is a apparent in 'Arch Priest' and reaches full force in the tall column-like corkscrew spiral of 'Zelah' (1963) in bronze. Likewise, the investigation of both internal and external aspects of form - both for Hepworth and for Mitchell the most effective means of introducing complexity into the minimal format of the carved monolith - led to an adventurous and indeed playful adaptation of Hepworth's famous 'polo-mint' cavity. Whereas she controlled the cavity, either by limiting its number in any single piece to perhaps just 2 or 3, or else by making it conform to an organic spiral, Mitchell sometimes used it with abandon. His cavities could be rectangular as well as circular. 'Carn' (1961) is a good example. In 'Carnellow' (1975) a 4 foot tall bronze, he uses no fewer than six large cavities, which have an unpredictable bubble-like movement up the central axis. The open embrace of early 'Maternal' themes is discernible in this exquisite late bronze: human content that is, however, all but submerged in the formal abstraction.

During the mid 1950's Mitchell's energies were taken over by duties at Trewyn, leaving his own output relatively meagre. The painter Dod Proctor gave John Wells a fallen cherry tree, and Wells passed it on to the sculptor, who went on to carve a so-called 'Primitive Figure' and a 'Cherrywood Form' in 1955. The tall column-like object has a thrusting upright movement and carries 3 cavities - a smaller one at base, a large one at 'middrift' and another in the form of an opened-up top. The twin pinnacles of 'Cherrywood Form' seem to correspond to raised arms, perhaps in ritualistic gestation. Soon afterwards the sculptor carved guarea, elm, iroko, and the superb African hardwood lignum vitae. The use of guarea culminated in one of his finest carvings, 'Porthgwarra' (1961). This horizontal piece has a pronounced linear movement that disappears into a large central cavity. The overall shape could suggest a dolphin head, a fish or a landscape. Either way timelessness and the gradual shaping of the form and material are the themes at play here. As is the case with the work of Bernard Leach, the suggestion is made of the play of natural forces, a kind of automatic overdrive that absorbs the processes of human interaction in the shaping of the material.

In 1956 Barbara Hepworth began working in bronze. Mitchell followed in 1958, and thereafter used bronze as his prime material. One innovation he can call his own is the way that rough bronze casts, returned from the foundries, were subsequently subjected to hours of laborious filing and chiselling. The results were extraordinarily beautiful surfaces containing a rhythmic interplay between the smooth and hewn, the polished and patinated, the convex and concave. Carving really was his forte, extending even to post-casting stages.

His most personal mode of expression, it conveyed that uncanny mix of tenacity and sensitivity. In the final analysis Mitchell's main contribution lies in the painstaking but rewarding perfectionism of finishing bronze. His first sculpture in this material, 'Zawn' (1958) has a zigzagging upward thrust that points to the aforementioned corkscrews of the early 1960's 'Zelah' series. Ready-made source material for the shapes lay with the implements such as fish hooks, screws, spades or drills that he had used in earlier fishing, mining or gardening activities. Thus Mitchell identified not only with the materials but also the tools with which he was working. The procedural influences that were brought to bear on the final outcome should not detract from the conceptual element, for Mitchell's work has a designed poise and elegance. Tom Cross wrote in 'Painting the Warmth of the Sun' about 'the oval standing form, flattened and pierced' and suggested that the sources may have been the 'abstracted flying forms of fish or bird, or those associated with man-made implements.' [1] Nowhere is the association with an implement more in evidence than in 'Porthcressa' an unusually tall asymmetric bronze of 1961 which resembles an anchor or hook, with its two forked upright forms.

Mitchell was gradually mastering his craft at Trewyn during the 1950's. 'I learnt that even on a very large scale carving, less than a hair's breadth rubbed

Denis Mitchell. Tresco. Slate, 1984.

58

off with emery paper could alter the whole sculpture.' He was thus prepared for the vital final workings on bronze, wood or slate. The professional imperatives of the Hepworth atelier induced on his own sculptural practise the quintessential principle of formal refinement. Between 1955 and 1957 he was chairman of the strife-torn Penwith; his association both with that institution and with Hepworth opened many doors. In 1959 he had a one man show at the A.I.A. galleries in London, followed in 1961 by a solo show at Waddington's. Since that time his principal exhibitions have been at the Arnolfini in 1967 - in those days showing contemporary art from Cornwall in a way it has ceased to do during the succeeding decades - with Marjorie Parr during the late 1960's, at Cyril Gerber's Compass Gallery in Glasgow in 1973, at the Glyn Vivian Art Gallery in his hometown of Swansea in 1979, and most spectacularly a large 80th birthday showing at the Penwith in the summer of 1992. This was a well-attended tribute to a half century of activity and in particular high-lighted the technical accomplishment, refinement and sheer beauty of his late work, those exquisitely perfected pieces of the period since the mid 1980's St. Ives retrospective at the London Tate. These works show how one of the less original sculptors of the 1950's and 60's could, through earnest endeavour and dedication to pure refinement within a limited formal range, hoist himself into the front rank of post-war British sculpture. He never felt the need to try out new technological materials for their own sake. By sticking to his guns within a narrow formal range the work never looks dated in the way that once fashionable avant-garde sculptures of the 1960's do.

Mitchell moved from St. Ives to Newlyn in 1969, perhaps as much to avoid the unprecedented onslaught of tourism as to stake his own claims as an independent sculptor. Yet in these later years he shared a Newlyn studio with John Wells. Together they perpetuated the abstract and constructive, yet also lyrical principles that Ben Nicholson and Barbara Hepworth, as sophisticated urbanites, first brought down to Cornwall in 1939. In 1967 Mitchell left part-time teaching at Penzance Grammar School and at the Redruth Art School to concentrate entirely on his work. Since then he used Delabole slate which was worked to great precision, a result of pre-designed concepts and the use of efficient mechanical tools. The slates often have the simple presence of the gravestone, seen in 'Carngarrow' (1984) or 'Tresco' of the same year. The rounded rectangle of 'Tresco' is bitten into with a large central disc which uses its rough hewn surface, fractionally below the perfectly smoothed outer 'skin', to radiate like a sun or the strings of a Gabo construction. 'Tresco' is a good example of the device, also exploited in the alternatively polished and patinated surfaces of the bronzes, that the artist employs in order to create textural and visual variety within the overall symmetry. The grain running across the lower part of 'Tresco' adds further play within a minimal format, and is exploited also in the wood and marble carvings throughout all phases of his work. He was no doubt alerted to the expressive possibilities thrown up by grains while carving some of Hepworth's pieces during the 1950's. During the mid 1980's Mitchell also produced a number of fresh, crisply carved, wood sculptures, such as 'Bolingey', mainly in lignum vitae. The cavities enter from the top and seem to all but open up the enclosed volume of the central mass to the outside world. At the same time the elongated shaping of the cavities reflects the actual movement and thrust of the chisel.

Breon O'Casey was another skilled craftsman who came to Trewyn studio as a sculpture assistant, replacing Mitchell in the early 1960's; the latter gave him a grounding in basic skills a few years earlier. By the 1960's Hepworth was too successful to have the time to teach assistants herself and, furthermore, by this later stage in her career, relied more than ever on delegating physical execution of the works to a team of trusted and competent helpers. It is a measure both of Mitchell's talent for imparting secrets of the trade and of O'Casey's manual gifts that he quickly graduated from Mitchell's studio into a 'heavy duty' Trewyn assistant. He worked there on a part-time basis for three years. He was not a sculptor, for the small metal objects he made developed from the craft of jewellery-making. O'Casey's obvious facility for working with metal was exploited by Hepworth, who asked him to make a number of sculptures in silver or bronze sheets based on her plaster or wood maquettes. As far as his own work is concerned, O'Casey enjoys the effect of pattern, both in etchings, paintings and weaved fabrics. These patterns integrate cubist silhouettes with ancient Celtic symbols. The paintings are spare and the soft rectangles or circles of colour carry an emblematic air; the intellectual clarity and calculated geometry of other St. Ives artists is absent. At the same time, O'Casey favours a slow and deliberate working process and for this reason began weaving in the 1960's. Weaving was the closest that painstaking craft could come to the more immediate and inventive orbit of pictorial art. The abstract colour shapes and patterns produced with wool and other materials emulated the visual creativity of contemporary painting while also fulfilling the demands and rigors of craftsmanship.

In both vertical and horizontal sculptures Robert Adams (1917-1984) also made use of abstract shapes that converge and enfold space. Meeting Adams by chance at Kettles Yard in 1983 enabled me to hear the sculptor explain how such simple pinching gestures informed the shapes of many of his abstract sculptures. Adams spent a year working in St. Ives and once owned the house in Pilgrim's Walk, Hampstead where Ben Nicholson lived during the final period of his life. Mitchell knew Adams well, and they respected one another's work, sharing many characteristics. Since 1952 Adams often visited Cornwall to see friends such as Mitchell, Barns-Graham, Leigh and Frost. But in the mid 1970's the Essex-based sculptor took on the post of Head of Sculpture at Falmouth and during 1975/76 rented a St. Ives cottage. As Alastair Grieve has pointed out in his comprehensive survey of Adams's oeuvre, he changed direction in his later work after the emergence of the St. Martin's 'New Generation' and the spectacular success of Caro's 1969 Hayward exhibition. Adams, a pioneer of British constructed steel sculpture in the 1950's, was outmanoevred during the next decade by the greater radicalism of Caro's huge, floor-based and plinth-free structures. Adams's welded pieces retained the more discreet, conventional format of Gonzalez's 'totems' - only when executing the few architectural commissions for which his talent was best suited did he work on a large 'heroic' scale, though even here his work was based on a predetermined design, for as Lawrence Alloway once explained he was not an artist to 'melt, bury or fracture platonic geometry.' Producing bronzes on a smaller scale therefore seemed a timely and integral way forward at the same time as fulfilling commercial imperatives. Grieve noted that 'his way forward lay in a return to traditional sculpture's materials and to techniques and forms which link him to the 'School of St. Ives' rather than the London or New York avant-garde. Adams's post '68 sculpture can be related to Nicholson, to Hepworth and to Hepworth's ex-assistants, particularly Denis Mitchell.' [*2] Indeed, Adams considered a move to St. Ives in 1968 but had been discouraged by the distance from London. Marjorie Parr, who exhibited Mitchell, Milne and other St. Ives artists also began to show Adams's later bronzes.

From the early 1950's onwards Adams's work walked similar paths to those of Hepworth and her assistants. The artist's early use of steel, brass and iron rods resulted in thin tripod-like figures whose gaunt, features and makeshift appearance expressed the anxiety of the atomic age. They employ a formal language suggested by Picasso's wire constructions of 1930. But in contrast to the more romantic or evocative sculptors of the period, (such as Butler and Chadwick), Adam's use of vertical and horizontal, of straight lines and arcs created an architectonic balance calculated to conform to that other side of post-war feeling - the construction of an ordered new world. In spite of a fondness for welding metal, Adams continued to share with his St. Ives friends a predilection for carving. Early wood carvings, in birch, holly and African woods, retained an association with the originating block. The late bronzes were cast in sand moulds at a marine foundry and treated with liver of sulphur. These created uniquely dark and uniform textures counterpoising untouched bronze surfaces. They were cast, not from the usual plaster models but rather from carved wood ones, a material that once again provided subtle resonance to the undulating surfaces of the final bronze shapes.

The early carvings have an affinity with tribal sculpture in terms of a simple, vertical frontality; the pirouetting, conical forms reflect an engineering sensibility. In the Tate's 1949 yew figure 'Dancer' Adams expores the structural behaviour of forms in a dynamic and unpredictable way not found in Mitchell's or Hepworth's contemporaneous monolithic carvings. Adams's use of tilted cones perched on tapered points show the pervading early influence of Brancusi. Through the exacting medium of woodcarving, Adams managed to convey what Grieve described as 'a flow of inter-locked forms down, around and throughout the entire work.' [*3] This was partly achieved by the additive process of jointing, wood's equivalent to the soldering or welding processes of the metal works. Although Adams was an individual and never worked for her, he was often in the shadow of Hepworth, particularly in those carvings like 'Bud' that used enfolding, wavelike forms reminiscent of the older artist's 1946 carving 'Pelagos'.

Adams was innovatory in his early adoption of bronze in 1953. He continued to pursue in this ponderous medium the earlier interest in counterbalance, and some of the cast pieces of the 1950's continue to enact, through a simple planar balance, the same balletic or cantilevered forms in space that had been achieved in the welded pieces. He also started to spray the steel constructs with thin coatings of bronze, to enrich and protect. By 1960 he used brazened rods to create spiral or triangular forms and later made semi-transparent screens welded from hundreds of tiny metal fragments. The playfulness of his sensibility characterised him as innovatory within his own terms of reference rather than within the overall development of modern sculpture. This playfulness was anchored to discipline, however, and to the dictates of the material being crafted. By the early 1970's he was creating the 'Slim Bronze' series that comes close to Mitchell. Grieve's assessment of Mitchell's sculpture as using forms that were often 'symmetrical, like Hepworth's, with circular hollows and cleavages suggesting very abstracted details of the human body' seems to be less true for Adams's more architectural bronzes. In a series of wave-form sculptures, among them 'Link' (1973) Adams echoes the crashing forms originally presaged by Hepworth, and since employed by Mitchell and Milne. In contrast to the latter pair, Adams was a sculptor whose main body of work, skirting the post-war British Constructivist school, was considerably less dependent on Hepworth's or Moore's reference to landscape sources. Nevertheless Grieve is correct in acknowledging her influence in Adams's later small bronzes. His 'Two bronze forms' of 1978 allows Grieve to point out that 'combining two sculptures on one base possibly derives from Hepworth' and that 'Adams was no doubt like her, also inspired by grouped, neolithic Standing Stones in Penwith'[*4] In a 1979 bronze 'Crescent' Adam bites into a circular bronze to create an enfolding, pinching effect that comes very close to Mitchell's circular slate 'Endoc', whose circumference is incised with a number of keyhole-shaped sockets.

After Denis Mitchell, John Milne (1931-78) was probably the sculptor who owed most to the example of Hepworth. Milne was born in Eccles. He studied art after the war at Salford Technical College. His sculpture sources are diverse, foreign and exotic, even while being formally indebted to Hepwoth's reductive precisionism. J.P. Hodin, author of a monograph on Milne, argued that Milne belongs to a classical strand of modernist sculpture. The classical character of his work, whether representational or abstract, could be clearly seen in early figures, which in swelling terms reveal an unmistakeable debt to both Dobson and Maillol. His interest in sculpture predated the classical, however, and he delighted in studying sculpture of past civilisations in the great museums of Manchester, London, and above all Paris. Later on, journeys to north Africa, Greece and the Middle East enabled him to use architectural features as originating ideas for his sculpture. Milne, who studied for a short time under Auricoste at the Grand Chaumiere in Paris, had a more cosmopolitan education than Mitchell. Milne's early terra-cotta figures such as 'Seated Figure' were swelling voluptuous forms, full of tactile reference and embellished with extra, anatomic details like the ripples of thin drapery across sensual, fleshy surfaces.

Milne's student work was based on wood or terra-cotta but after his apprenticeship to Barbara Hepworth in 1953 he opted for carving and bronze casting as favoured modes of expression. In common with Mitchell he specialised in a use of bronze that exploited to the full the contrast of polished and patinated surface; perhaps on occasion he emulated Hepworth's rather unsure and belated use of bronze. Surface pattern persisted in Milne's work from the early terra-cottas onwards, while a predilection for pronounced, linear stylisation, for streamlined arabesque reflected the suave elegance of the man himself. In the rectangular format of his metal reliefs, sparkling shapes, suggestive of the organic, vie with ribbed or striated surrounds. The shapes, both in the reliefs and in many of the free-standing sculptures, recall petals, boats, rigging or architectural features like temples, viaducts, arches or obelisks. The reliefs culminate in the beautiful 'Icarus' of 1967 - in the cold cast aluminium whose use he learnt that year from Allan Dunn, technician at Falmouth Art School. This fine relief uses a pair of shapes derived from anchors. The intermittent reliefs are among his most personal creations. He followed Mitchell's example in chiselling, filing, patinating and generally perfecting the object after it had left the foundry.

Drawing in charcoal was another of the ways in which Milne distinguished himself from his contemporaries, for he used charcaol generously, confidently, and with a broad feeling for rubbed texture. Linear precision held less interest for him in his graphic work, which is planned while also being expressionistic. Control and exuberance characterise his charcoal drawing. The compositions adhered to a systematic geometric order that sometimes emphasised a spiralling, linear energy. A sweeping, rhythmic energy animated these drawings, promoting Hepworth to detect relatively early on that his drawing was advanced. She told him that, 'When your sculpture is as good as your drawing you will have arrived.' Hodin wrote that in Cornwall, 'he started to think in large compact forms', in response to the chunky outcrops of the Cornish landscape. His drawings were not precise plans for three dimensional work nor experiments in the spatial dynamics of figurative form, but rather ran parallel to the sculpture as independent expressions of his broad feeling for surface, movement and direction.

During the 1950's Milne displayed in his work the lessons of direct carving in wood and stone that he had learnt in the ineluctable presence of Trewyn, (in a sense he never left for he became a neighbour and later executed a large bronze 'Monolith' sited as a memorial to the revered Hepworth in nearby Trewyn Gardens). Thus he produced a 'Vertical Form' in Nigerian guarea in 1954, a carving that comes close to Hepworth with its upright curvatures and undulating continuities. The Brancusi-inspired 'Kiss', (the title is Rodinian), in Portland stone was notable for the way the artist retained correspondence between the image, with its neo-cubist scarifications, and the form of the originating block. Milne squared off the forms, avoiding roundness or prettiness in a way that suggests his main source of inspiration were the pillar-like forms of Egyptian and archaic sculpture rather than the sweet naturalism and rotund classicism of later Greek art. This was probably a conscious effect, given the early studies that he had made in the ethnic departments of major museums. The cube-like form of this inchoate sculpture points forward to an increasing simplification and abstraction. In 'Gnathos' paring down to essentials has reached an advanced stage, for in this large, polished bronze of 1966 we have to rely on the title, (Gnathos is a Greek word meaning jaw), to give us any sense of what two protruding forms, that almost touch in a pinching posture, may mean. This is one of the artist's most accomplished works and was included in the Tate's 1985 St. Ives retrospective.

In 1967 Milne visited Morocco, a country where, according to Hodin, 'the majesty of the desert, an endless, wavy sea of sand the vastness of a space filled with a beauty unknown to him', made a huge impression. New bronzes, unorthodox in the degree to which landscape was directly evoked, resulted in works like 'Atlas' and 'Corinthos'. The latter is cut into by two vertical shafts,

John Milne. Bronze, 1970's.
Photo: Robin Davies.

as if alluding to a canal. However, the degree of abstraction is such that it takes a title to fully alert us to the fact of what the source material may be. More axiomatic are some of the bronzes, upright and totem-like, produced in the late 1960's and early 1970's where he uses 'C' or 'U' shapes as components in stacked configurations. In 'Hera' or 'Phobus' (1971) he uses pure alphabet forms, shed of normal associative functions. These ingenious devices, which anticipate Roger Leigh's ceramic letters of his 'potplant' sculptures, owe a debt to the stacked totems of Smith's late cubes and Brancusi's Column. In a more textured sculpture like 'Easter Island Form' Milne responded to a pre-historical context in an attempt to discard sophistication and any hint of modernist academia. How successful the attempt may be is open to debate. By the 1970's the abstract bronzes only disclose their sources through titles or through the broadest allusion to architectual form. Perhaps the artist was looking for an equivalent to Hepworth's megalith and standing stone sources when he used similarly ancient, if more exotic, middle-eastern pyramid or aqueduct forms. Throughout the 1960's he visited Greece each year, where he gathered many ideas. Hepworth also loved Greece and her carving 'Pelagos' of 1946 is recalled in a late Milne bronze of thirty years later, called 'Wave Turning'. The choice of theme is similar though Milne's sculpture uses flat facets and a squareish format with which to create a similarly determined interplay between internal and exterior form.

Unfortunately John Milne never lived long enough to effectively develop his art out of the magnetic shadow of Hepworth. He was an unhappy man, though a popular and social one. He was a renowned host who never set up a snob barrier between artists and the rest. His death in 1978 at the early age of 47 was a loss to St. Ives, particularly coming so soon after Hepworth's. He produced some elegantly designed and refined bronzes during his twenty-five year career in the town. He mixed the local marine influence, epitomised in large bronzes of anchor forms, with a more sophisticated and exotic interest in Arabic culture. This resulted in a subtle intonation to the essential orthodoxy of the Hepworth school.

Roger Leigh, who was six years older than John Milne, also entered the Hepworth atelier armed with a visual education that, in his case, gave him a knowledge of modern architecture. Leigh, who served in the RAF, succumbed to the will of vocation-minded parents and studied architecture at Liverpool University. He saw Hepworth's work for the first time there. A staff member of the architecture school was given one of her ovoid sculptures dating from the late 1930's as a retiring present. The minimal design and smooth, refined surface were too subtle to make much of an impression on a young student although in 1948, on the way to Italy on a Liverpool architecture school trip, he saw the work of Moore, Hepworth and Epstein at the Battersea Park open air sculpture exhibition. This experience was a catalyst, triggering a desire to make sculpture. Thereafter he started to carve stylised figures from cherry woods picked up near his parent's home in Gloucestershire. There was little time to pursue carving on the course in Liverpool, though, so he had to restrict the furtherance of sculpture to holidays. Nonetheless, Leigh gained valuable artistic experience from the Liverpool years; he attended Arthur Ballard's Saturday morning life drawing sessions at the art school, where June Furlong was the model, and he also learnt to throw pots with Stan English at the college. This introduction to pottery was significant for an artist who later made close friends with Bernard Leach in St. Ives and later still made ceramic sculptures based on alphabetical shapes. These broke down the distinction between utility craft object and fine art by functioning also as plant containers. The Bluecoat provided a lively artistic and social centre in Liverpool and there he saw the best of local art.

After Liverpool, Leigh sought work in an active sculpture studio and, having failed to secure a place in Henry Moore's workshop, was accepted by Barbara Hepworth, who valued his architectural background. She felt this would be compatible with her reductive approach. They met at the Tate opening for the Unknown Political Prisoner exhibition - Hepworth was runner-up to Reg Butler - and a time was fixed for Leigh to begin work at Trewyn. He lived in her cottage opposite for the first few months, which was 'rather like going into Kettles Yard'.[*5] He worked four days a week for a period of a year. His partner was Denis Mitchell, who guided him and seemed to understand exactly what she wanted even though instructions were often as vague as a scant chalk outline on a stone or wood block, or else general instructions by word of mouth. Leigh's first job was 'Monolith', the large blue limestone which was shown at her retrospective at the Whitechapel in April 1954. The carving of 'Monolith' was done by Mitchell and Hepworth, though Leigh finished the job by smoothing off the surface with files. Like everyone else who had entered Hepworth's working life, he was impressed by her dedicated professionalism. Plans for sculptures were conceived in her mind. 'She had an incredible perception of what she wanted from the start,' Leigh later recalled, 'and we saw no working drawings'.[*6] If absent for a week or more, she left her team of helpers with a demanding schedule of tasks. Unaided by mechanical tools, Leigh and Mitchell, sometimes supported by the Welsh wood sculptor Tom Pearce and the South African abstract painter Stanley Dorfman, would execute wood carvings entirely by hand. Later on, however, stone surfaces were finished with high speed grinding discs and a rock percussion drill.

Duties extended beyond studio carving; assistants broke normal working hours on occasions, working into the night if presented with a deadline. Leigh and Mitchell stayed in London a whole month while preparing for her large Whitechapel show. They even did gardening at Trewyn and were called upon to move large works onto a lorry. Leigh once went by taxi to the Morris Singer Foundry in London, where he took a plaster to be cast.

The professional atmosphere that so impressed newcomers had the disadvantage of leading to an over-serious working ambience. At the best of times she lacked natural or spontaneous humour. The proceedings were fairly brisk and business-like; her children were not allowed to talk to the assistants, who were often moved out of the way to do some gardening or plasterwork in the greenhouse studio if important visitors came. It was a rare occasion when she paid attention to their work. Worldly success was everything to her, and perhaps therefore the serious note had something to do with economics. Even in the mid-fifties she threatened to lay off assistants as an economy drive, and she had to sell a Mondrian grid painting for £11,000 to stave off debts. Whistling and singing were generally frowned upon. If she went away they let their hair down for a while, though sweated it out to ensure that allocated tasks were completed in time for her return. Tom Cross draws attention to the serious atmosphere by alluding to the 'terrifying intensity' of the studio. Cross went on to identify that 'singlemindedness and insistence on the highest standards in her work gave the impression that she was lacking in humour.'*7

After lodging in Trewyn Cottage, Leigh moved into a cottage owned by Endell Mitchell in Hick's Court and there began the earliest of his St. Ives carvings. Sven Berlin, the self-styled sculptor of carved figures in the Gaudier/

Roger Leigh. Axil. *Bronze, 1964.*

Epstein mould, left St. Ives in 1953 almost as a refuge from the ethos that had taken root in the Hepworth atelier. Berlin abandoned some lignum vitae and alabaster in his Cripplesease studio. Leigh rescued the material with Mitchell and from it made some small alabaster carvings. Hepworth, visiting Leigh for supper, admired a stylised bull that she saw. She later gave him an informal 'crit' of carvings that he brought to show her at Trewyn. She sponsored him for his first few appearances in Penwith exhibitions, and soon after proved helpful in his becoming a full member.

Roger Leigh's spell at Trewyn was formative, though he wanted to practice as an architect and was not fully committed to sculpture. He moved to London and worked for the L.C.C. until 1957, designing warehouses and old people's homes. He made small sculptures in the basement of his Chelsea flat, works that he sold, and through this private activity the desire to make more sculptures returned. Meanwhile Hepworth was evidently missing her assistant; she even phoned a friend, Priaulx Rainer in search of Leigh's address. The telephone operator, Yankel Feather overheard the conversation, and the former Liverpool artist interrupted. Leigh later recalled that 'Priaulx eventually gave Hepworth my phone number, but she was so affronted to have her conversation interrupted by a telephonist, who even knew the answer to her query.'[8] Much required by Hepworth, Leigh returned to Trewyn in 1957. With earnings from London, he purchased a cheap, rundown cottage in Nancledra and acquired a car, which enabled him easy access to St. Ives.

Roger Leigh. Tump. *Painted clay, 1990.*

Leigh began constructing with wood or steel units, creating an intriguing complexity from a simple range of forms. He also modelled concrete across steel mesh. Such processes indicated an interest in the architectural and a commission for Mutley Properties in Bootle, Merseyside resulted in the large 'Sagitta II' (1965). The thrusting lines and interlocking chevron units of the piece matched the supporting stilts of the building. On a smaller scale, too, Leigh constructed with the same simple chevrons that extrude like branches at variously tipped angles from the sculpture's central stem. A vertical bronze of 1964 'Axil' shows how complexity can result from variations on a simple formal theme. These structural units fulfill a quasi architectural role in the language of sculpture. Suggestions of the organic stemmed from the displacement of form; the same use of repeated units characterise the later ceramic sculptures, like 'Tump', (1990), that also function as plant receptacles. The use of alphabet shapes carries Duchampian overtones especially in the way that familiar form, when seen in new and unusual settings, sets off mystery.

The wood pieces constructed in his Nancledra garden were coated with bronze, copper or zinc powders. Polyester resins were also used to seal, protect and give a uniform skin to varying hard or soft woods. Encouraged by Brian Wall, Leigh started welding steel and was inspired by the Spanish sculptor Chillida, whose work he had seen in magazines and which offered a healthy and much needed alternative to Hepworth. He learnt from Chillida the importance of forms reaching out into surrounding space with expressive force. Leigh's efforts to branch out on his own did not go unnoticed at the time, and he was visited by Philip James, director of the Arts Council, as well as by many contemporaries and artists.

But he was unable to live solely from his sculpture, and taught architecture and town planning at Camborne for a number of years around the turn of the 1960's. He also taught pottery at a school in Camborne between 1961 and 1963. Jack Pender was an art master at this school. Originally introduced to practical pottery by Bruce Taylor in St. Ives, Leigh had for sometime felt drawn to potters and had befriended the Leach family, (he played Hockey for Penzance with David Leach). His new wife Pat worked for the Leach pottery throughout most of the 1960's. During the middle years of that decade Leigh practised as an architect again, this time locally in Truro, though he continued to produce some sculpture. Indeed he showed during the late 1950's at the Drian and Waddington galleries in London and in 1964 had a show at Denis Bowen's New Vision Centre. He also taught for the first time at an art college, in the foundation sculpture department of Falmouth art college. In 1966 he felt the need for a change and left Cornwall for Wiltshire. At the suggestion of Michael Snow he successfully applied for a teaching post at Exeter College of Art, where he taught for the next two decades until retirement.

Leigh used the Holman foundry in St. Just to cast bronzes. During the second half of the 1950's metal suddenly assumed greater significance in local sculpture, and Hepworth, as well as producing her first bronzes, also created some elegant pieces from folded zinc sheets, curved and cut and stringed. Leigh could not fail to be swayed by the new age of metal, but it was Brian Wall who most forcibly waded into the medium, using steel as an exclusive material and the processes of welding as his key process. Wall, born in London in 1931, was appropriately the son of an aircraft mechanic. Probably this influenced Wall's adoption of steel as a favoured sculptural material.

Roger Leigh, Bruce Taylor, Gwen Leitch, Denis Mitchell, Brian Wall and Misome Peile at Drian Gallery, July 1958.

Evacuated to Yorkshire during the war, where he would have gained some appreciation for the same bareknuckled landscape that had earlier inspired Moore and Hepworth, Wall later returned to the south east. Before his national service in the Air Force in 1950, he had commenced drawing studies at Luton Art School. After military service he pursued a growing interest in art by visiting Paris, where he studied drawing and painting at the Cité Université. He met César, Germaine Richier and Brancusi in Paris, thanks to a letter of introduction from Michael Seuphor. César, Richier and Brancusi offered contrasting examples of modern sculptural practice ranging from brutal expressionism to the poise of traditional forms of craftsmanship. But at this early stage in his career it was the experience of coming face to face with Brancusi's work that meant most to him. The strong, creative urge, rooted in the physical dimension of work, pointed the way forward and showed how art could express the life force. After the Paris experience, Wall sought other artistic environs, and followed the well-worn path to the Cornish art colony. His painting was abstract at the time and had more in common with the St. Ives milieu than with the figurative and expressionist painting of the so-called School of London artists.

In common with several others of scant means and limited experience who came down in the 1950's to make a contribution to the 'St. Ives School', Wall relied on part-time hotel jobs. He worked at the Treganna Castle Hotel with Robert Brennan, who introduced Wall to the leading artists in the town. Peter Lanyon, whom Wall met casually, helped obtain a small studio for the new recruit, who began waitering for the Pandora Cafe in 1955. He served Barbara Hepworth many times, with the result that the famous sculptor requested that he join her growing team of assistants at Trewyn. Socially, Wall advanced his case through frequenting Endell Mitchell's pro-art Castle Inn in the middle of Fore Street.

Hitherto, Wall had been a painter, making use of the familiar St. Ives motifs of abstracted boat and quayside shapes. Terry Frost, a relatively inexperienced painter himself at the time, seemed to speak with the clear-headedness of a mature artist when advising a number of fellow travellers, Wall among them, to pursue new directions. Moreover, Frost was the first to recognise that Wall should make sculpture, and if Frost frequently stepped out of the four-sided pictorial arena in order to make brightly coloured, free-standing geometric collages or reliefs, then he always stayed a painter and never made sculpture in its own right, (in spite of working for Hepworth in the early 1950's on her 'Contrapuntal Forms' piece for the Festival of Britain). Frost recognised a sculptor in Wall, and put his money where his mouth was by purchasing one of the artist's earliest pieces. The New Zealand painter John Forrester, then in favour with Nicholson, also influenced him. Forrester's contemporary wood constructions used pronounced stripe patterns. But Wall's working two days a week at Trewyn exerted the greatest influence. He worked on wood and stone carving and also on her less convincing copper sheet constructions. She took a shine to him, giving advice of an artistic, as well as personal, nature. He worked on the pre-cast preparations for Hepworth's large bronze 'Meridian' now located at State House in London. It was appropriate he should work on this, one of her largest commissioned sculptures. 'Meridian', an orange peel shape, 'explored the use of a swinging line of bronze, a total expression of interior form',[9] according to Tom Cross. It represented the way that metal's special versatility allowed the complete opening up of sculptural volume to accomodate outside space. The adoption of bronze casting, an outcome of both modelling and carving processes in the original plaster, followed on from tentative experiments in constructing with fragile planes of sheet copper.

By this time Wall was starting to impose an independence on his own work; indeed, by the end of the decade he was producing novel 'three dimensional de Stijls', as he was to call them, using thin rods and planes of steel. This open linear scaffolding created a dynamic contrast of open and closed spaces. The vocabulary was basically classic and precise with little of the shattered surfaces or lumpy inconsistencies that characterised the romantic, expressionist sculpture of the time. Instead, his works related to the neo-plastic world of Mondrian and modern architecture. In addition, Wall began to bridge the gap between Hepworth's pre-war European modernism and the later American-influenced St. Martins group. He sought emotional content through non-representational form; visually intricate, his rectilinear

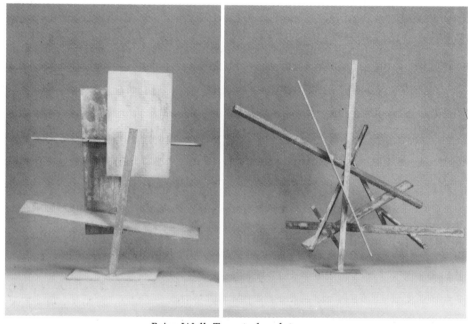

Brian Wall. Two steel sculptures.
Courtesy: Suzanna Pollen, Sothebys.

constructs in space were self-referring objects, a product of the existential imagination. Art was an inner expression, however much it may have received the input of modernist codes. A symptom of felt expression was spontaneity, even when using cut, 'found' or pre-determined components. There was never any question of preliminary maquettes or drawings; however compact or self-sufficient the final outcome may have looked, it was the result of that spontaneity, and indeed of welding's ability to be a subtractive as well as additive process. Fired up by the influence of Hepworth's dedicated professionalism, Wall went on to produce hundreds of linear constructions, most extending in scale to arm's length. He tended to work in series, seeking an ongoing creative dynamic with variations on a theme, an idea suggested by his interest in Zen. No wonder he ended up on the West Coast of America.

In 1959 Wall left St. Ives and returned to London, where new artistic developments, not to mention career opportunities, presented themselves. He set up a studio in Kensington and was visited by Roger Hilton who, ever alert to the significance of the present moment, told Wall about Anthony Caro, then the hottest thing in British sculpture. Hilton and Wall made an impromptu visit to Caro's house in Hampstead, where the impression was of an ambitious and determined innovator moving the frontiers of sculpture a step towards architecture and the environment. Whilst impressed with the structure and lyrical poetry of Caro's forms, Wall steered clear of his coloration, which he felt to be an American affection, and kept paint away from the oxidised surfaces of his own constructs. Caro saw Wall's early exhibitions at the Grosvenor and Grabowski galleries and as recently as 1992 Caro visited the opening of one of Wall's by now rare London showings, at the Francis Graham Dixon gallery. Wall purchased a house in Islington with Anthony Benjamin, but in 1969 left Britain to take up a teaching post at the University of California. This followed a spell at the Central School. During the course of the 1960's Wall's sculpture changed; he used large, open box shapes. These works, with their probing interplay between volume and open space, interior and exterior form, ran parallel to much British sculpture of the 1960's, in which scale, formal enhancement and explorations into new spatial concepts were 'in'. Yet never one to feel his back to the proverbial wall, he drew from his own wellspring, and if the new works hinted at, or ran parallel to, the effects of New Generation steel sculpture and American hard-edged abstraction of the sixties and seventies, then certainly he was not directly indebted to either Smith or Serra or the Minimal sculptors. Nevertheless, during the 1970's and 1980's, installed in a San Francisco studio, Wall's sculptures grew larger.

Keith Leonard, (1921-1993), originally an art student who came down from Birmingham in 1955 to work at Trewyn, was another sculptor owing much of his early development to Barbara Hepworth. He worked for her part-time between 1955 and 1959. He teamed up alongside Mitchell, Dicon Nance and Wall, and worked on Hepworth's 'Meridian'. Unlike Denis Mitchell, Leonard gained a solid training in the cosmopolitan hub of London and Paris. At Trewyn Leonard could not have found a more different approach to the one he encountered under his Slade sculptor tutor, Professor Alfred Gerard. Gerard was as alert as Hepworth to subtleties of direction, to nuances of surface, yet his approach was to build form outwards from an armature, and for this he used the additive mode of clay modelling. This contrasted with Hepworth's reductive carving from blocks of wood, marble or stone. Hepworth thought Leonard an original artist and a natural candidate for carving marble. Before he began working at Trewyn, Leonard had spent time in Ossip Zadkine's studio in Paris, an experience that further broadened the terms of reference for someone fast becoming a cosmopolitan artist.

Leonard looked beyond the frontiers of academic practice, however, for sources of inspiration. Far from being a hermetic formalist, he did not produce work for the sake of it and never catered to commercial demands. He worked slowly, perhaps too slowly, pursuing ideas gained from his love of musical and architectural structure. He developed a keen interest in the abstract structures of music and architecture, finding in these art forms a

Keith Leonard. Design for a Monument to Pavlova. *Fibreglass.*

correspondence with the expressive conceptions of sculpture. Observations of dancers in movement or of figures trapped in bags gave him ideas. So did the steel structures of buildings, apparent in the processes of architectural construction. A linear approach in the constructing of Leonard's three dimensional form therefore resulted. Leonard's interest in the simple tension created with vertical and horizontal marks was influenced by the neoplasticism of Mondrian. Gerard had placed such emphasis on the importance of direction in the building out of form from a central axis that in the late 1950's Leonard created a number of large paintings composed with 'sticks' of colour stacked across one another to create a dense web of crisscrossing lines, their expressive energy a product of contrasting colour and direction. One foray into the realm of the multi-directional resulted in a huge composition of intersecting star shapes; created with white lines across a pale blue ground, it was shown at the 1964 World Fair in New York. The infinite quality implicit in the Cornish landscape, the unboundedness of the Atlantic clearly moved him to produce these strikingly beautiful paintings. He also painted a number of white, minimal pictures carrying simple curved arcs of charcoal. An influence on the paintings was Pátrick Heron who, at the time when Leonard was living as caretaker in Heron's newly acquired home 'Eagle's Nest', was making colourful calligraphic pictures from short stabs of truncated but interactive brushmarks. Leonard's pictures were less gestural than Heron's, the static lines and intersecting rhythms belonging to a sculptor's conception of space. These pictorial exercises were rehearsals for the sculptural realisation of form in space; the subtleties of direction and movement, realised through curvilinear planes, were fulfilled through use of appropriate materials in the third dimension.

Leonard creates these curvatures in the third dimension from a graphic exploration of space. He achieves what Mondrian called the 'spiritual equipoise', a not insignificant factor for an English artist who, friendly with Winifred Nicholson, shared her belief in Christian Science. The curvilinear planes of pieces like 'Monument to Pavlova' are created by wrapping cloths around wire structures and spraying them with fibreglass resin. This delicately cantilevered, flowing, upright piece clearly aims to mime the poise of a dancer gyrating on the tip of a single toe. The final fibreglass surfaces were smoothed down with tools. Although drawn to the inherent beauty of materials, he is an artist whose work is dictated by conceptual factors, by the idea rather than physical process. Leonard was a good communicator of visual ideas and he taught at Farnham in the early 1960's before teaching spells in London and the north-east. He returned with his wife, the painter Charmian to live in Cornwall in 1984. A later interest in wood enabled a new range of tall forms, anatomic as well as geometric in character, to slowly emerge from his Penwith atelier.

NOTES

1.   Tom Cross. 'Painting the Warmth of the Sun' Alison Hodge. 1984.
2.   Alastair Grieve. 'The Sculpture of Robert Adams' Yale. 1993.
3.   Alastair Grieve. 'The Sculpture of Robert Adams' Yale. 1993.
4.   Alastair Grieve. 'The Sculpture of Robert Adams' Yale. 1993.
5.   Roger Leigh. Conversation with the author. Wiltshire. December 1991.
6.   Roger Leigh. Conversation with the author. Wiltshire. December 1991.
7.   Tom Cross. 'Painting the Warmth of the Sun' Alison Hodge 1984.
8.   Roger Leigh. Letter to the author.
9.   Tom Cross 'Painting the Warmth of the Sun' Alison Hodge 1984.

CHAPTER 5

From Naive to Expressionist

Though not unique to St. Ives, a tradition of naive painting, emulating the innocence of children's art, took root there to the extent of forming a distinctive and popular strand in the ongoing story of art in the famous colony since 1930. The fortuitous discovery of Alfred Wallis, the lone primitive and former mariner on that fateful August afternoon in 1928 is a story that now assumes legendary proportions. The phenomenon of Wallis forged a moral

Alfred Wallis.
Courtesy: Montpelier Studio, London.

and aesthetic link between naive painting and sophisticated modernism, and in the process close-circuited the spurious modernity of inter-war, post-impressionist landscape painting. Sven Berlin wrote that these leisured academic painters often 'looked down like condescending giraffes'*1 on artists of Wallis's unschooled ilk. According to Charles Harrison, Wallis was responsible for the idea 'That real creativity was somehow direct and innate, that the imagination was fettered by training, that a painting was more importantly a thing in itself than a representation of something else, that strength of expression and vitality of working were more important than accuracy of description and technical skill, that the child, the primitive and the modern artist were somehow joined.'*2 After Ben Nicholson, a younger generation of sophisticated artists pursued the same virtues of innocent directness. Roger Hilton's gouaches, produced as final, bedridden statements in defiance of approaching death, consciously strove to create humorous and highly decorative images of animals and figures with the unaffected directness of children's art. Bryan Wynter looked to invest his flickering and calligraphic pictures with the eye's initial landscape perceptions, untainted by the rationalising process of the intellect. Inspired by the mystical writings of Aldous Huxley and the experience of the mind-expanding drug mescalin, Wynter looked for the sudden innocence of bombshell enlightenment.

Although the years following Wallis's death in 1942 were characterised by the growth of abstraction - both constructivist and informal - something of the personal energy of naive, primitive and childlike art continued to enliven St. Ives art. Expressionism, at first unpopular in the anti- German post-war climate, contained the same power of subjectivity found in naive art. It was a northern, humanistic, even romantic art, and one that countered the precise classicism of Nicholson with a poetic regard for the contingencies of Cornish custom and life. A prominent vein of expressionistic painting always existed in Cornwall, offering an alternative to excessively formal paths of the modern movement. The rich colour and robust forms of expressionism convey feeling in direct ways and eschew the rules of classical and academic art while retaining - in marked contrast to the abstractionists - the conventions of, and commitment to, representational art. The original expressionists in Germany were moved by the primitive directness of tribal art. The content also took the form of a return to nature, as in Otto Muller's nudist sand dune pictures. Naive and primitive currents therefore run through much expressionist painting.

Differing kinds of artistic naivety can be argued about at length. The fact of being self-taught is a symptom, if not cause of naivety. An expressionist like Francis Bacon was self-taught, but his raw vision is anything but naive, even while it is deeply personal. Bacon spent a winter painting in a Porthmeor studio in 1959 and he fitted in well. The critic John Willett, writing the essay for Alan Lowndes' 1972 Stockport retrospective - and Lowndes' work encompasses both naivety and expressionism - distinguished between three types of naivety. The first category means 'incompetence, a childish or primitive inability to see at all deeply into things, combined with a lack of technique.' Wallis fits here even though a lack of technique was a source of strength. The second naivety, according to Willett, was 'a sophisticated imitation of the same quality, as practised by highly trained artists who have become dissatisfied with the conventions of their training.' Willett identified this with 'the charming but slightly unconvincing naivety of 1920's Paris.' Ben and Winifred Nicholson, as well as Kit Wood, had been in Paris during the

1920's and in their inimitable English way displayed a self-conscious will to assimilate naivety into the sophisticated context of their own painting. Willett's third and salutary kind of naivety is reached with 'the kind of simplicity which takes things as they are, without prettifying them, and goes directly to what may be a quite complicated and difficult point.' Implicit in this is a will to realism, whatever that may be, though this does not preclude poetic licence or lyricism in the picture-making process, so long as such qualities are unaffected and unobtrusive to the expression of objective reality.

The current line of enquiry is further complicated by wayward or eccentric examples within the naive to expressionist axis. There may be illogical, paradoxical, or contrary reasons to explain an artist's absorption into one or other category. If Wallis's illiteracy in the formal, academic means of painting had something to do with starting to paint late in life in order to keep himself

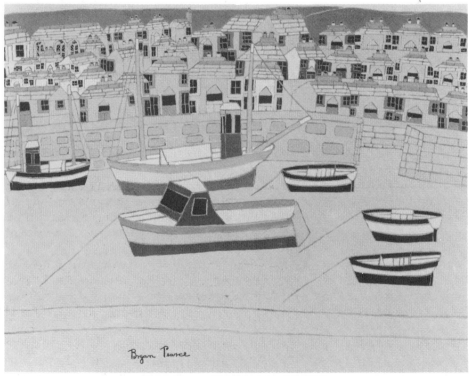

Bryan Pearce. Porthleven. *Oil, 1970.*
Gordon Hepworth Gallery.

company after the death of his wife, then Bryan Pearce's latter day St. Ives primitivism is the outcome of imposed circumstances beyond his control. Suffering since childhood from the now almost extinct disease phenylketonuria, the cerebral disorder that prevents a child's normal mental development, Pearce was condemned to living in a world 'a little apart from the rest of us'. With more than a tinge of fatalism Peter Lanyon wrote that it was 'necessary to accept these works as the labour of a man who has to communicate this way because there is no other'. Indeed, the 'reality' that his paintings transcribe is inherently and chronically childlike.

Born in St. Ives in 1929, the son of a local butcher, Pearce was encouraged to paint for therapeutic reasons by his mother Mary, also a painter. In contrast to Wallis, Pearce began painting early in life and between 1954 and 57 studied the rudiments of the craft at Leonard Fuller's school. Until 1957 he painted only in watercolour and these early tentative efforts in essaying the medium are unbelievably stiff but appealingly simple. Grasp of perspective and illusionism was an impossibility for this genuine naive, uninfluenced by the world around him. Gradually, through painstaking and mechanical application, Pearce unwittingly turned a weakness into a strength. He honestly portrayed St. Ives in crisp compositions based on flat design of compartmentalised units and pristine colour that is uncanny in its evocation of, and association with, the clear bright light and clean unpolluted environment of his native county. Some argue that Pearce's rise to prominence has been stagemanaged and choice of subject dictated by the un-innocent, commercial minds of others. Certainly, after his early success at the 1961 John Moores Liverpool exhibition, Pearce went on to exhibit at the St. Martin's and New Art Centre galleries in London. In 1975 he even had a retrospective at M.O.M.A. in Oxford. But Pearce's oeuvre follows a remarkably consistent path, independent of any worldly success, where the years of painting are palpably, if silently embedded in the paintings in terms of patience, control, and a serene simplicity usually achieved only late in life, in the so-called second childhood, by more sophisticated artists. Matisse's call for an art of serenity and balance, promoting well-being, is certainly fulfilled in the humbler context of Pearce's art. Indeed, Alan Bowness noted that, 'simply by the practice of painting the artist has developed a great sureness of touch and sensitivity to colour.'*3

Pearce's working methods are a transparent feature in the final outcome. He begins to draw in with pencil faithful, if flawed observations of St. Ives townscapes, Cornish landscapes or domestic still lifes. Next the graphic line work is meticulously gone over with ochre paint, and finally the vividly demarcated forms are filled in with evenly applied strokes of clear colour. These sometimes have a jewel-like intensity, as in pictures featuring the stained glass of the parish church or in floral subjects. On other occasions an even balance is struck between warm ochres for the buildings and cool, light blues for the sea. The colour can no more be credibly anchored to naturalism than the drawing can be accurate. Thus Bowness remarks about 'preferred blues for the sea and sky' and 'preferred greens for fields and trees'.*4 But whereas Wallis was literal in his use of sea colours, being aware for instance of the 'colourless' colour of seawater in a bottle, Pearce is trapped by sheer technical and conceptual limitations. But he is alert to the rhythmic possibilities of recurring objects and the pictures often make play on, for example, the multitude of windows across a townscape, the mosaic-like patterns of brickwork, the stripes of jugs and tablecloths, the veins of leaves, or a succession of moored vessels anchored in stillness to the uniform blue of the harbour. Both in terms of its emphatic design and its quintessential aura of something unique and precious, Pearce's work possesses the 'common touch' and mass appeal of tourist art yet also the loftiness of the St. Ives fine art tradition. His work has been rescued from the harbour-front trinket shops, however, and has been widely collected by those able to afford the fixed prices. He takes his place alongside Wallis as a naive picked up and promoted by the sophisticated aesthetes who have played so prominent a role in dictating the taste of that tradition.

Mary Jewels with Cordelia and children, Newlyn, Christmas 1966.

If Pearce is wholly a St. Ives product then another naive artist of quite different persuasion represents Newlyn. Like Wallis and Pearce, Mary Jewels was a native of Cornwall and having lived and worked in Newlyn her entire life leaves behind a body of work that is sympathetic and loyal in its evocation of the duchy. She once wrote that, 'I am influenced by nobody and entirely self-taught, a true Celt loving my Cornwall, its lovely stone hedges and the beautiful blue sea, with puff ball clouds and little fishing coves.' Jewels uses rich, thick colour; her seas are choppy with churned up aquamarines and the skies are breezy with clotted whites scudded across light blues. The work is painterly, like Wallis, but has none of the design quality of Pearce. A love of Cornwall, which she seldom left, accounts for a seasoned freshness. Her work maintains directness by eschewing preliminary drawing or other distractions to the spontaneously felt in a landscape motif. Using memory or imagination, she could vividly recall a scene without the reportage of exact drawing. She learnt to paint alone, encouraged by Augustus John and Cedric Morris (whose own art often integrated the awkwardness of the naive with the rich colourful handling of the competent expressionist). They were frequent visitors to her home. Indeed she and her sister Cordelia, (first wife of the sculptor Frank Dobson), played host to many artists, not least Ben Nicholson who, during the war, motorcycled over from St. Ives to spend evenings with them. Perhaps for this reason Alan Bowness has suggested that Jewels is not 'the popular conception of a naive painter - an illiterate peasant working in a vacuum of ignorance - but a woman, by no means out of touch with artistic circles, whose great natural gifts for art have gone untrained and remained unspoiled'.*5 She was supported by sophisticated artists, who could see the danger of exploiting her innocent talent for commercial reasons. Furthermore, unlike a contemporary woman painter like Shearer Armstrong, she never joined Nicholson's crusade against the traditionals of St. Ives landscape painting. Having a firm sense of her own position as if decreed by the stars, she never revealed the kind of touching delusion of a more technically gifted painter like Rousseau, who one remarked to Picasso that he was 'modern' by virtue of depicting aeroplanes in his painting while Picasso's cubist language of planes and angles made him an 'Egyptian' artist.

Newlyn later provided home for another self-taught painter who brushed with varying modes of naive art. Bourne's 'savoir faire' also puts his work into a more sophisticated orbit, one where positive, interacting colour rejects the grey tonalities of much English painting. He is not afraid of large scale formats either, and his interiors and landscapes, full of the anecdotal warmth of human incident, have an air of confidence in spite of imperfect drawing and composition. He constructs and expresses himself through colour. Figures vie for attention in his colourful interiors. The drawing is wobbly, rudimentary and even childlike but there is nothing uncertain in colour planes that fulfil expressionism's independence from naturalism. The walls of Bourne's interiors hold paintings of a lyrical kind - reminiscent of fauvism or expressionism - and these 'pictures within a picture' devices add extra weight to the aura of self-conscious artfulness. The flattened perspectives and disrupted illusionism of the interiors owes something to Matisse - particularly famous works such as the 'Red Studio'. The ornate, sumptuous quality of the French master is missing in the plainer context of Bourne. An awkwardness of technique results in discordant pictures that are salvaged and pulled together by an intuitive feeling for colour's psychologically healing and formally harmonising energy. Flaming oranges, pinks, blues, greens and reds breathe life into pictures that celebrate the simple poetry of the everyday, as is evident in the work of his friends like Yankel Feather or Rose Hilton.

Bob Bourne's painting also witnesses a lifelong association with the sea, and in common with Wallis, while in marked contrast to Pearce or Jewels, his is a peripatetic biography. Born in Exmouth, he was raised in Brighton but evacuated during the war to Bermuda. This and a spell in Australia during the early 1970's brightened the palette, though the Americanised sophistication and functionalism of the west coast of Australia was anathema. He yearned for a return and in ironic reversal to the legend of Gauguin, relayed by Somerset Maughan in 'Moon and Sixpence', Bourne returned to the mother country and the old world in order to attain the necessary simplicity of lifestyle. His painting blossomed upon returning home. In 1976 he settled permanently in Newlyn following half a year in central France.

Bourne's association with Cornwall dates from 1960, though his existence was an impecunious one in those early days of caravaning and working in hotels. In 1967, with some help from mother, Bourne purchased a small house in Paul. Here he developed an independent use of colour seldom matched in other figurative painter's work, though reached in the more sophisticated art of the abstract painters. Bourne was never out of touch intellectually from the art scene about him, and he admired Lanyon and Hilton, above others, for unorthodox pictorial construction that replaced conventional perspective with an intuitive mise-en-page. By 1973 he was enjoying an exhibition at Tooths in London, an experience that unnerved an artist not conditioned to such success. But further success followed (he lived for two years in west London, near to Elena Gaputyte), and Andreas Kalman purchased the first of many pictures. In the mid 1980's Kalman's acquisition of Bourne's paintings grew from a trickle to a torrent, buying them in bulk for a ready market on Brompton Road. During the 1980's he also consolidated his exhibiting position on the home front with regular contributions to Newlyn and Penwith shows, while having a solo show at the Salthouse Gallery in St. Ives.

Charmian Leonard, who exhibited with the Penwith Society at the height of its eminence, perpetuates colour as a central feature in the art of painting from nature. Her background is part Greek and part Cornish, and perhaps for this reason she portrays the place of St. Ives with the bright colour of Cornish summertime. The timeless poetry of secluded beaches, transparent seas and clear azure skies are evoked in these pictures. Perhaps unconsciously, she hints at the Mediterranean aspects of Cornwall. Her work has the deceptive simplicity of Winifred and Kate Nicholson, both of whom were friends. Sidestepping the tonal and descriptive tendency of much British art, she composes with colour and creates a conceptual significance of almost mystical dimensions. Colour's inherent energy is enhanced, in pictorial art, in terms of temperature contrast, modifying juxtapositions and tonal variation. Aware of subtle auras surrounding objects she tries to attain the 'unknown colour' that Winifred Nicholson spoke of as lying at the far edges of the natural spectrum. In a still life by Leonard, the leaves are painted with multifarious shades of green in a way that expresses the individuality of each within the wider context of the plant as a whole. She sketches wherever she goes, though the drawing of plants fulfils her feeling for natural form and pure colour. 'Much great art is based on conviction', she writes, 'the wonderful order, precision and infinite variety we find about us, the tides, the stars even each blade of grass is different'. Leonard was taught at Chelsea by Ceri Richards and Vivian Pitchforth, among others, and the lesson of her training was that the academic rules of painting need not exclude ambitious visionary content. She was also taught by Carel Weight, but instead of following Weight's ethereal narrative, she delved into the metaphysical possibilities beyond the formal vehicle of colour. She later taught at several art schools and makes annual visits to Greece, which she paints with a pronounced feeling for pattern and subtle arid colours. Schematic compositions based on simplified wave forms are the nearest she comes to abstraction.

Romantic expressionism resided in the work of Crypt artists like Sven Berlin and Adrian Ryan. Berlin wrote the definitive biography of Alfred Wallis, whom he never met, during the mid 1940's. It was published in 1948, (the later book by Edwin Mullins never emulated Berlin's pioneering achievement). Berlin became something of a thorn in the side of St. Ives's avant-garde establishment by virtue of a rugged bohemianism, a déclassé stance, and an anti-intellectualism that at once made his work accessible to the layman. Berlin attacked élitism in art by painting folky subjects and by championing Wallis in his book as a people's painter rather than as the modern artist's 'pet primitive'. Yet the simplicity of Wallis's vision was lost on many 'laymen' and a bundleful of work by the recently deceased artist was burnt. It took a sophisticated audience to nurture Wallis's work in those early years and Berlin, the ethical champion of Wallis in print, went on to disperse dozens of Wallis pictures, giving them away as gifts to fellow artists or friends, a naive gesture in view of their later commercial value. Berlin was a gifted, self-taught artist (he studied briefly with the watercolourist Arthur Hambley in Redruth before the war). His unorthodox and wayward streak challenged the academicism of both modern and traditional practice. Ideologically he also entered ethical debate with Hepworth and Nicholson, taking the form of a lengthy correspondence, concerning the alleged exploitation of Wallis's work for commercial reasons at a time when the old man was neglected and left to die a pauper's death in the Madron workhouse.

Sven Berlin's autobiography 'A Coat of Many Colours', published by Redcliffe in 1994, indicates a colourful character with talents in many directions. His draughtsmanship displayed the same bold outline of the 'savage messiah', Gaudier, that romantic figure in early twentieth century art who, like Wallis, had been assiduously collected by Nicholson's friend and founder of the Kettle's Yard collection in Cambridge, H.S. Ede. Berlin's harbour scenes, agricultural genre pictures, self-portraits, or sketches of fishermen have an almost mythological intensity at times, though the location is never in doubt. They are expressionistic in tone, flamboyant in colour and exploit to the full, surface texture. The rich colour is laid down over coarsely brushed undercoats which show through, giving a transparency to the work's physical processes. A naturally rich palette increased during the long course of Berlin's career, all the more so after leaving Cornwall in 1953 in order to pursue a romantic, and indeed naive interest in the gypsies of the New Forest.

Berlin's romanticism, explained in part by some Jewish and Welsh ancestry, was encouraged by Augustus John, whom he had occasionally met in Mousehole pubs. John became a beacon for the younger artist, who by the early 1950's was increasingly at odds with the abstract formalism and Art-for-Art's sake classicism that Hepworth and Nicholson were imposing onto

Sven Berlin. Irish King. *1978.*
Photo: John Paddy Browne.

St. Ives. The new Penwith Society, by discriminating between abstract and representational, gave disagreeable official tone to this development and prompted Berlin's early resignation, along with Peter Lanyon. But whereas Lanyon exploited his Cornish heritage and tapped into the vein of art history in his home county by forming an alternative grouping at the Newlyn Gallery, Berlin looked for a total Cornish exit, and John's wandering bohemianism gave him his cue. The other Crypt member who came within John's orbit was Adrian Ryan, Berlin's co-exhibitor at the final Crypt exhibition.

In contrast to Berlin, Ryan received a solid training at the Slade. Holidays at Padstow bit him with the Cornish bug and he lived with his first wife at Mousehole from 1945 to 50. Mousehole was much frequented by artists after the war. Jack Pender was a native who used the local motifs of boats and harbour. As well as attracting John, the small harbour with its distinctive double pier and views across Mount's Bay, was the subject of William Scott's attentions. Nicholson produced a composite still life landscape subject of Mousehole at the time, while Berlin and Heron visited and invited Ryan to participate in what turned out to be the final Crypt exhibition. Ryan knew John in London, where he maintained a Tite Street studio (opposite John) throughout the 1940's and 50's. He painted a portrait of Augustus, and the John family generally supported him to the extent of buying pictures. Augustus's son Edwin was friendly with another romantic Cornish-based painter George Lambourne (1900-1977). Living for many years in rough circumstances on the Penwith moors, Lambourne later purchased St. Clement's Hall in Mousehole and painted figurative compositions with a theatrical sense of the drama of everyday life. During the war, he had been mentioned in dispatches for bravery, and a series of fighter pilot compositions expressed both war experiences and an expert level of graphic ability, gained through studies in the 1920's at the R.A. Schools. His later career was motivated, however, by a desire to shed this academic conditioning. While friendly with the whole John family (often visiting Fryern), he wished to branch out as an artist and made unconvincing experiments with differing paints and supports. He even painted on glass and made some attempts at gestural painting. For all this, he was essentially a romantic artist of limited, figurative intentions. His evocations of a densely moored Newlyn quayside, of colourful huts on Hayle Towans, or of grouped figures symbolising vulnerability, characterise him at his best. He made some strikingly personal interpretations of human tragedy, such as loss at sea, one notable example being 'Lost Fisherman', a subject of sombre mood and dark blue colouration that owes something to the stylistic and emotional qualities of Picasso's wailing, Blue Period figures.

If Lambourne's striving to shed the academic was motivated by a romantic impulse to paint in a more emotional and cogently expressive manner, then Ryan's rebellion against Slade training was more discrete, taking the form of a French expression in the use of heightened naturalism. Ryan's art was mostly inspired by two adopted 'Frenchmen', Soutine and Modigliani. During the 1940's he owned examples by both artists. He also owned a White Period Utrillo. Years later in 1991, Ryan wrote that such influences 'did not lead me to abandon the disciplines of drawing and composition which my father had been taught, but did encourage me to use bright colours and a freer handling of paint.'[*6] Once an architecture student, Ryan remained forever drawn to buildings, particularly churches, which he painted with bright, breezy and loosely handled paint. Ryan turned Utrillo's Montmartre churches into the more prosaic, but no less animated, images of Paul church, and in so doing alluded to propinquity between Cornwall and France that had been evident since the plein-airists first colonised Newlyn in the 1880's. It was

Adrian Ryan. Portrait of Polly Walker. *Oil.*

never Ryan's intention to be an innovator, however, and he seldom looked to appropriate the emperor's clothes in the way that an equally French-inspired contemporary like Patrick Heron did. Instead, Ryan's natural breeding (his father had been an academic portrait and landscape painter), and his absorption into the spirit, as opposed to the style, of French art enabled him to maintain traditional standards of drawing while indulging in freely expressive, if still naturalistic colour. But naive art also had its appeal. He admired Kit Wood's work, seen at the Redfern Gallery, where he also frequently exhibited after the war and then again in the 1980's. He knew Mary Jewels, and admired the candour of her uninfluenced work. In spite of living in Suffolk during the 1950's he returned to live in Mousehole during the first half of the 1960's, purchasing a cottage with the Cornish painter Joan Gilchrist.

Gilchrist's distinctive pictures of people going about their daily business are recorded with an affectionate eye for detail, an eye that is naive in its literal, flat, mechanical transcriptions of complex townscape imagery. She does not simplify or filter imagery through a sophisticated editing of visual information, but rather creates a flatness of composition, an awkward flatness as akin to Pearce as it is distant from the kind of non-illusionistic flatness used by the abstract painters. Her people have the naive charm of Lowry's matchstick figures and inhabit similarly uniform white surfaces. But she creates pictures with the control and rigour of a professional, symptomatic of a formula-bound approach betraying a spurious naivety.

During the 1950's, a number of émigré painters came to live in Cornwall for varying lengths of time and brought with them an imaginative richness and sense of colour unusual in English painting. Among them were Peter Potworowski, a much-travelled Polish painter who taught at Corsham with some of the leading Cornish artists of the time, Albert Reuss, an Austrian refugee who settled permanently in Mousehole during the late 1940's, and Patrick Hayman, originally from New Zealand. They introduced a mid-European introspection and with it a heightened sense of the visually poetic in their unassuming and often innocent figurative imagery. Their work was imbued with that psychologically charged, even metaphysical quality through which fleeting impressions, memories and subtle perceptions were conveyed with a pervasive sense of mystery or melancholy. The sadness, typical of the Jewish wanderer, found outlet in Cornwall's western peripheries. With the region's sense of looming vastness and isolation, painters like Reuss or Hayman responded with uncompromisingly personal work that also made sense within the Celtic lexicon of Cornish art. Their symbolic statements were coloured with a deeply subjective vision that touches a common spiritual essence.

Peter Potworowski (1898-1962) lived in England from 1943 to 1958, after which he returned to his native Poland for the remaining few years of his life. As well as succeeding as a teacher - Margo Maeckelberghe later confirmed how popular he was with the students - he also made an impact with regular exhibitions at Gimpels, the Redfern and other venues. During the 1920's he had studied art in Warsaw and had lived in Paris, while the 1930's saw him based in Poland but branching out with regular visits to many other European countries. He arrived in England via Sweden and Scotland and helped form a loose grouping of Polish emigré artists - Josef Herman and Jankel Adler among them - who made such an immediate and colourful impact on the dry English art scene, whose centre ground then offered only the alternatives of Bloomsbury or Euston Road styles. Exposure to the Cornish-based fraternity on the staff at Corsham undoubtedly spurred him to visit Cornwall and during the 1950's he spent part of each year painting in Penwith, staying in a rented cottage at Sancreed. Imagination was an important ingredient in Potworowski's pictures, which seldom represented situations or environments with any degree of sharply focussed credence. In the Tate's

'Forest Cornwall' (1954) Potworowski responds to nature's looming presence in Cornwall by using symbols drawn from natural motifs. Tree, fern and cone shapes are abstracted into spiky forms, while discs denote sun or moon. In a manner similar to that of a contemporary like Roy Turner Durrant, he follows a neo-romantic path into abstraction, though the pictographic sign language of Klee, and later on the oval compositions of Cubism proved the most abiding formal influences.

Potworowski was a talented teacher who shunned academic approaches in general and art historical pigeonholing in particular. Indeed, his non-hierarchical view of art of all periods, in its refusal to be taken in by historical status, was essentially innocent of ethnocentric or culturally mediated value. Wide travels fuelled the artist's imagination with memories and spectral impressions, and much of his imagery is formed with that lyrical and fleeting handling of paint that expresses the transitory nature of much of his life. An interest in loose rubbed or scratched textures enabled him to recall memorable experiences of places visited, such as Warsaw ghettos, west country interiors, Cornish landscapes or waterfalls, without the high finish of pedantic transcription. Frequently, a composite of memories or perceptions in a picture by Potworowski allowed him, in the words of his colleague Adrian Heath, to 'endow a familiar room or landscape with the qualities of an indelible dream.'[7] Sometimes a muted range of hues was employed and a series of domestic subjects, such as nudes in a bath, views through a window, or music lessons in the living room, recalled in stylistic and thematic terms the art of Bonnard. Potworowski was a natural painter in the way that naives or primitives often are, and his creative energy took the form of relaxed paint handling, unconventional uses of texture and colour to express the inexpressible, and a range of images culled from his experience but expressed with an entirely subjective charm and innocence.

Although the work of Albert Reuss (1889-1976) shares with Potworowski's a mood of subjectivity, the feeling is more contemplative. Reuss's way of constructing a picture is quite different. He uses a simpler language of flat planes of light, harmonious, pastel hues. He also differs from Potworowski in being self-taught, though his works have an obvious accomplishment that has much to do with wisely playing to his strengths. He composes with a linear stylisation and the forms are coloured in with hues that give a correctness of mood and schematic harmony to the nature of the subject. Music is clearly important, not only in the sense that the colour is sonorous, but also in the way that guitars, mandolins or clarinets are the subjects in a number of portrait compositions. Reuss models forms with subtle gradations of tone, and creates a quiet sense of volume that rescues the linear and stylised quality of the imagery from a dead pictorial flatness. There is certainly a quiescent, introspective poetry in his work that sometimes touches a vein of surrealist enigma, as a spare repertoire of recognisable objects like blankets, ladders or rocks are amplified and put in discordant contexts. This makes us see pure shapes with a visual freshness, shorn of normal functions. The abstract significance of these shapes for a moment takes over from normal associations and in the process evokes a mysterious and pictorially pleasing mood of reverie. The unusual juxtapositions of commonplace objects in the art of Reuss reflect the story of an Austrian émigré whose early life was an uprooted one. He was forced to seek sanctuary in England. Although happily married and settled in Mousehole from 1948 onwards and in spite of enjoying regular teaching and exhibiting opportunities in England, Reuss never fully belonged. John Halkes wrote that the artist's 'increasing deafness, his uncertainty with modernism and his rejection of academicism had left him isolated …single figures in the paintings inhabited empty rooms and the landscape portrayed barren deserts.'[*8]

The 'strength of expression and vitality of working' that Harrison saw as Wallis's enduring legacy also informed the melancholic and nostalgic art of Patrick Hayman. Wallis's evocations of early life at sea were taken further by Hayman, who tapped collective memories of common Jewish experience. The paint handling is intuitive and by academic standards seems clumsy. The style is in fact a convincing mixture of the cultivated and the naive. The colours are rich and poetic rather than naturalistic. 'He had a natural colour sense', wrote Barbara Hayman, explaining how he 'often painted one colour on top of another, suggesting a feeling of violence.' The colours also evoke an introspective mood and the images and symbols allude to the artist's experience of a vastly looming nature. They also symbolise his hopes, fears and loves. His distinctive misshapen style has the primitive lopsidedness of Wallis, an artist who greatly intrigued and inspired him. But Hayman's work is also full of expressionist angst, particularly apparent when crucifixion imagery, fork-tongued creatures, battleships, warplanes or swastikas occur. The artist's painful introspection finds outlet in the political sentiment of protest. In this mood he is far from naive or primitive.

Although Hayman was born in London and educated at Malvern during the early 1930's, he spent a decade in New Zealand. He did not return to England until 1947. Native Maori culture had an inevitable influence on him. In particular, he was moved by the primitive directness of form that expressed tribal society's accord with nature. Voyages between New Zealand and England also gave him an intimacy with, and understanding of, the sea. Boats plough through his seas as they do in Wallis, and the image of lovers by the sea, dogs, early aeroplanes and fish also recur in his work. He lived in Cornwall during the early 1950's, first at Mevagissey then at St. Ives, where he was befriended by Lanyon and many other artists in the town. He even exhibited in an abstract show at Gimpels in 1951, though he developed a richly associative symbolism and imagery that soon distanced him from the abstract formalists among his contemporaries. His was an intuitive and therefore expressive approach to image-making. His work had an abstract quality in the way that one form suggested another in the unpredictable working process, but the poetic idea was always uppermost. This unpredictability gives his work an air of mystery and enigma that is surrealistic.

Hayman enjoyed the ancient, wild, edge-of-the-world quality in Corwall, which he described as giving him 'a feeling in miniature of New Zealand.'[*9] Instead of Maori art he found Wallis, though he had known about both Wallis and Wood through magazine reproduction in New Zealand. He appreciated

Wallis for being a 'visionary, unsuspected artist persevering against all odds, transforming bits of detritus into vehicles of expression.'*10 Hayman made three dimensional paint constructions which he 'transferred with witty ingenuity into magical objects' according to Barbara Hayman. But Kit Wood, who had also been educated at Malvern College, meant even more to Hayman. Hayman's work does not always bask in the tranquil world of

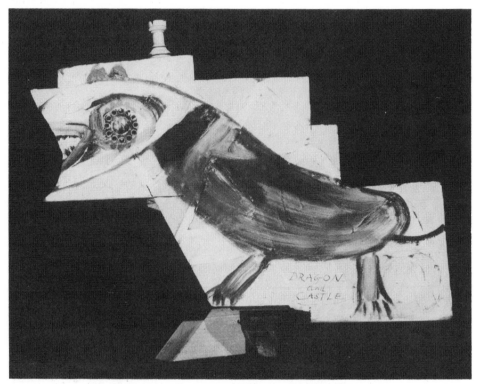

Patrick Hayman. Dragon and Castle. *Oil and collage, 1982.*
Blond Fine Art.

Cornish or Breton harbours, however, and frequently introduces the disturbed imagery of a politically conscious cosmopolitan. Like William Blake, Hayman also made watercolour poems, associating poetic narrative with visual image. In 1988 Louise Hallet published Hayman's book of painted poems. Hayman's painterly evocations of poetic symbols also recall Munch, Nolde and Chagall. During the late 1950's and early 60's he produced an influential quarterly magazine 'The Painter and Sculptor', which upheld figurative art in the eye of the storm of international abstract art. He lived again in St. Ives for a year in the mid 1960s and continued to make annual visits from his west London base. As well as enjoying solo shows he participated in the important Tate exhibition of St. Ives art and also in the touring exhibition 'Alive to it All'. He died in London in 1988.

A younger painter, Michael Rees, continues the vein of paintery expressionism and personal, ever quirky subject matter typical of Hayman. Rees is alive to it all, in the sense that he uses the scale, crudeness and brash colour of much fashionable figurative painting of the 1980's.

Although Yankel Feather came into his own as a painter during the 1980s, he had been involved in the art scene since the 1940's, motivated by a Jewish

Yankel Feather. Interior. *Oil.*

love of painting and a natural gift for expressing his keen perceptions through the visual medium of art. Such were his natural gifts that as early as 1950 Erica Brausen discussed the possibility of showing him at the Hanover Gallery and he exhibited at the meretricious, if provincial Academy of his native

Liverpool. Feather's work has that deceptively relaxed handling of pigment which strives to suggest imagery of an elusive and fleeting kind. He brings to still-life, landscape, nude or genre themes a lightness of touch and a fluency of colour that is French, even Renoiresque in feeling. Abstraction in the hands of this resolutely figurative and poetic painter merely means simplification of an experienced motif. Along with his friends Rose Hilton and Bob Bourne, Feather forms an enclave of talented and natural colourists within a Cornish art scene that since 1980 has seen genuine talent as being thin on the ground. There is no laboured narrative in Feather. He evokes poetry through simple means that are always tied to use of the paint medium. The visual idea that spurs him can be a dream-like scenario, a contre jour figure arrangement against a light expanse of sea, or a series of animal compositions. Stylistically, his work uses many oblique influences though these are intuitively grasped and are not textbook renditions, copies or homages. Like Potworowski before him, Feather has a good visual memory that enables him to create imagery from his imagination. Drawings made of cattle near Zennor formed the basis for richly coloured oils of cattle. Expressionistic in feeling, these works touch the soul of the animal kingdom and perhaps remind one of the pictures of Compendonk and Marc.

In 1977 Feather moved to Cornwall and began a serious engagement with the adventure of painting. Early Cornish visits as a young man after the war saw him take temporary jobs in local cafes and hotels. He was encouraged by Terry Frost and visited Leonard Fuller's school. But a restlessness prevented his concentrating on painting alone and Liverpool continued to draw him. In 1960 he opened a club in Liverpool, run by his sisters in his absence. This made some money at the height of the Merseybeat boom. He later opened an antique shop so that by the time he came to live in Newlyn in the late 1970's he was a man of independent, if not wealthy means. Shortly before leaving Liverpool he had a solo show at the Bluecoat, exhibiting painterly beach scenes and boat subjects that were a little self-consciously Lowryesque. Although he had visited the famous old man's Mottram home and was affected by Lowry's looming presence in northern art, he was more inclined towards the kind of lyrical and colourful English painting that Hitchens practised. Another artist who composed with touch, Soulages, also impressed, though the Liverpool artist had no use for the Frenchman's degree of abstraction. Feather was also inspired by Bomberg, an expressionist who, like Matthew Smith, had a spell painting landscapes in north Cornwall, employing a hot range of exagerrated colour. When, in the late 1980's, Wilhelmina Barns-Graham visited Feather's studio near St. Just she was struck by the sheer diversity and volume of work in the studio of someone who never 'pushed' himself. Beholden to no-one, contemptuous of art world politics and independent by nature, Feather is an artist full of surprises and delights. His progress as an artist was on slow burn for many years but by the 1990's was flowering fully.

Landscape painters who developed individual expressive styles in response to studying under Peter Lanyon included Nancy Wynne- Jones, Jeremy Le Grice (who had intensive spells with Lanyon at the St. Peter's Loft school in St Ives) and Margo Maeckelberghe, who assimilated his influence at Corsham. Born in Penzance, Maeckelberghe invariably strikes the mood and energy of the Cornish coastline, which she paints with heartfelt rapport for the sea and its mysterious movements. Climate and behaviour of the elements add to the tonal condition of light in giving her work a compelling richness of content. The intensity of blue in the pictures resembles Lanyon's 'Offshore', 'Silent Coast' or 'St. Ives Bay'. In the sense that blue is a dominant feature of all her work, she is not a great colourist. Rather she is a talented draughtsman, drawing with paint in strident, energetic and confident mimicry of the action and movement of the sea against hard rocks. At Corsham she learnt the gift of painting with arm instead of wrist. Drawing is the key to understanding the fast streaky impressionism that expressed emotional responses to the sea rather than tame descriptive ones. Essentially a marine painter in the sense that the sea forms the dominant subject throughout her career, Maeckelberghe is not tied to the academic conventions of pre-war seascape painting exemplified by Napier Hemy, Julius Olsson and Borlase Smart. Smart instructed the young Lanyon, though Smart's preference for painting outdoors was shunned by later artists who, like Maeckelberghe, opted for studio practice using plein-air sketches only as aide memoire. Maeckelberghe also differed from the earlier artists in that her approach to the difficult task of representing something in perpetual motion resulted in a gestural equivalent to the motif. The long expressive streaks of saturated blues and viridians identified with the elusive forms of waves and currents lapping over rocks. With an expressionistic brio she never attempted the older analytical approach to depicting wave formations and movements.

At Corsham Maeckelberghe found favour with William Scott as well as with Lanyon. Scott even employed her as a studio assistant. She learnt from him the value of discipline, which in her teacher's case spelt a restricted palette of dark blues, greys, blacks and browns, and an austere, pared down composition that yet embodied lush pigmentation. She also used a restricted range of colour, in her case a characteristic blue, with black, white and yellow. Lanyon was more forthcoming than Scott concerning the secrets of the painter's trade and demonstrated to students like Maeckelberghe the chemistry and application of paint. Nevertheless, Scott probably exerted the greater influence on the young painter. His emphasis on maximum expressive effect through economy of means instilled an important professional principle. Maeckelberghe's fluent draughtsmanship used to locate structure in landscape is clearly seen when a painting's main forms retain traces of dark outlines. Drawing is absorbed into the painting process, and revealingly she once wrote that 'Drawing lays bare the bones of the landscape for me; it's like a map into a strange country, it helps to build an image, but it can never be the complete image. One constantly rejects, selects, searches again.' Sometimes she is inspired directly by objects like stones, seaweed or lichen, while elsewhere a picture begins as 'a logical development of a previous painting.' Landscape even becomes a metaphor for the way passion confronts reason. Like Lanyon she searches for mythic dimensions to landscape, not by associating landscape with the figure, but by identifying with the lost age of

Atlantis. She certainly evokes the wild, mysterious, even mercurial character of Cornwall. Yet she does not sentimentalise the pagan, barren and ancient aspects of this landscape.

Margo Maeckelberghe. Zennor Zawn. *Oil.*

Cornwall was not, however, the only landscape to impress its 'genius loci' on her sensibility. Married to a Belgian doctor she made annual trips to

Belgium, resulting in a series of Ostend boat subjects. She lived in Gibraltar in the mid 1950's and some Spanish pictures were produced. Visits to Italy were responsible for some Tuscan landscapes while later on Greece, which she found to have the same maritime magic of Cornwall, exerted its inevitable hold on her sensibilities. Greek pictures provide a much needed break in the sequence of Cornish landscapes. During the late 1980's she ventured further afield, holidaying in Hawaii, whose fully tropical colours of turquoises and purples entered her work and made it sing even louder. A visit to India led to a few Indian subjects. She avoids focussing on aspects of human geography and instead looks for a broad structure of topography seen from elevated positions, and in this case she comes close to a Liverpool painter Clement McAleer. She is at her happiest when painting from clifftops and looking out to sea, as is provided from Zennor Carn, Bryan Wynter's former home, that she purchased. It is not unusual, either, for the artist to use composite imagery culled from several topographical sketches. This enables typical Cornish landscapes to emerge from her easel that do not belong to any exact location. She aims for an immediacy through fluent use of oil paint sensually wrapped around the bones of landscape structure first plotted by a conscientious, if rapid, output of in situ drawing. During the 1960's Maeckelberghe, as a mature and independent artist, became an active exhibitor and member of both Penwith and Newlyn galleries, though sensibly steered clear of rancorous politics by keeping a healthy distance. But she did exhibit with a loose-knit group of like-minded artists who were generally opposed to orthodoxies of Penwith abstraction or middle generation expressionism. She exhibited with Alan Lowndes, Derek Guthrie, Jack Pender, Michael Canney, Ithell Colquhoun, John Miller and several others. At the time of writing she is Chairman of the Penwith Society.

Jeremy Le Grice, another native of Cornwall, started painting as a schoolboy at Eton. This unlikely place was one where his obvious gift for portrait painting was encouraged. He later gained a place at Guildford art school. But it was back on home territory in Cornwall where he found the source material to ignite an artistic temperament. He was 'hit sideways'[*11] by seeing Lanyon's painting 'Harvest Festival' at Newlyn Art Gallery in 1953. Soon after he studied under Lanyon at the St. Peter's Loft, and had also visited Lanyon's Attic Studio. Later describing Lanyon as 'incredibly benevolent', Le Grice went on to receive much encouragement from the fellow Cornishman. Association with Lanyon enabled Le Grice to confidently relinquish a laboured academic style and reach for a more personally expressive one. He was a full-time student during the first summer of the school's existence. Lanyon encouraged him to give everything, both physically and emotionally, to painting and put his principles to the test by painting among the students. Emphasis on exploring the country in physical terms through engagement with it was 'absolutely seminal' for Le Grice's emerging expressionism.

After a spell of painting in a spare corner of Michael Canney's Newlyn Art Gallery, Le Grice won a place at the Slade. He had hardly known his father and so took to heart the guidance received from the likes of Lanyon and Canney. Coastal subjects in a dark, brooding expressionistic style reflected the sense of loneliness and isolation that is an aspect to life on the westernmost edge of England. If at first he felt uneasy with London then student life was enlivening after the restrictions of boarding school. He enjoyed the tutelage of Rogers, Coldstream and Vaughan, large figures whom Lanyon had encountered before the war during a brief interlude at the Euston Road School. Coldstream, well known for being a sympathetic teacher, made 'witheringly apt' comments and with a catholic taste took interest in students' work, even though Le Grice's at the time betrayed an as yet not fully digested preoccupation with Bomberg. But Cornwall was never far away from his thoughts and he organised a visit by Lanyon and the critic John Berger to the college.

Le Grice was feeling homesick, and in 1961 came back with his first wife Mary Stork to live in St. Just. The Slade discipline of measured draughtsmanship and composition gave the work an authentic basis against which he might react. Strong expressionistic landscapes resulted during the ensuing St. Just years of the 1960's. Karl Weschke was an influence during the period; older, experienced and versed in the German expressionist tradition (Weschke had known Otto Dix before the war), this gifted artist's work, superficially reminiscent of Francis Bacon, conveyed loneliness and desolation through solemn landscape visions. Weschke encouraged Le Grice to darken his palette and also to look for the monumental and grandiose in landscape forms. In 1967 he enjoyed a commercially successful solo retrospective at Plymouth Art Gallery, opened by Bernard Leach. The other influence that filled the gap left by Lanyon's untimely demise was Roger Hilton. Hilton promulgated the virtues of economy, of saying the most with the simplest of means. Sentimentality had little role in Hilton's work, which, with a frequent dose of humour, invested the spontaneity of mark-making with a philosophic as well as visual significance. Exposure to the high point of Cornish modernism had its price, and an impressionable Le Grice felt his work inadequate in the loftier context of his mentors. He wished to get away from the now stifling effect of Cornwall, and changed his work in response to a move to Gloucestershire. He taught at local art schools, had contact with Alan Lowndes who had also moved there, and responded to the area's softer pastoralism with work of lusher feeling. Little painting was produced during a period of introspection. In 1983 he returned home with his second wife and felt free to paint again on his own terms. The intensity of work produced after 1986 made up for lost time.

Nancy Wynne-Jones was born in Wales in 1922 and was therefore only a few years younger than Lanyon, under whose tutelage at the St. Peter's Loft she first found her feet as a painter. Her earliest pictures, with loose handling of landscape motifs and fusion of abstraction and naturalism, have the mark of someone close to Lanyon in a personal as well as artistic sense. Indeed her pictures allude to the kind of direct influence that could not be achieved through more distant text book assimilation. Like Maeckelberghe and Le Grice she maintains the single viewpoint of traditional landscape painting. A spontaneous use of paint bids to express the most fleeting of experiences. Also like Maeckelberghe she creates variety, not in terms of formal

Margo Maeckelberghe. Birdwind Thermal. *Oil, 1992.*

Patrick Heron. The Harbour, St. Ives. *Oil.*
Wills Lane Gallery, St. Ives.

Martin Lanyon. Harbour Storm. *1991.*
Courtesy: Gordon Hepworth Gallery.

John Tunnard. Untitled. *Oil, 1945.*
Paisnel Gallery, London.

Bryan Ingham. Large Oval Still Life. *Relief painted, 1992.*
Private Collection.
Courtesy: Francis Graham-Dixon Gallery.

Michael Canney. Marine Collage, Newlyn. *1957.*
Belgrave Gallery, London.

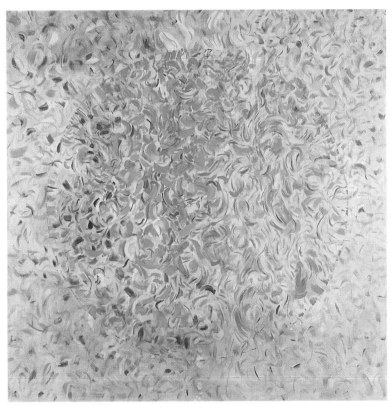

Michael Snow. Leaf Flight. *Oil, 1989.*

Patrick Heron. Portrait of MD. *Oil, 1951.*
Graham Gallery, Tunbridge Wells.

Margaret Mellis. Still Life. *1952.*
Graham Gallery, Tunbridge Wells.

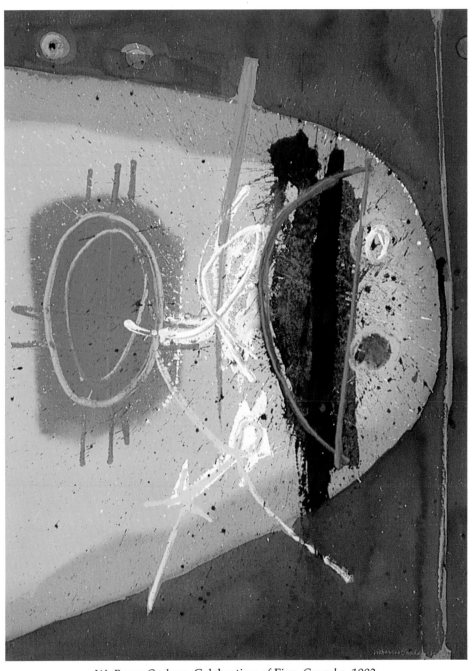

W. Barns-Graham. Celebration of Fire. *Gouache, 1992.*
Collection: The Artist.

Rachel Nicholson. Pig 'n Fish. *Oil.*
Montpelier Studio, London.

Clive Blackmore. Still Life. *Oil.*

Morag Ballard. Icarus. *Oil, 1992.*
Courtesy: England & Co..

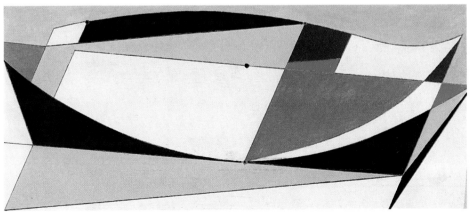

George Dannatt. Boats. *1989.*

Patrick Hayman. Harbour and Fishing Boat. *Oil, 1951.*
Blond Fine Art.

John Park. Sailing Boats St. Ives. *Oil.*
Montpelier Studio.

Michael Strang. Cornish Harbour. *Oil.*

William Gear. St. Ives June, 1948. *Watercolour.*
Graham Gallery.

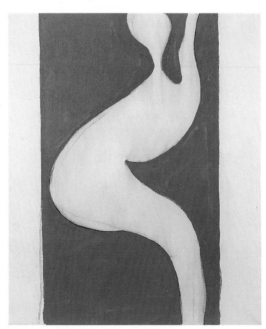

Roger Hilton. April 1968. *Oil.*
Paisnel Gallery.

Karl Weschke. Gordale Scar. *Oil, 1988.*
Redfern Gallery.

Lawrence Isherwood. St. Ives Harbour. *Oil.*
Graham Gallery.

Eric Ward. The Yellow Hat. *Oil.*
Sims Gallery, St. Ives.

Maurice Sumray. The Hunchback. *Oil.*
Sims Gallery, St. Ives.

Michael Canney. Fourfold I. *1988.*
Belgrave Gallery.

Charmian Leonard. Near Zennor. *Oil.*

Joan Gillchrest. Mousehole, Cornwall. *Oil, 1977.*
Sims Gallery, St. Ives.

Joan Gillchrest. Porthleven Setting Off. *Oil, 1975.*
Sims Gallery, St. Ives.

experimentation but rather through changes of subject made possible by leaving Cornwall for Ireland in 1972. In painting the lusher landscapes of Wales and Ireland, Wynne-Jones extends the range of her work. The

Nancy Wynne-Jones. Levant. *Oil, 1958.*

sharpness of Cornwall is replaced by the softer, diaphanous effects of Snowdonia and by what the Irish critic Brian Fallon described as 'the fierce, sappy green'*12 of Ireland. Furthermore, visits to the Mediterranean unleashed a rich palette more in keeping with the vivacity of French art than the tonal rationality of much English art.

Wynne-Jones paid homage to Lanyon by painting his portrait in a way that integrates the separate genres of landscape and portrait painting. In this depiction of the revered young master of St. Ives painting, she substitutes facial verisimilitude for a broad summarising style. The flesh tints become a beach, the black of Lanyon's beret a headland attacked by seafoam. Whisk-like brush-marks have an immediacy and freshness. Wynne-Jones relies on the monumental aspect of the artist's head and characteristic beret and smock to give personality to an otherwise anonymous visage of smudged paint. The metamorphic use of paint in this 1957 example has a cutting, creative edge - more so than in other portraits of artists, such as she made of Roger Hilton in 1957 and of Tony O'Malley in 1965. Entirely in terms of imaginative handling of paint and colour she strikes a quintessential St. Ives correspondence between figure and landscape.

By 1960 she openly adopted the breezy manner of her teacher. In 'Sea and Land', broad gestures and sweeps convey the interaction of sea foam and green headland that was an immediate feature of the maritime view on her doorstep in St. Ives. At the start of the 1960's she lived in 'The Battery', an old coastguard station on the 'Island' in St. Ives, an outpost like Sven Berlin's 'Tower' had been on nearby Porthgwidden. In another local view, 'Waveboat', she once again creates a composite visual image, at once an incoming wave and a boat. In the earlier 'Levant' the artist alighted on a favourite early Lanyon theme, the disused copper mine near St. Just that drops down to and under the sea. The chasm of mine shaft, the surrounding cliff edge and the bleeding of copper rust into the sea are details that are treated with broad and rapid paint handling. The haemorrhaging of copper is indicated through a long, red slash of paint beneath the dark chasm form at the heart of the composition. In 'Levant' Wynne-Jones follows Lanyon in working up and across the picture plane. She creates tactility by feeling out form with gesture; unlike a fellow Welsh landscape painter, Peter Prendergast, she does not use line as an uninterrupted structural framework. But by the latter half of the decade her palette brightens as she searches for new territory, both literally and artistically, as if in response to the recent death of Lanyon. In spite of this sad event the mid 1960's was an exciting time; in 1965 she had a solo exhibition at the New Vision Centre in London and in 1966 married Conor Fallon, the Irish sculptor. This event pointed to her future in Ireland. The last decade of her Cornish years was spent in a large house in Gulval, near Penzance, from where she entertained extravagantly and extended great hospitality to fellow artists.

A common motif in later pictures is that of the roadway leading into a landscape. 'I generally paint a road', she has written, 'to announce that there is deep space in the picture, but I bring all the landscape to the surface of the painting, flattening, intensifying.'*13 An awareness of the virtue of perspective (instilled during drawing studies at Heatherleys and Chelsea in the early 1950's) as an illusionistic device for construction of landscape imagery, does not preclude a literal or expressive use of surface. She later introduced naive or expressionistic distortions of conventional pictorial composition in ways that reflected Lanyon's appropriation of Wallis's unique multi-directional approach to forming landscape imagery. Cézanne also became relevant here for the tension that could be struck up between the flatness of surface mark and the illusionism of space.

Wynne-Jones produced charcoal and pencil drawings - exploiting the medium to the full - throughout all phases of her career. A rapid, confident execution relies on a searching, meandering line to literally 'feel' out form, and zigzagging, hatching and eddying add further twist and visual, graphic variety to the surface. She is a natural draughtsman whose thickly inscribed and strongly delineated landscape studies like 'Botallack' (1965) echo Lanyon's late Clevedon drawings and Elena Gaputyte's charcoals. In a number of later drawings depicting the 'Road to Bandon' (late 1970's) Wynne-Jones continues the theme of the roadway entering the landscape and, perhaps more significantly, perpetuates the virtues of graphic fluency and visual immediacy. These are 'alla prima' graphic statements, strongly designed yet full of movement. They breathe with a liberated energy and seem to imply colour even where none exists. This confident, exhilarating air also animated later oils like 'Kinsale Harbour' (1988). Here she portrays the pearly light on a southern Irish estuary that is sandwiched between green headlands. The paint is applied with a sensual delight and is not tidied; drawing is absorbed into the painting process and a feeling of the mutability

Rose Hilton. On the Terrace. Oil.
David Messum Gallery, Cork Street, London.

of landscape, as perceived through our senses, is conveyed with a loose yet satisfying completeness. She does not embellish the works with the ritual of human activity. She retains the emotional directness of expressionism at the expense of the control of figurative and abstract academicism. She later wrote that 'the truly vital painters and sculptors of the 50's and 60's - and they through Lanyon, mostly exhibited at Newlyn rather than the Penwith - were the ones who were not interested in turning out correct modernist works, but who worked out of their own visual experience, and attempted to find their own way of expressing it. Lanyon towered over everyone in terms of originality and breadth.'*14

Rose Hilton and Louise McClary make colour their primary expressive vehicle and both retain the human form, though in very different ways. Rose

Louise McClary. Sacred Supper. *Acrylic.*

Hilton's nudes and figures use the soft focus of Post-Impressionist art. In her use of soft pastel colours and blurred edges she conjures a lyrical and atmospheric feeling of wellbeing. There is a domestic ambience that recalls much French art but Bonnard in particular . There is too, an implicit feminine quality that, in spite of herself, has flowered since emerging from under the

100

shadows of her husband Roger Hilton. Louise McClary's contemporary-looking work reflects in more robust terms the figurative work and expressionist revival of the late 1980's. Her art is more Germanic than French

Bob Bourne. Conversation with Roger Hilton. *Oil.*
Sims Gallery, St. Ives.

and a psychological drama, seen in 'Sacred Supper', attends distorted or disturbingly amplified mask-like images painted in bright, rich colours.

101

John Emmanuel, self-taught and from the north, also has a Porthmeor studio, where he produces a spate of reclining nudes, embodied in thick, gleaming glazes of textured paint. In common with Josef Herman he paints figures with a physical, almost sculptural gravitas. The sensuality of surface, with textured inlays, suggests the iconic significance of the human figure.

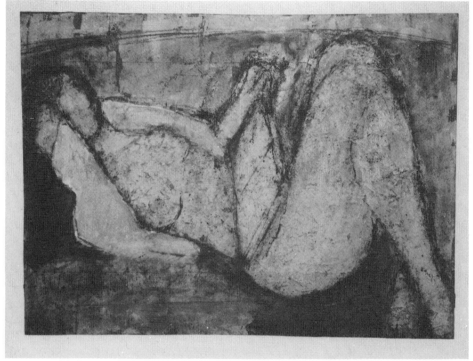

John Emmanuel. Figure Reading. *Oil.*
Photo: Roger Slack.

They have an almost religious aura, aided by occasional use of gold paint. Such striking figurative images seem suitable for mosaic, though they conform to the mainstream St. Ives tradition, with its predilection for order, for variations on a predetermined theme, for careful craft and for tasteful formal arrangements. With their smoothed surface patinas, these paintings also seem to hint at the association between the figure and landscape that we have seen as a recurring feature in all phases of St. Ives art. The large figure, full of classical gravity, fits into the picture with an encased certitude; the subject is thus a support prop, governed by aesthetic qualities to do with paint, colour, tone, surface and drawing.

Emmanuel likes his images to carry the process of time on their shoulders - they are worn fleshes and again in common with much St. Ives art, abstract and figurative, they seem to allude to time-worn antiquity. Perhaps he is struggling to say something about the human condition. Early in life Emmanuel, as a Barrow decorator and sign writer, discovered that wallpapering and house painting were relevant skills for someone wanting to paint pictures. This probably explains his habit of using paper alongside paint in the construction of textured surfaces. Pen became an instrument for drawing and a pronounced ink line characterises and gives definition to the shapes of limbs. The model is usually his wife or a close friend. Whatever the case, individuality is subsumed; instead he creates a generalised image entirely expressionistic in tone. His works have an obsessively worked intensity, sharing the work ethic of those artists, like Kossoff or Auerbach, that he so admires.

The figure is also uppermost in the monumental but darkly toned landscapes of Karl Weschke. An enveloping mood of apprehension does not stop the emergence of powerfully defined form. Weschke is the expressionist painter par excellence of modern Cornish art. His background is German and with a Teutonic accent he paints on a large scale, emphasising the bulk and weight of forms such as the human figure. Weschke's scenarios of washed up corpses are dramatic, theatrical, even sentimental. His dogs are similarly harrowing, barking at some western disturbance, while in the Gordale landscapes he confirms an involvement with the volume and spatial weight of inanimate as well as animate form. His colours are restricted to dark browns, greys, blacks and ochres. He shifts tone with incredibly subtle attention to the prevailing mood and atmosphere of the scene at hand. The artist's debased visions of human corpses clearly recall the more domesticated visions of Francis Bacon, who lived and worked in St. Ives in 1960 and knew Weschke. However, the openly heterosexual feeling conveyed in Weschke's 'Four Women and a Dog' contrasts with Bacon's enclosed homoerotic world. Born in 1925, Weschke's German childhood was unstable and disrupted, reflecting what was going on in German society at large during the 1930s. For this reason he later adopted pessimistic subjects. Largely self-taught, Weschke came to live in the refugee's haven on the western-most tip of England, where his outward-going nature enabled successful entry into the artistic milieu, and where personal charm assured many friendships with fellow artists. Weschke's secret lay in a winning blend of the convivial and the retiring. This mixture of gregariousness and isolation helped artists like Wynter or Weschke through the at times tricky world of a close, competitive artists' colony.

Weschke's first solo show was at Denis Bowen's New Vision Centre in London in 1958. Soon after, in 1960, he moved to a remote cottage at Cape Cornwall. The rugged, treacherous coastline of this stretch of Cornwall suited an imagination that was neither fanciful nor optimistic. The vulnerability of the human in the context of this awesome and grandiose environment became the thematic source material, and dominant emotional element, for images of dumped or lonely figures, tall cliffs, vast beaches, screeching dogs, horse riders or moving water. His forlorn figures are not, however, dwarfed by their

Karl Weschke. Four women and a dog. *Oil, 1973.*
Collection: Prantl.

vast surrounds; these figures therefore invest the picture with a large psychological presence, and with it an emphatic dimension to experience. Moreover, the artist's interest in the relationship between the human and animal world takes a leaf out of the book of soulful expressionist art, especially that of the Blue Rider. The impersonal figures often have an ambiguous air, for as Tom Cross observed 'The lying figure may be sunbathing, or it may be sacrificial.'*15

NOTES

1. Sven Berlin. *'Alfred Wallis, Primitive'* 1948, Republished 1993.
2. Charles Harrison *'The Modern, The Primitive and The Picturesque'*. 1987. Scottish Arts Council p.10.
3. Alan Bowness. Introduction to Bryan Pearce exhibition at M.O.M.A. Oxford 1975.
4. Alan Bowness. Introduction to Bryan Pearce exhibition at M.O.M.A. Oxford 1975.
5. Alan Bowness. *'Mary Jewels and naive painting'*. *'The Painter and Sculptor'*. Autumn 1958 p.4
6. Adrian Ryan. Catalogue statement for exhibition at Galerie Tew. Atlanta, Georgia. 1991.
7. Adrian Heath. Catalogue introduction for Peter Potworowski exhibition. 1982. University of London and Royal West of England Academy, Bristol, 1982.
8. John Halkes. Catalogue introduction for Albert Reuss exhibition, Newlyn Orion 1980.
9. Philip Vann. *'A Voyage of Discovery'* p.10 South Bank Centre 1990.
10. Philip Vann. *'A Voyage of Discovery'* p.13 South Bank Centre 1990.
11. Conversation with the author. May 1993.
12. Brian Fallon. *'Nancy Wynne Jones Retrospective Exhibition'* University of Cork. 1992. p.11
13. Brian Fallon. *'Nancy Wynne Jones Retrospective Exhibition'* University of Cork. 1992. p.11
14. Nancy Wynne Jones. Letter to the author 9.7.93.
15. Tom Cross. *'Painting the Warmth of the Sun'* p.180. Alison Hodge 1984.

CHAPTER 6

Peter Lanyon

Peter Lanyon's early death in 1964, at the age of forty-six, leaves behind the question of how his art might have developed. There is evidence in the last five years of a searching, passionate career, that he sought the direct vitality of American art. He made several professional trips to the United States and the late canvases, which still used Cornish themes also adopted new American ones; these are painted with the brighter colours and broader handling of contemporary American art. This hard-won confidence suggests that late on he broke through to a more relaxed and powerful mode of expression that enabled him to respond to new environments. The wit, energy and easy manner of his late works simplified the structurally complex, even chaotically jumbled imagery of the artist's earlier pictures. He was not an intellectual painter, but was rather an artist for whom experience was of paramount importance. He experienced landscape to the full, identified with it physically through his own bodily responses, and infused the results of his encounters and findings into the independent activity of painting. There is certainly a Rauschenbergian will to bridge the gap between art and life, in all phases of Lanyon's work. During the 1950s his normal Cornish subject matter was supplemented first by Italian, then Devon, Dorset and Derbyshire themes. By the 1960s, however, he responded to American culture, from rock'n'roll to urban consumerism and the brashness of pop. It is even possible that he may have become more of an American artist than a British one. He thought himself a provincial painter, however, and consciously resisted the easy allure of cosmopolitan fashion if it was not relevant to his most personal imperative, that of expressing experience. Yet his art belongs to the mainstream; he was perhaps a provincial person rather than artist, having always lived in a rural location.

At the time of writing, Lanyon has been dead for slightly longer than the twenty-five year duration of his professional life as an artist. His work has been carefully managed both by family and the Gimpel Fils and latterly Bernard Jacobson galleries. He has not been let out onto the market too quickly, and the intermittent showings of his work have been carefully considered affairs, mindful of not overcooking his growing esteem. Consequently his work has been exhibited in modest or provincial settings, often on the Arts Council circuit, and no major retrospective has followed the 1968 exhibition at the Tate. Books and catalogues on his work have likewise been of limited value and scope. Andrew Causey's 1971 book (Aiden Ellis) surveyed the main oils, but was accompanied by a concise, though far from comprehensive, text without much biographical flesh. Specialist catalogues,

106

like Causey's Whitworth study of paintings and related studies or Haydn Griffiths' study of his graphic work, opened up his lesser-known drawings and prints for a market created by the sharply rising prices of the oil paintings. Andrew Lanyon's 1991 book about his father, published new biographical material, ranging from letters, unknown sketches and statements, to family reminiscences. This collector's book on handmade paper fulfilled the need for biographical information. He has also been inadequately covered within the wider context of the 'St. Ives School', in books like Val Baker's 'Art Colony' (1959), Cross's 'Warmth of the Sun' (1984), or my own 'St. Ives Years' (1984). Apparent in all this is that his posthumous reputation has been skilfully nurtured in a gradual way - hype would be counterproductive to an earnest artist whose radical modernity has continued to gain new admirers and adherents as time has passed. Far from looking dated, his work has a constant meaning to new generations of students and artists who, even in an age of figurative revival, are often committed to plastic inventiveness and painterly values. His importance as an innovator in British landscape painting of this century is now widely recognised, and the prices for his best works have risen more than ten-fold since the early 1980s, to reach six figure sums.

Lanyon's work is full of movement, either depicted literally with gestural brushwork or emblematically, through allusion to 'unrestricted lateral movement across a surface'*1 The latter was first seen in the seminal 'White Track' (1939) with its distinctive central sling shape. Even in this early pre-war work Lanyon evokes landscape through tactile surface and a curved profile that recalls a hilltop silhouette. The artist always made constructions and drawings as ways of exploring space in preparation for the final image constructed in paint on the surface of the board or canvas. He was interested in the dualities and opposites of nature - male and female, surface and depth, opaqueness and transparency, concrete form and illusionism. He did not want an all-out abstraction but rather an associative abstraction full of naturalistic evocations, and here lies the central paradox of his art, making him so compelling and poetic an artist. The late paintings incorporate the materials once used in the constructions - coloured glass, perspex, tubing, found objects, metal, wood bars and so on - into the actual flat two dimensional field of the painting surface. This enabled him to evoke the tactile and visual experience that a physical engagement with the landscape gave him. The elemental flux of nature was expressed with a textural and gestural handling. By 1959 Lanyon emulated, in paintings like 'Gunwalloe' or 'Lost Mine', de Kooning's or Kline's handling, in which form and content became synonymous. In 'Lost Mine' he used fluid, spontaneous brushmarks to express the swallowing up of a mine shaft by an encroaching sea. Purchased by the Tate in 1992 for a six figure sum, 'Lost Mine' sees Lanyon create a sexual metaphor for the encroaching of the sea into a breached mine chasm. Since 'Europa' (1954) Lanyon dipped into mythic sources in order to imbue landscape imagery with the charge of human drama. He wrote that, 'my work has returned frequently to the shore as female, and the sea as male.' His wish to associate landscape with the female figure became increasingly apparent.

Lanyon's formal and thematic developments during the late 1940's went on display in the three Crypt exhibitions of the 1946-48 years, then in 1949 at the inaugural Penwith exhibition and at the artist's first solo show in London, at the Lefevre. The year 1949 was a threshold for his painting career; he was about to launch on a distinctive style that showed how the influences of first Smart, then Nicholson and Gabo had been absorbed but transformed. In the first Crypt show, Lanyon exhibited 'Generator', a colourful configuration of planes and curvilinear segments that conjured up a machine image while also evoking a figure. In this Lanyon is investigating, in an almost sculptural diagram, the relationship of interior and exterior forms. The influence of Gabo is still apparent as it is in many other works, (particularly in 'Generation' 1947) and related studies during this time. Small diagrammatic drawings using transparent planes, geometrical rhythms and curvilinear elements were produced in pencil during the war, and were sometimes made with ink, watercolour, and wax. These Gabo-influenced works radically supersede the academic sketches of 1937-8 when, under the influence of his studies at the Euston Road School, he concentrated on realistically depicted figures at work, or reclining in deckchairs. But these sketches show Lanyon well in control of conventional drawing - hatching, visual editing and tonal construction have reached a fluent level. The decision to explore non-figurative form after the war did not therefore pre-empt a mastery of basics.

The influence of Gabo is so fundamental a feature of Lanyon's formative, early development that it is instructive to ponder on the artistic relationship between them. The younger artist later declared that he found Gabo's sculptures 'such complete things that their very presence is paralysing.'[*2] The Gabo influence was dynamic and later furnished Lanyon with something to react against and thereby find his own identity, a unique blend of innovation and influence. The relationship between the two never descended into the rancour that clouded interactions between Lanyon and Hepworth and Nicholson. The Cornish artist later visited Gabo's Connecticut home, and the latter felt great 'sorrow' at Lanyon's early death.[*3] There was often a personal element in Lanyon's preferences, though not to the extent of compromising his main artistic choices. Michael Canney recalled how, 'Lanyon also used to talk much more frequently about Gabo than Nicholson, and had a higher respect for him. Peter was very contrary in his opinions and would of course enthuse about a sculptor rather than a painter, but I think that in this case, the Gabo-worship was genuine.'[*4] Canney was also, 'also struck by the fact that Gabo was far more of an influence on his own development and that Nicholson, the painter, was not the principal influence.'[*5] Canney found it odd that Lanyon's primary influence should be a sculptor rather than another painter, but went on to explain that 'Peter's work during the war in the R.A.F., cannibalising aircraft and converting the parts to other uses, is essentially a tactile and practical act, closer to sculpture than painting, and very much concerned with a three dimensional world - certainly a long way from the painter's concern with the flat surface, or with illusionism.'[*6]

Although Lanyon's high reputation is founded on innovations made within the traditional English genre of landscape painting, his oeuvre is underscored by the constructions that are 'more strikingly original than the paintings' and also 'totally personal', according to Lanyon's fellow Cornish contemporary. The 'totally personal' nature of what Canney described as 'those crazy structures of broken glass, plastic, Bostik, aluminium, discarded fragments of his life, and even rejected portions of his paintings'*7 is based on their

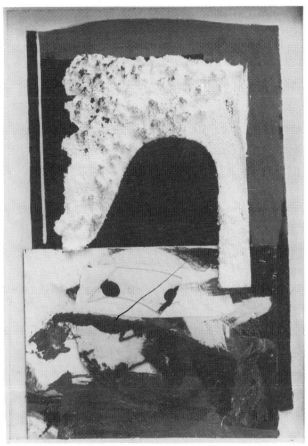

Peter Lanyon. Pendeen. *Plastic, glass and oil. 1964.*
Sheila Lanyon.

Cornishness. Canney explained that 'Lanyon's constructions seem to grow naturally out of the materials used, so that the constructive process is a spontaneous one, not as sophisticated as the paintings, but having the appearance and feel of the rough and tough world of the tin miner - totally genuine and uninfluenced artefacts - and very Cornish in their improvised nature ... they constantly remind me of the tin streamers' raw and crude workings - old metal castings, planks and gulleys, assembled spontaneously and with a certain genius for 'making do' with what is at hand.'[*8] It is this mixture of a native Cornishness, expressed through a spontaneous manipulation of materials closest to hand, (a quality that had first attracted Nicholson to Wallis), together with the 'conscientious researches under a superlative master' that makes Lanyon such a versatile, interesting and double-edged artist. Here lies the uncanny blend of the local and international.

Another, very different kind of influence at the time was Adrian Stokes, who lived at Little Park Owles (Lanyon's later home) and was responsible for bringing down to Cornwall Hepworth, Nicholson and Gabo in a bid to escape

Peter Lanyon in studio.

war-torn London. He was better known as a writer than a painter. Stokes's influential book 'Colour and Form' was published in 1937 and followed on from 'Stones of Rimini' (1934). At the very centre of Stokes's thesis in his book is the distinction between carved and plastic as the two fundamental modes of artistic expression. As relevant to sculpture as much as to painting, the concept was further developed by Stokes to include the role of colour. He advocated a use of colour to support and enhance form through simultaneous contrast 'at all angles and directions throughout a picture'. He went on to prefer 'Colour that comes out from form, rather than colour merely 'Stuck on', carving as opposed to plastic.' Stokes's notion that colour was a primary instrument for generating form fell on fertile ground in Cornwall - the early Gabo and Lanyon paintings used the tonal and chromatic properties of colour to stress the inherent and essential luminosity of form. Lanyon's colour, seeming to emanate from form in the way decreed by Stokes, possessed a luminosity that pertained to the transparent curvilinear planes of his 'Gaboid' paintings of the late 1940's, but extended to the painterly, abstract landscapes of the 1950's, like 'St. Ives Bay' (1957) where the shine and sparkle of blues brings the maritime picture to life in an extra-ordinarily moving and evocative way.

The artist used the stuff and form of paint to evoke experience of landscape. He associated the rich medium of paint with flesh or used the scraped down textures of paint and hardboard to evoke the geological sandwich of rock strata. Later on, his incorporation of collaged material into his paintings signified the unifying of form with content, as the debris of his environment was used to satisfy both illusionistic and concrete aspects. The incorporation of found objects into his work illustrated the importance of outdoor experience, for these objects were the umbilical cord tying Lanyon's work to experience of nature. Early in his career he relinquished the plein-air painting practices learnt from Borlase Smart in 1936 and was driven indoors by the force of the elements. 'When I began to paint', he declared, 'the cliff edge and winter storms put more pressure on me than I could absorb. My pictures became so messy and dispersed that I was driven indoors and settled for experiments in the technical problems of painting.' The constructions, while using the debris of the outside environment, were made in the domestic arena of the studio, and so were models of the spatial and structural dimension of his experience of nature. Although he was driven indoors, Lanyon continued for the rest of his career to draw in outdoor locations, a practice that culminated in the late Clevedon drawings. These were executed in the company of Bristol art students, whom he had taken to the resort on a sketching expedition. But sketching excursions in the company of other artists, like the one to Geevor Mine in 1946 with Wells and Berlin, lessened as Lanyon matured and preferred to pursue private artistic problems alone. Cross has remarked how, when in the studio, no one was allowed in and 'he would shut himself away for days or weeks while a particular problem occupied him.'*9

The highly evocative use of naturalistic colour owes something to Alfred Wallis, with whom Lanyon identified both for ethnic and artistic reasons.

Indeed, the influence of Wallis seems all but obvious. Lanyon's use of local colour to express the green grass, grey and brown granite, gorse yellow and lichen greens related to the older artist's use of landscape-evoking colour. Wallis used varnish paints and yacht paints which were based on stand oil. Lanyon used half stand oil, half turps in which to grind his colour. This enabled him to work relatively fast, because of stand oil's fast drying properties, and he was thereby able to exploit accidental painterly smears in the image-making process, as new layers of paint were dragged across tacky undercoats. The artist wrote in 1952 that, 'Paint represents experience and makes it actual. My source is sensuous ...plastic form is arrived at ...by sensory paint manipulation.'

In view of Lanyon's later dissension with Hepworth it is not fashionable to link his work with her sculpture, though the 1947 'Generation' presents a

Peter Lanyon. Construction for Bojewyan Farms. *1952.*

112

madonna-like figure that echoes her hollowed out figure carvings. But it was in his attempt to break out of too close an involvement with Gabo's constructive mould that Lanyon began to create an identity for himself. Margaret Garlake wrote how 'the intractable problem of distancing himself from a revered master was a compelling stimulus for Lanyon to alter the course of his work.'[*10] In horizontal landscapes like 'West Penwith' and later 'Bojewyan Farms' Lanyon took the pure planar language of Gabo and superimposed naturalistic impurities. He explained, 'It is these references and impurities which I developed and so opted for a richer and in fact more local vein.' In 'West Penwith' and 'Portreath' of 1949 Lanyon felt he had succeeded in shedding the tight influence of his mentors, for he considered these works represented 'the initial breakthrough from Gabo-Hepworth-Nicholson abstraction, and the basis of all my painting since.'[*11] Lanyon, the proud Cornishman, probably felt more charitable and certainly had less to lose in acknowledging the influence of Wallis. The horizontal format of several late 1940's works like 'Fishboat' or 'Bicyclist in Penwith' may well have been influenced by Wallis's 'long' paintings, two of which were owned by Stokes and which Lanyon would certainly have known.

Lanyon's 'distancing himself from a revered master' took other forms than those to do solely with the development of style. As early as the 1940's Lanyon revealed a self-willed, even headstrong tendency to plough a lone furrow; he wanted a separate identity for himself that did not compromise with others. He had definite ideas about what he wanted and in numerous letters to his dealer Peter Gimpel, spoke about his struggles to reach an authentic expression. He also described what he saw as harmful influences in the work of other less sure artists. He occasionally supported others in his letters, even recommending John Wells to Gimpel. In one letter, written in 1951, he saw 'a very big gulf between what I am doing and what we know as abstract. I would show today for instance with Nicholson white reliefs and Gabo and Mondrian and be honoured to be called 'abstract' but what is really happening is that there is a perpetuation of alphabet searching - a new sleazy research into development forms beyond the usefulness of it. Even Gear is looking for roots. What the abstract means is a continuation of a cosmopolitan culture which is dead.' A dead cosmopolitan culture probably meant the demise of the International style and the absolute programmes of the pre-war Circle group. It was in his own interest to develop art through the objective channels represented by a return to nature even while relying on a degree of abstraction in order to retain formal toughness.

In St. Ives, Lanyon's quarrel with Nicholson and Hepworth about their perpetuation of 'cosmopolitan culture' extended also to others. In a 1948 letter to Sven Berlin, Lanyon reveals a desire to get on with his own career and not get bogged down in a too close group identity. He wrote 'I am greatly disturbed by lack of real co-operation among the Crypt members. It appears to me that my position as founder and director of the Crypt leads to responsibility being left to me. I therefore intend to discontinue the organisation of the Crypt but will be perfectly willing to show if anybody decides to organise it.'[*12] Lanyon believed the Crypt shows had completed the intended revolution within the old Society of Artists. The new generation's presence in the Society's basement took on the metaphorical guise of a gunpowder plot. In the same letter Lanyon went on to say, 'The differences of opinion and feeling amongst us being the healthiest side of the whole organisation, I do not wish to be in a position of administration at a time (the next three years) when my own ideas are crystallising and therefore, my opinions hardening.' He continued by stating that, 'the possibility of creating something real are greatest' but he also felt unable to speak to his London contacts on behalf of Crypt members because of 'too many doubts about the response I shall obtain from the members about any arrangements I may make.' There is thus sense in this letter of an uneasy alliance among Crypt members. Lanyon's ideas were certainly crystallising at the time and so he did not want to become distracted by responsibilites such as running an exhibiting group, particularly one that had such conflicting approaches.

The possibility of 'creating something real' came to fruition in the year following the last Crypt show, with the final schism between the younger artists and the older Society, and the subsequent formation of the Penwith. But even here Lanyon soon felt his interests compromised by the problems of belonging to a large group of artists. Nicholson's manipulation of the Penwith angered Lanyon, who felt a rule distinguishing between representational and abstract art in favour of the latter was 'inhuman'.*13 He had a keen sense of artistic tradition in Cornwall and felt the Penwith would easily become 'a way to personal fame or common advertisement' among as yet immature artists. Tom Cross explained how, after resigning from the Penwith, 'Lanyon had little to do with the art organisation in St. Ives. He became a member of the Newlyn Art Society and was at pains to choose his friends from those who were more independent of St. Ives, either by geography or by personal preference.'*14

The strength of feeling against the orthodoxies of a semi-official Penwith group style matched the sureness of Lanyon's own artistic principles. In an essay for 'Arts' (New York) in early 1956 Patrick Heron summarised his colleague as an artist for whom total abstraction 'holds less interest than an art which abstracts from visual reality in order to communicate that reality to us more forcefully.' This was the essential point about his motive as an artist. Heron's apt summary was echoed in 1963 when Lanyon insisted on painting being an active force 'looking forward and assisting in a positive constructive view of the world.'*15

The instruction that Lanyon received from Ben Nicholson gave him a vocabulary of concrete form, but so absolute were the terms of Nicholson's composition that the younger man soon felt compelled to rebel. He sought to camouflage Nicholsonian austerity and abstract formalism with the trappings of associative naturalism in a bid to express the declared subject of his art - the landscape of his native Cornwall. Lanyon's early work shared what Tom Cross explained was a similar 'use of cubist form and muted, scraped down colour.'*16 But Lanyon wanted to go further and create a metamorphic poetry and a richness of reference in order to reach the desired 'Sense of atmospheric mystery and movement.' The heightened sense of mystery and atmosphere accompanied old places, and was attained in the very earliest paintings such as the wartime 'Ruins at Capua'. Movement was expresed in terms of time as well as space. A sense of humanist as well an existential presence compelled the artist to express both the human history of Cornwall and the development of landscape through geological processes.

Implicit in the work of St. Ives artists is a preoccupation with the factor of time as an agent of landscape evolution. Wynter's 'Sandspoor' paintings, for instance, recorded the aftermath of animal migration in terms of deposited footprints. Hepworth's sculptural surfaces are likewise scoured and marked with the suggestion of once dominant natural forces that have long since passed. Wynter was interested in Aldous Huxley's mystical insights into time and read 'The Doors of Perception'. He also experimented with the mind-expanding drug mescalin. Ultimately these interests led to the late 'Imoos' - mobiles that expressed themselves not only through spatial movement but also through time. But Lanyon's interest in time was less philosophic or mystic. Rather, his interest was a practical one, as a way of reaching greater understanding and perception of geology and landscape structure. Lanyon's constructions were therefore static entities, encouraging movement from the spectator who could walk around and experience his transparent, planar and spatially open works from different angles in a microcosmic equivalent to the manner that the artist adopted active ways of moving about a landscape in order to gain intimacy with it.

Cross pointed out how Lanyon's three early masterpieces, large pictures of Portreath, Porthleven and St. Just, were each worked up after elaborate preparatory studies. These studies took the form of freely executed charcoal or pencil drawings produced on the spot, though investigating the subject from as many angles as possible, and constructions in which the artist explored the structural and spatial elements, in order to help him gain full and intimate understanding of the subject prior to painting it on canvas or board. The use of constructions in the preparation of a painting was proof of how plastic and formal were Lanyon's approaches even while wanting to deal with the incidents of nature. He wanted space to be a dynamic element in the composition and it had to be explored in literal three-dimensional terms before the two dimensional painted image was tackled. This gave the final image greater cogency and authenticity. Lanyon's first solo exhibition, at Lefevre in the autumn of 1949, won him acclaim and he was invited to produce a large painting for the 1951 Festival of Britain. The increased scale of these new pictures in itself prompted the kind of investigative preparations just alluded to, and contrasted with the very earliest work, such as the 'Yellow Runner' or 'Fishboat', which have the intimate scale and neo-romantic air of much early post-war British art. Although the forms of 'St. Just' and 'Porthleven' were still dense and jumbled, these environmental works nonetheless looked away from the 1940's and forward into the 1950's. 'Porthleven' was also the name of a painting produced that same year by Barns-Graham, whose severely linear and scraped down approach to the buildings and harbour geography is indebted to Nicholson. All the same, Lanyon's assembled forms - clocktower, pier, boats, sea and sky - are stacked in an independent and neo-cubist way to satisfy strictly formal requirements. In so doing, the shapes are tilted up in a similar way to Nicholson's device of presenting still life objects frontally, through tilting the tabletop in a way that meets the picture plane.

In his large 1951 painting of St. Just, Lanyon used a style and approach to form that also departed dramatically from the treatment given to the same subject by another former Crypt colleague, this time David Haughton. Haughton's approach, like Barns-Graham's, was linear, and used a single static viewpoint with which to construct exact and measured renditions of the derelict mining town. Haughton had been trained at the Slade. Forms and shapes as perceived through space were pinpointed within the conventional vanishing point of Renaissance perspective. Lanyon's pictorial space, which used landscape markers like telegraph poles as 'space articulators', relinquished set procedures with which to locate form. He was encouraged in his autonomous approach by Nicholson's tilted cubism, Gabo's spatially open, transparent constructivism, and by Wallis's primitive assembling of landscape shapes that were fitted in willy nilly to the pictorial arena without any sense of topographic or naturalistic credence. In the same way that Wallis, and his later naive successor Bryan Pearce, could string a row of cottages upside down along the edges of a painting for decorative ends, so Lanyon grouped various references around the central, black axis. The axis in 'St. Just' reads as both a mineshaft chasm and a crucifix, while topographic imagery jumbled to the left and right of the central axis conjured up a pair of figures, male and female, in a way suggestive of rebirth through procreation. The figurative images are diffuse, secondary and often hard to decipher, being embedded in primary topographic information. The correspondence between landscape and figure was not developed into a literal metamorphosis, of the kind created by Dali in his 'paranoia criticism' phase. But the figurative presence fulfilled the artist's desire to create a human dimension to landscape, which was now able to carry mythic, social, psychological and even political meaning. In one single monumental picture he thus succeeded in producing not only an atmosphere of place, a sense of the 'genius loci' that was as fundamental to British landscape art as was what Burke's 18th century treatise called the sublime and picturesque in landscape, but also comment about the exploitation of landscape by capitalism. His work therefore contains a political dimension, too, and has continued to gain relevance in the present day's growing ecological consciousness. The loss of Cornish lives in mining accidents drove Lanyon to equate the mineshaft with a crucifix. 'St. Just' was shown in London in the 'Space in Colour' exhibition at the Hanover Gallery in 1952. Its showing in the metropolis elicited cosmopolitan reviews and John Berger spoke of the cartographic quality in Lanyon's work, distinguishing it from an ordinary descriptive role.

In 1953 Lanyon revisited Italy on an Italian government scholarship. (He had spent part of the war there on active service). He visited the British School in Rome and then went up into the hills where he became fascinated with the same close relationship between human settlement and natural geography that had moved him in Cornwall. Anticoli Corrado became Lanyon's equivalent of Bomberg's Spanish Ronda, and both here and in the hill town of Saracinesco Lanyon made drawings that were later used to produce large and colourful paintings. The southern light and classical sharpness of form led to a 'more intense use of colour,' but as Cross also remarked, encouraged still more an interest in classical myth, and especially an enhanced association between landscape and the female figure. Although this had already been dormant in his work, it assumed larger prominence in the classically-influenced 'Europa' of 1954, and reached sublime proportions in the 1957 'Beach Girl', in which the reclining figure of his mistress on a beach also doubled up as a section of coastal landscape. Gouaches and charcoal drawings of this time examined the reclining figure as a motif replete with landscape associations, and the example of Henry Moore's craggy, pierced and eroded figures reinforced the lesson. He used the life model at Corsham, an exercise that encouraged the stark image of the life model to form the iconography of a number of independent and worked up oils and gouaches during the late 1950's.

The New American Painting exhibition at the Tate early in 1956 came as a reassurance rather than challenge to Lanyon. Indeed, the exporting of abstract expressionism was not the sudden revolution that is sometimes believed. Gestural and spontaneous painting had grown out of surrealist automatism and had gradually created a school of post-surreal abstractions in Paris as well as in New York. As Patrick Heron later pointed out in his epic 'Guardian' essays, St. Ives was abreast with developments coming out of America. Nevertheless, Lanyon's viewing of work by Rothko, Kline, Motherwell and Pollock greatly encouraged him. Already Lanyon's work had seen a move away from the themes of earth and fertility and had become atmospheric, concentrating more on the elements of sky and sea. In January 1957, exactly a year after the New York painters were shown at the Tate, Lanyon had his first solo show across the Atlantic at the Catherine Viviano Gallery in New York City. Here he made a great impression among a group of like-minded artists, and he made frequent visits to the United States thereafter, reflected in his late work's use of American sources and imagery. In 1959 he enjoyed a second exhibition at Viviano's.

The picture that perhaps most clearly showed the effect of New York painting was 'Silent Coast' (1957). Although it was inspired by a famous Lanyon theme, the high aerial perspective where everything 'was still and slow moving, as on those days when after stormy weather one gets extreme silence and restfulness on the coast of West Penwith.'[*17] the picture did in fact resemble Rothko in terms of a diaphanous frontal plane of atmospheric blues. The solitude of being high up, among the clouds and thermals, reinforced Lanyon's sense of painting being a lonely, existential activity, where the artist was left alone to confront the universe. Nevertheless, the adoption of gliding in 1959 and the subsequent glider paintings led to an imagery with a very specific source for 'air is a very definite world of activity, as complex and demanding as the sea.'[*18]

Gradually, the distinction between construction and painting broke down, in a way suggesting that Gabo's early Constructivist influence was being superseded by a less serious tenor, in the wake of pop and neo-dada modes that were perhaps best exemplified by Rauschenberg's open-ended notion of painting that bridged the gap between art and life, and also the gap between painting and sculpture. Collage and the introduction of found objects from the artist's personal experience of 'reality' were the best ways of achieving this synthesis. Lanyon was a curious mixture of the cavalier and the traditional, for he never fully broke out of the chronic pastoral tradition at the root of British art, and furthermore his professional approach had, if not a predictability then an implicit logic. He tended to work in series, exploring and exhausting ideas together. The artist's 'Built Up Coast' (1960) was part painting, part collage, and contained coloured glass, fragments of painted board, ceramic tile, and a metal grid. He dragged white paint thinly across a rough dark blue underpainting, creating, through textural association, the feeling of wind across the ocean, whipping up surf and foam. The ceramic tiles incorporated in this painting were certainly used from tiles that the artist had made in Mary Redgrave's kiln in St. Ives, for his large ceramic mural of 1960 'The Conflict of Man with the Tides and Sands'. By working in series Lanyon would improvise on one painting by using materials or imagery overspilling from another. This fulfilled the plastic spontaneity and flow of energy that was an imperative of avant-garde painting on both sides of the Atlantic at this time. In some ways Lanyon was able to bridge the gap between Robert Motherwell's philosophic distinction between psychic and plastic automatism, proving what a versatile, energetic and broad artist he was.

Another instance where free-standing constructions - one hesitates to call them sculptures because the artist viewed them as incomplete preparatory studies - were absorbed into the pictorial arena is in 'Coast Soaring' (1958). The painting is set within a deep box frame, the inside edges of which are painted in an evocative blue. The prominent framing and glazing increases a sense of the work's object quality, making it akin to a wall-bound sculptural relief. Across the central area of the painting are two arcs, made of copper and red plastic tubing, which curve across most of the painting's vertical height. While echoing the sling trajectory of 'White Track', these collaged arcs also anticipate the metal bars screwed into the red and green surface of the late painting, 'Glide Path', (Whitworth Art Gallery, Manchester).

Lanyon desired to transmit his experience of nature through a dynamic and sensuous engagement with the materials of his art, and he also wanted the spectator to participate in the process by confronting him or her with unusual modes of presentation. A measure of Lanyon's success on both sides of the Atlantic came with mural commissions at Liverpool and Birmingham Universities, then at Stanley Seeger's home in New Jersey. This important commission resulted in a huge thirty foot painting 'Porthmeor' that revealed enlightened patronage from a private American collector. Lanyon produced a painting 'Lake', depicting the large grounds at Seeger's Frenchtown New Jersey home. Lanyon used bright and crispy delineated primary colour for this. Colour indeed grew brighter and less naturalistic after 1960, in response to Pop art and Post Painterly Abstraction. The compositions use broad and clearly defined areas of a single colour even while continuing to depict landscape subjects such as stretches of coastline. A good example of this is 'Fistral', where the components of a glider window merge with a clear, if flatly rendered, evocation of the bay near Newquay.

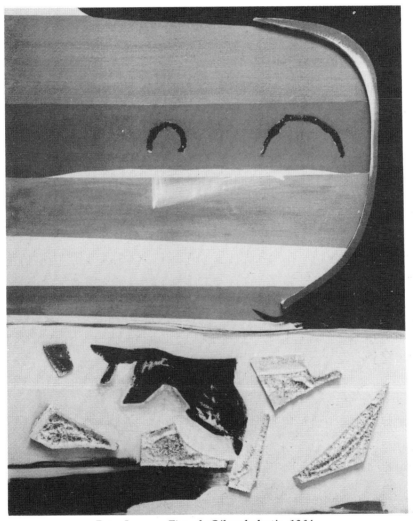

Peter Lanyon. Fistral. *Oil and plastic, 1964.*

In 'Heather Coast' (1963) Lanyon uses a vivid purple and red to structure most of the composition, while the late Clevedon canvases also use primaries.

The Whitworth's 'Glide Path' likewise presents red and green in a starkly drawn zonal juxtaposition without any modulating textural or coloristic incident. The effect of American art is surely apparent in 'Colour Construction' of 1960, in which transparent pyramids of blue glass are lit from

Peter Lanyon. Clevedon and Pier. *Gouache, 1964.*

inside by a circular electric tube light. The late construction 'Field Landing' presents a free-standing red plane of irregular though hard-edged geometry and related in terms of colour and planarity to 'Glide Path'. A new humour had entered his art, which displayed the virtuosity of the carefree assembler. Although this confident, even flippant ingenuity with materials was not new, harking back to its greatest practitioners like Picasso and Schwitters, the wit, stridency and lightheartedness of these works relates to the new consumer-orientated hedonism of Pop art. Lanyon was assuredly seeking to break down the boundaries between media, merging painting with assemblage, and creating through differing disciplines, materials and processes the broader synthesis which gave ample justification to the totality and passion of his all-consuming experience of the world. In 'Playtime' (1964), an aptly named painting containing glasses, sockets, screws, door hinges, broken ceramics,

120

spoons and car mirrors, Lanyon reveals a childlike delight in assembling with ordinary everyday bric-a-brac. The effect of Johns as well as Rauschenberg is undoubtedly present in the random recycling of consumer objects. Had Lanyon lived and pursued such processes perhaps he would have eventually made installation works like the ones Richard Long or Tony Cragg later produced.

Another instance of Lanyon's late involvement with the man-made sphere of consumer culture came with the gouache studies of American automobile numberplates, although in gouaches like 'Village Maidens' (1963) the artist returned to a rustic source. But the pronounced frontality of these images typified his late work. In 'Eagle Pass' (1963) he painted an automobile steering wheel, in a picture representing the experience of driving in Mexico. Andrew Causey wrote that the 'parochialism of Lanyon's immediate sources was complemented by his receptivity to any innovation that he could put to good use in his own painting. This is especially true of his openness to modern American painting and his love of America itself.'[19] His final picture on an American theme was 'Lake' (1964) which according to Causey 'represents a marked change of direction in Lanyon's late work, which is in general richer and less naturalistic in colour, more thinly painted and less dependent on Cornwall alone as a source of ideas: it is characterised by a greater urbanity, conceding something to elegance.'[20]

NOTES

1. 'The Constructions of Peter Lanyon' Margaret Garlake. South Bank Centre. 1992. p.50.
2. Letter to John Wells 31.3.49
3. Conversation between Miriam Gabo and the author. London 1982.
4. Michael Canney to the author. Letter dated 27.12.92.
5. Michael Canney to the author. Letter dated 27.12.92.
6. Michael Canney to the author. Letter dated 27.12.92.
7. Michael Canney to the author. Letter dated 27.12.92.
8. Michael Canney to the author. Letter dated 27.12.92.
9. 'Painting the Warmth of the Sun' Tom Cross. Alison Hodge. 1984. p.127.
10. Garlake. South Bank Centre. 1992.
11. Peter Lanyon. Recorded talk for British Council. 1963.
12. Letter in collection of Eric Quayle, Zennor.
13. Peter Lanyon. Letter to 'St. Ives Times' 15.4.55.
14. Cross. p.128
15. Peter Lanyon. Notes on painting. 30.9.63. See Andrew Lanyon p.245.
16. Cross. p.123
17. Peter Lanyon. Recorded talk for British Council. 1963.
18. Peter Lanyon. Recorded talk for British Council. 1963.
19. Andrew Causey. 'Modern Art Exhibition' Poole Arts Centre. 1980.
20. Causey. Poole Arts Centre. 1980.

CHAPTER 7

Through the Eye of a Circle and Square

It is possible to see the Cornish landscape exerting a softening effect on the fully resolved abstraction of artists like Ben Nicholson and Naum Gabo. In Nicholson's case this resulted in the merging of the shallow space of cubist still-life with the deeper landscape space framed within the four sides of a window motif. Nicholson made a play of surface design and illusory depth, exploiting an essential tension between two and three dimensions that seems to enliven pictorial art. The younger artists who pursued Nicholson's cubism and Gabo's constructivism did so using an even greater mixture of geometry and soft naturalism. They included John Wells, Barns-Graham and Alex Mackenzie, whose use of line, plane and overlapping geometric form alludes to topographic or tectological landscape features. Still younger practitioners like Michael Snow, George Dannatt, Michael Canney and Morag Ballard used compass, ruler, set square or else simple visual judgement to create compositions of emotional richness as well as rational precision. The contrast between static and dynamic form elicited a lyrical poetry of great distinction and subtlety. Yet, Nicholson, Gabo and their 'followers' were not alone in forging a mid-century Cornish modernism. Artists like John Tunnard, Marlow Moss and Ithel Colquhoun also brought down with them international ideas, and their contribution deserves greater appreciation.

The mature art of John Tunnard (1900-1971) integrates the opposing extremes of surrealism and constructivism - the parameters that staked out the ground of progressive art during the 1930's - in an unusual and individual synthesis of visionary proportions. During the war, when he was a coastguard in Cornwall, Tunnard invested hybrid compositions of organic and geometric forms with the specific maritime shapes, textures and images that were absorbed from the landscape of Cornwall. He moved to Cornwall during the early 1930's, though his education had taken place in the cosmopolitan atmosphere of London. Born in Bedfordshire and educated at Charterhouse, Tunnard studied design at the Royal College in London during the 1920's. Later he taught design at Penzance, and it was through an ability to organise a surface that Tunnard wove together a wide assortment of images, of alternately dream-like or concrete proportions, that broke out of normal perspectival schemes.

Tunnard absorbed many influences during the 1930's. The biomorphic and architectural aspects of modern art - seen in the art of Klee, Calder, Miro and Tanguy - made a great impression on the mind of an artist who had a curious interest in both the natural world and in technology. The abstract language of music also had its role to play, for Tunnard frequently played drums with a jazz band. Some of his string, disc or curved forms clearly evoked musical instruments. But the actual look of his art - the interlocking semi-transparent planes, the fantastic glimpses of land, sea and sky, the taut lines, curvilinear segments, fusions of geometry and naturalism, balanced fancies and the scraped, smoothed or striated layers of paint texture - derived from the disciplines of a designer who, during the 1930's, ran a textile business. The weaving and dying processes therefore played as much a part in moulding the artist's characteristic scraped surface as the use of surrealist techniques like decalcomania, frottage or other rubbing effects.

By the end of the war Tunnard was an artist of confidence whose superbly poised painting 'Forecast' (1945) brought together these strands. The work has a futuristic mood of new inventions on the horizon and of technological progress to come. The mystery of natural form gives way to speculative prototypes of space age machinery. As far as style is concerned, the drawing weds the automatic, biomorphic energy of Miro with the rigid planning of the surveyor's drawing board. But the colours and textures are generally naturalistic, moving from the ocean bed biomorphs reminiscent of Tanguy to the aerodynamic forms of Calder and Gabo. By 1945 Tunnard had been collected by the Tate in London and by the Museum of Modern Art in New York. He had also been feted by Peggy Guggenheim, who found his work musical, delicate and gay. With carefully composed structures and designs, and with naturalistic palettes, Tunnard's paintings exuded the energy of 'an English Romantic whose imagination combined modern art, technology, personal experience and knowledge of nature.'[*1]

Tunnard's work evolved from an early conventional landscape style which geometricised prominent landscape features like telegraph poles, roads or stone walls. Lanyon, who was inspired by Tunnard's work, later referred to telegraph poles as 'space articulators' in a landscape; images of telegraphs are used as formal and spatial markers in his preparatory studies. Tunnard is likely to have divined the telemechanical significance of such objects. With the enquiring mind of a scientist, he created schematic symbols of energy lines in his work. There came a point during the late 1930's when Tunnard decided to invent rather than represent what he saw, though the general mode of presentation of his imagery was based on sound illustration and design. All this resulted in an articulate fusion of the imagined and the seen in his work. Such was the breadth and diversity of his formal and imaginative powers that he had won the respect of Henry Moore, as well as Guggenheim, before the war, and exhibited with front rank Surrealists at the A.I.A. galleries in London.

In spite of these successes, Tunnard was loath to associate closely with other artists, either in London or in Cornwall. He entertained lavishly and was sociable but he worked alone, pursuing an individual vision with a variety of stylistic influences. Though these styles were essentially based on pre-war avant-garde developments, Tunnard managed to keep his work in touch with the mood and conditions of the times, and in particular his work ran parallel to the spirit of discovery that accompanied technological progress during the 1950's and 1960's. In 1958 Michael Canney wrote an article in the scientific magazine 'Discovery' about what he called the proper and significant relationship between science and art. In it, he cited Tunnard as an example of the painter who uses the intuitive vehicle of art to share in modernism's scientific spirit of discovery. Canney even argues that radar forms occurred in Tunnard's work before their actual invention in the practical arena of technology. Canney wrote how, 'the vast distances in John Tunnard's paintings seem to herald the space age'*2 Certainly the realm of extra-terrestrial space, expressed as cosmological symbols in the intuitive orbit of Surrealism, assumed the full authority of objective science in Tunnard's later work. The 1969 composition 'Messenger', for example, is dominated by a large radio telescope disc, and the surrounding space tilts from the violets of the upper atmosphere into the blue blacks of outer space. This late work accompanies the historic moon landings of the same year.

John Tunnard's exploration of deep, even infinite, space distinguishes him from Nicholson's, shallow space. The planarity of Tunnard's compositions obeys the requirements of sound surface design while allowing a rich poetry or Surrealist enigma and fantasy to emerge. He pushes the frontiers of consciousness and scientific understanding. In 1953 he moved to Lamorna, a part of Cornwall where two other similarly isolated modernists, Marlow Moss and Ithel Colquhoun lived. During the subsequent two decades of his life Tunnard introduced an extravagant mixture of symbols and fragmented images that included ants, bolts, utensils, plants, machines and landscape features. These have the random quality of the dream. His electric cable biomorphism integrates technology with nature in the same way that he had earlier associated machines with insects. When mundane objects are launched into the realm of the fantastic through chance association, Tunnard's work looks a prototype for that of 1980' artists like Graham Crowley and Maurice Cockrill. Ithel Colquhoun also evokes a fantastic aura through chance effect and metamorphosis, though her means are different. She belongs to the wing of plastic automatism whereby the marvels of chance and transformation are reached through the physical processes of working materials. Frottage, decalcomania and other rubbing techniques create textural evocations of the natural world. Elaborate, soft, swelling natural forms based on plants, rocks or segments of anatomy are elevated to levels of iconographic significance. She explored the occult in order to enrich the imagery of her art with the full transformative power of hallucination and alchemy. Like Tunnard, Colquhoun has an international following, due to links with Surrealism and her belonging to the canon of Feminist art.

Marlow Moss settled in Penzance in 1941 and later exhibited on several occasions with the Penwith Society. She had lived in Cornwall as early as 1919 and attended sculpture classes at Penzance art school during the 1920's. In the late 1920's she lived and worked in Paris, where contact with Mondrian and Leger became of prime importance for her development. Michael Canney, who at the time of Moss's death in 1958, was curator at Newlyn, made the following recollections:

'In retrospect I find it difficult to credit that Marlow Moss, perhaps the closest follower of Mondrian, could have lived and worked in the midst of a colony of artists in west Cornwall for so many years, and have still remained a private figure. It is true that she was frequently absent on the continent, and that she deliberately led a secluded life at Lamorna, where she had a small studio like a mission chapel. But I do recall one fleeting image of her on a pony and trap, riding in style on her way to Penzance market, with Nettie (Njihoff) beside her. On another occasion she appeared in Newlyn Art Gallery, striding from picture to picture, small, alert, and attired it seemed as a kind of jockey. I did not know then, and indeed nobody was aware, that her work was respected by Leger and Ozenfant, by Max Bill (a particularly close friend), by Jean Gorin, Herbin, Vantongerloo, and a host of other European artists of note. She had even been sponsored by Mondrian himself as a founder-member of the 'Abstraction-Création' group.

As an artist, Moss has been dismissed as 'Too close to Mondrian for comfort', an indication that her critics are prepared to ignore the favourable opinions of Max Bill and Mondrian regarding her contributions to Neo-

Michael Canney. Wreck. Oil, 1960.
Graham Gallery, Tunbridge Wells.

125

Plasticism. Her introduction of the double line into orthogonal compositions was sufficiently important to provoke Mondrian into writing and asking why she had done it. Moss, the rational artist, justified her innovation as a rhythmic and dynamic device, and summoned mathematics to support her case. Mondrian replied …'Figures don't mean much to me', but he nevertheless introduced the same double line into his own work.'*3

Michael Canney, better known as a writer, broadcaster, curator and art lecturer, produced a sizeable body of painting in the shadow of these other activities. Painting confirmed his identity as one of the most versatile, intelligent and distinguished voices in the west country art scene. Slowly, he established a more authentic and personal voice for himself, and did so, paradoxically, by developing in his art a highly impersonal language of geometric systems, mathematic proportions and constructed harmonies. A lucid vocabulary of hard-edged forms were either collaged, constructed or painted directly onto generally small square boards, a scale and medium that best suited his intellectual temperament. The principal early influence was his friend Peter Lanyon, with whom he spent much time. For a time he shared Lanyon's constructional style of energetic paint handling, sensual collaging, and cheeky metamorphosis. The Lanyon-inspired works at the turn of the 1960's, like 'Wreck', retain individuality because Canney plays to his strengths, which are best relayed through a modest scale and a disciplined involvement with shallow cubist space. Furthermore, as Canney explained 'Lanyon's intensely individual approach was too personal, the pursuit of the 'genius loci' too elusive, and the informed automatism of the painting process too exhausting for me.'*4 This statement highlights the clear-headed rationale that enabled Canney to create an authentic way forward for himself as a creative artist. Later, in response to teaching, Canney embarked on a visual exploration into hidden harmonies and rhythms elicited by systematic analyses of form and colour. Particularly after retiring from teaching in 1982 and moving to Italy, he created variations on the theme of dividing, cutting, overlapping, folding or rearranging parts of the square. Sometimes using a uniform surface of white, reducing any external 'impurities', he also introduced colour as a plastic element of the composition. He looked to Josef Albers, among others, for basic colour principles. Albers's theories about the relativity of colour, its interactions and tonal or chromatic contrasts, became useful at this juncture.

The earliest works, dating from the early 1950's, are representational images of Cornish terraces or of Newlyn's harbour. They use a simplified language of colour planes that are harbingers of more abstract things to come. The choice of subject reflects the artist's biography. From an early age an interest in art was encouraged by his father, a Cornish clergyman, and his mother, an amateur painter, and Canney attended annual St. Ives show days in the 1930's. During the 1930's he came under the tutelage of Arthur Hambley at Redruth, Bouverie Hoyton at Penzance and Leonard Fuller at St. Ives. At the latter's school he was close at hand to Alfred Wallis's cottage in Back Road West, which he visited. More significantly, he met major artists of the modern movement like Hepworth, Nicholson and Gabo during the war. The war saw

126

him on military service in Italy, a country that he loved for its formal classicism, elegant style and mood of melancholic nostalgia. He met the master of metaphysical painting, Georgio de Chirico, and drew a telling likeness of his memorable face. Though not influenced by Surrealism in a stylistic or even thematic sense, he was intellectually drawn to the mysterious essence of much of its art, wrote an authoritative article on it in 'Art International' in 1966 and organised an exhibition of leading Surrealist artists, while spending a year on the west coast of the United States as director of the University Art Gallery at Santa Barbara.

War service was followed by a return home, where he saw the Crypt exhibitions. He described the experience as marking 'my first encounter with certain aspects of Constructivism, a movement that was to play an important

Michael Canney. Sixty Paper. 1990.

part in my own art and thinking some twenty years later'.*5 During the late 1940's he studied illustration and graphic design at Goldsmith's, a factor that was to imbue his painting of all subsequent phases with a concern for basic surface design and pure interacting relationships of line, plane, form and colour. More particularly, the shallow space of Cubism informed his work, whether representational landscapes of the fields surrounding the Hospitalfield Art School in Arbroath, (where he convalesced in 1951 from tuberculosis) or later simplified compositions of Cornish harbour or roof motifs. A phase teaching in London was followed, in 1956, with his becoming curator at the Newlyn Art Gallery, a part-time position that put him in touch with the whole Cornish art scene and allowed him to paint. The most ambitious of his works at the time added thick, knifed pigment to rigorously designed, rectilinear surfaces. The influx of Abstract Expressionism made itself felt in terms of a looser handling and a more visually daring use of collaged material like corrugated card, sack cloth, or strips of painted board. These works were accompanied by cool, hard geometric reliefs, complete and self-referring entities representing the logical conclusion of a formal distillation from the cubic houses, pyramidal roofs, conic lighthouses and rectangular piers that had inhabited earlier compositions.

Canney was intellectually amenable to reductive programmes in art. From the romantic figure of Roger Hilton, who was working in Newlyn, he learned that colour needed a tough significance in pictorial art and that a restrained range of beige, grey, ochre, blue, dark green and brown was desirable. Canney's lifelong association with Cornwall was tempered by an outgoing cosmopolitan interest in the international scene, and he looked as much at Albers or Max Bill as he did at local Constructivist strains. Between 1966 and his retirement in 1983 he taught at the art college in Bristol. The Bristol years put him in touch with younger artists whose influence proved invigorating. In particular, the style-conscious artists grouped around 'Artscribe' magazine drew attention to surface and design as ongoing issues in modern painting. This proved relevant to Canney's own preoccupations, which had become hermetic and uncompromising. 'The essential principle', he later wrote, 'is that the painting or relief is ultimately constructed from the original material alone and that nothing extraneous is added. In this limitation lies the creative challenge.'[*6] The unvarying format of the square is used in the Albers manner, for 'its non-associative properties, its mathematical simplicity and its formal neutrality'. The image is likewise derived from a square sheet, folded over, divided, cut or rearranged according to numerical systems, classical proportions or simply according to the judgement of the naked eye. He transfers the image onto the surface of the picture by drawing and stencilling around the prepared sheet. A degree of personal choice is allowed in the use of hue, and chance visual effects can occur as a result of the working process, as for instance when one area partially crosses another, creating a third hue that synthesises the previous two. Film colour is used, an approximate mix of the two preceding colours. Colour can be as systematic as the formal organisation - the principles at play in the use of colour have to do with psychological, optical and formal effects. Canney is not a colourist because his palette is systematic rather than intuitive, and planned rather than emotional. Yet, unlike many better known artists, he is not afraid of colour.

John Wells (born 1907) also absorbed the influence of modern Constructivist art as it grew out of the soil of his home county. Trained as a doctor, and practising on the Scillies during the war, Wells developed an abstract style in his spare time. Visits to the mainland were rewarded by meetings with Nicholson, Hepworth and Gabo, artists who particularly inspired him. He had known Nicholson for over a decade, having met him and Kit Wood at Feock in 1928. Gabo detected a romantic temperament at play in the work of an artist who sought to express, through a precise visual language of line and geometry, the invisible energy behind the movements of insects, birds, plant growth and other natural phenomena. This was the artist who wrote to his friend Sven Berlin, 'how can one paint the warmth of the sun, the sound of the sea, the journey of a beetle across a rock, or thoughts of one's own whence and whither? That's an argument for abstraction'. Gabo called him the 'Paul Klee of the Constructivist movement'. The influence of Paul Klee is apparent when Wells creates a dynamic and lyrical poetry of straight, intersecting lines embodying geometric forms like triangles, squares, and sliced segments of the circle. These forms evoke kite, cottage or boat imagery, while straight or undulating lines recall hills or sea horizons as in the part neo-romantic part constructivist 'Landscape under Moors' (1948). A grainy and dry tactile surface is analogous to the hard, granite textures of Cornwall.

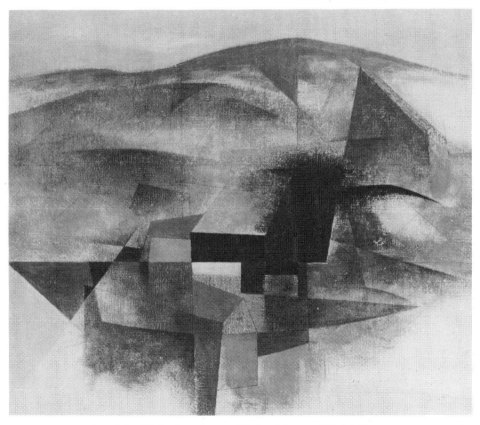

John Wells. Landscape Under Moors. *Oil, 1948.*
Courtesy: British Council.

129

On occasion, Wells uses a light atmosphere to float forms in playful aerodynamic sequences. In 'Aspiring Forms' (1950) or 'Landscape and Flight

John Wells. Landscape and Flight Forms. *Oil, 1958.*

Forms' (1958) he uses a vertical trajectory and balances a number of spiralling crescent or wing forms. The composition hinges on a light tension between straight and curved lines which hover around a central axis. These forms are thinly painted and have an airy transparency suggesting ascent throughout air and space. The notable early work, 'Aspiring Forms' was hung alongside Denis Mitchell's similarly composed bronze sculpture 'Turning Form' (1959) in the St. Ives Tate's inaugural installation, during the summer of 1993. The pair were close friends in later years and shared a Newlyn studio where they perpetuated the lyrical and constructive styles first introduced to Cornwall by sophisticated urbanites like Nicholson and Hepworth in 1939.

Although Wells was always a private, retiring man, suspicious of the outside world and particular about whom he let into the studio, he was aware of the significance of his work and the mantle it took on from his predecessors. During the 1950's he enjoyed two exhibitions at Durlacher's in New York, a prestigious gallery where Alex Mackenzie also exhibited. Durlacher provided a more eminent location than the Bertha Shaeffer Gallery, where Frost and Heron later exhibited. The importance of the Wells and Mackenzie forays into New York has been unfairly eclipsed in official histories that prefer to see Frost and Heron in the forefront of British transatlantic invasions. In 1960 and 1964 Wells had two exhibitions at Waddington's in London, the second one an installation of smoothly painted, geometric compositions shorn of romantic

Alexander Mackenzie. Levant Zawn. *Oil, 1960.*
Courtesy: George Dannatt.

131

associations with the natural world. Wells normally works on a modest scale and the mood is restrained. He shares none of the brash exuberance and expressionist energy of Terry Frost. The work celebrates an introspective world of latent harmony and balance, in distinction to Frost's sensual banquet celebrating the splendours of the outside world.

Alex Mackenzie's roots lie in a systematic, visual abstraction from nature. His background is an academic one, so that his art springs from visual experience of looking as much as from intellectual concepts. The landscape is a source for all his imagery. He is drawn to an austere, rocky topography such as he finds in Cornwall, Wales or Yorkshire. He is fascinated by ancient contours, whether they be stone circles, burial mounds or hill forts. Such forms provide dramatic reminders of the element of time and the remoteness of past civilisations. Like Wells and Tunnard, Mackenzie strikes a balance between the textures of nature and the linear structure of culture. In 'Levant Zawn' (1960) alternatively smooth, churned or scraped paint imparts a rich tactile and visual experience. Mackenzie has changed with the times. The thorough-going abstraction of the 1950's softened during ensuing decades so that so-called abstract and figurative elements merged in later work. 'All my

Alexander Mackenzie. Cornish Coast. *Oil, 1959.*
Gordon Hepworth Gallery.

painting has its origins in visual experience', he wrote for an exhibition with Wells and Dannatt in Penzance, 'although a balance between intellectual and emotional demands must be resolved'[7] As a draughtsman Mackenzie is second to none; his line moves with a steady precision but also with an unpredictability across rubbed or scratched textural surfaces. In 1963 Herbert Read and Roland Penrose wrote about him as 'a painter who possesses great sensibility for atmospheric and subtle gradations of tone.'*₈ A restrained palette of nature-evoking hues like blues, greens and greys, gives a landscape feeling to work, even when tangible imagery is absent. Read and Penrose went on to state that through 'his discrimination and the well-ordered arrangements of his canvases he is able to evoke that mysterious blossoming of colour from overcast skies and the deep perspectives seen through haze that belong inevitably to his native landscape.'

The late 1950's were perhaps the high point of his career. He had exhibitions with Durlacher in New York and with Waddington in London. The formal components of his pictures were reduced from landscape. He enjoys scraping and scratching surfaces to capture the gritty textures of hard rock. Ben Nicholson encouraged him at this vital stage in his development, when the findings of his youth - he had an excellent training under notable draughtsmen like Timmis, Wiffen and Martin Bell at Liverpool College of Art - were consolidating and hardening into a mature, personal language. Mackenzie draws from the landscape wherever he goes, and from spare line work creates a sense of form in relationship to the blank areas on a sheet of paper. Interval, sequence and movement are important qualities. He produces precise compositions of farmsteads or rows of cottages alongside the

Alexander Mackenzie. Untitled. *Oil, 1960.*
Graham Gallery, Tunbridge Wells.

133

more abstract compositions. With greater experience and a superb talent for visual editing, he makes line come alive as a conceptual as well as descriptive, spatial element. A gift for placement also gives his work a satisfying completeness.

Mackenzie became an influential teacher, running the art department at Plymouth until retiring in the early 1980's. He returned to Penzance, where he continues to work with assurance. He uses a sketchbook on frequent expeditions to Wales and Yorkshire. As well as distinguishing himself as a teacher, Mackenzie conducted his duties as vice-Chairman of a stormy Penwith Society with a typical and admirable magnanimity. In the artist's later work experiments are made with collaged paper or card, montaged imagery, and with large scale. He frequently uses a foreground rectangle as a geometric foil against which he paints more naturalistic colour. The textures in these later works often relinquish earlier abrasive surfaces and become smooth and consistent.

In his influential book 'The Modern Movement in Art' R.H. Wilenski distinguishes between what he sees as the fundamental categories of art. He reproduces an early Wilhelmina Barns-Graham landscape abstraction and uses the architectural category to identify the strong, formal qualities of pictorial art from the weaker modes where content and subject matter, often of a popular, sentimental or derivative kind, hold sway. Barns-Graham's work, in employing an emphatic line to gouge out decisive form from the crisp, blank surfaces of paper, canvas or board, clearly belongs to Wilenski's architectural billing. Wilenski's use of the term architectural is, however, more metaphoric than literal; he is speaking not of an art about buildings - though St. Ives rooftops, curvilinear harbour walls or cube-like cottages occur frequently in her art - but rather about one constructed on the visual principles of dynamic formal relationships.

Regular practice of drawing is of fundamental importance to an artist whose work has a vital linear quality. Drawing is not simply an exercise, plan or rehearsal, though inevitably she uses resolutions worked out with graphic means on paper in the larger, worked up context of the paintings. The process of drawing is a sensual one, and she has spoken of a great excitement and tension in being faced with the stark blankness of white paper and a range of graphic choices and differing media. A suffused sensuality broods in her work - she is always alert to the mood and atmosphere of place while never wishing to pedantically describe it - and coexists with the intellectual clarity of crisp drawing, immaculate spatial organisation of the picture plane, and a strong compositional balance.

Significantly, Barns-Graham views drawing as 'a discipline of the mind' and with this comes the notion of an inner journey, counterbalanced by an almost scientific search for the visual, structural principles that organise, govern and give form to natural phenomena. In this sense her work belongs to the intellectual yet also mystical tradition of Mondrian's theosophy or the Nicholsons' Christian Science. In a work like 'Meditation East' (1968) the artist creates a direct metaphor for the effulgent effects of consciousness. She uses hundreds of miniature squares to compose a mosaic-like image of sun shining in every direction. Mondrian's development - from the early 'supernatural' colours of the Dutch landscapes through the experiments with line and space in the pier and ocean series and finally on to the resolutions of de Stijl - was based on a visually reductive experience of nature and an almost mystic sense of what lay behind it. Barns-Graham's also searches for inner rhythm related to such natural phenomena as an incoming tide or a giant gust of wind across a stretch of sand. She is motivated by intellectual factors as much as by purely visual and sensual experiences of nature. A discrete range of colour in her early work - including siennas, ochres, viridians, greys and blacks, - absorbs into the context of abstraction the naturalistic complexion of beach, rock, lichen, ice, water or field imagery. Her later work, however, tends to confound the theory that she is another grey landscape painter influenced by Ben Nicholson's linear precision and un-adventurous palette. It is true she was influenced by him and went sketching with Nicholson in the 1950's, but she is an independent spirit. In large paintings and related gouaches like 'Barcelona, Celebration of Fire' (1992) she uses an explosive palette of vibrant orange, red, and dark blue colours. A gestural language of splashes, lines, eddies and stains embodies the intuitive immediacy of her working process. She even attacks the canvas or paper from different sides, yielding a composition that could hang vertically or horizontally. Even when limiting herself to a strict visual theme, as in some of the earlier sequential forms and collages, Barns-Graham works against rules with a spontaneous relish for the unknown. Her work has an unpredictability as it enters into new phases, exploring the limits of pictorial expression. In the sixth decade of her serious endeavour as a creative fine artist, this courageous Scottish painter embraces relatively large scale and a strident painting language of visionary intensity.

For fifty years after 1940 Barns-Graham frequently hid herself away in an outcrop high above Porthmeor, drawing on paper. She has written of the 'importance to be in union with nature'. This distinctive, if influenced, artist is ever mindful of the rich tradition of St. Ives painting. In these instances she pursues the 'plein air' disciplines of an early supporter, Borlase Smart. But a contemplative observation of nature is a means to a more conceptual and plastic end - the development in the studio of a range of appropriated shapes, originally culled from the 'outside', but now refined through the transformative power of intelligence. Abstraction for Barns-Graham is akin to an inner and personal identification with, and amplification of, the rhythms and hidden relationships of natural form. It therefore comes as no surprise, that in the working process, Barns-Graham uses a mixture a control and spontaneity, imposed order and improvisation. Thus a thinly pencilled grid is a foil against which arcs and circles float freely like balloons. In the aptly named 'Mirage' series of the early 1980's she used the transparent properties of watercolour to express the mysteries of light and air. Unpredictable variations on mathematical principles like the Golden Section give such compositions an implicit strength and an equilibrium between chance and order. This dynamic balance and inner rhythm gives such work a silent yet lively presence. An early influence was Paul Klee, whose notion of taking a walk with a line greatly impressed the poet in Barns-Graham.

Though graphically planned, her art is therefore essentially intuitive. The chief influences in her long career always came about as a result of a happy convergence of professional and private factors; the contingencies and biographic incidents of her private life coinciding with pertinent local influences. Thus her decision to come to St. Ives, as a frail and diffident student in need of a healthier climate, led to a timely entrée into a growing artistic phenomenon. Even earlier than this she enjoyed the formative influence of D'Arcy Thompson, whose book 'On Growth and Form' (1917) 'is concerned with the application of precise mathematical models to the morphology of organisms according to their laws of growth.' Thompson was a well-known scholar in St. Andrews during her youth, when she met the eminent scientific philosopher. According to Martin Kemp, Thompson's ideas influenced many artists, particularly her later St. Ives colleagues, 'who were seeking to reconcile the new art of abstraction with the kind of homage to nature which has been central to the British tradition.

W. Barns-Graham. Sleeping Town. *Oil, 1987.*
Graham Gallery, Tunbridge Wells.

Barns-Graham's art does not, however, carry rigid philosophic or aesthetic doctrines. In her dry way she wholly belongs to the empirical and experience-based approach to landscape painting that is so prominent a feature of St. Ives art. Her own art is a necessarily imperfect striving, using a healthy dose of intuition, after complete and absolute terms of reference. The phoney distinctions between abstract and representational break down. This is fitting for an artist who was one of the founders of the new Penwith Society and whose work absorbed the early influence of Borlase Smart and Alfred Wallis. In her work a dualism exists between the abstract compositions and the representational drawings. She was wise in taking a leaf out of Ben Nicholson's book.

Coinciding with themes explored by Cornish contemporaries like Hepworth and Wynter, Barns-Graham records the process of development of a landscape as it lies apparent today. Wind patterns, ocean current rhythms, bird migrations, giant glacier formations, as well as great lava flows in the Lanzarote series, point up the action of natural agencies across a landscape. In common with Nicholson, her art is devoid of people and even the elegant and painstakingly recorded town views, most frequently of St. Ives, are composed with the linear geometry of the inanimate. Possibly, people are deemed imperfect, or perhaps human activity disrupts some aesthetic or even ecological balance in the overall vision. Barns-Graham went on a number of sketching excursions with Nicholson in the early 1950's. She clearly gained from this experience confirmation of a style and working ethos already in the process of maturation. Her Edinburgh tutor, Hubert Wellington, recommended St. Ives because he felt her work was of the right ilk. Never a juicy painter, she always understated, and this understatement is as visible in terms of scraped down, tonally bleached paint surfaces, as in drawings that employ a supremely economic line leaving expanses of untouched paper. She often leaves a linear pentimenti as evidence of the graphic processes at play in the rendering of the image. In this mood she wishes not to tidy up with a rubber but instead create chiaroscuro through smudging. She creates a feeling for the antique through inlays of ochre or pale washes that simulate the effect of ageing paper. This is an affectation taken from Nicholson, though the idea of partial ground colouring behind the pencil 'scaffolding' is traceable to pre-war Parisian artists like Chagall and Miro.

In common with the revered Nicholson, a much travelled Barns-Graham exploits themes to do with Italian architecture (the towers of San Gimignano (1954) or the turrets and domes of Assisi). In later works she finds more personal subjects in the form of cottages and headlands in Orkney, jagged volcanic topographies in Lanzarote (late 1980's and early 1990's), or the patterns of cultivation on the lower slopes of Lanzarote's conical peaks. Roofs and field patterns are the closest she gets to describing the impact of human geography on landscape. On occasions when an Orcadian, Scillonian or Cornish landscape contains a cottage or a ship at sea it is as a poetic device to give resonance to an otherwise static scenario. Curiously, the silence or emptiness of Barns-Graham's drawings does not relay tranquillity (a more pastoral attribute?) but rather the clinical and sterile qualities of purity and clarity. What unites the early Swiss glacier compositions with the perennial rock studies of the Cornish coast and the later Canary landscapes is a concern with monumentality, with transparency and opacity, and with open and closed form.

The artist maintains firm control over contour in landscape drawings. She is a precisionist when it comes to formal execution. The areas of tonal smudge or inlaid wash are partial phenomena, judged in respect of their relation to the greater areas of virgin paper. She has an exquisite sense of what is enough. Line can either have uniform thickness and emphasis or else can fluctuate from the light and tentative to the heavily inscribed. In a classic drawing from 1968, 'St. Ives from Salubrious House', she chooses to alternate linear thickness according to the nature of the forms they describe. Thus the rectilinear roofs call into play an emphatic and straight line in contrast to the thinner, organic curvature of trees. In a number of Lanzarote drawings of 1989/90 she reverses the relationship of dark graphite on white paper by drawing with white chalks onto dark paper or acrylic grounds. Opacity and transparency, positive and negative space, open and closed forms are thereby evoked through plastic processes. Expression becomes one with the materials and means of creation, paralleling the formation of a landscape through geological process and the hand of time.

In her non-representational work, a repertoire of jostling circles, squares or rectangles is either directly painted or glued onto the surface as pre-painted collage elements. The use of collage is frequently miniaturist, and is certainly more intimate and discrete than Terry Frost's use of applied papers or canvas cut outs. Yet on occasion an elan more easily associated with Frost can dominate. Splash and gesture then govern the tempo, particularly in large gouaches of the late 1980's and early 1990's that scream with exotic, tropical colour. 'Lanzarote Red Slash', shown in her 80th birthday show at William Jackson in 1992, is full of the chromatic stridency of Heron and the brisk mark-making of Frost. Also in common with Frost, her most abstract compositions can directly evoke the mood and atmosphere of time and place, notably night on harbour waters. These gestural gouaches hark back to a lesser known phase of her oeuvre from the late 1950's when, under the inspiration of artists recently met, like Poliakoff and Giacometti, she introduced a new tachist flavour, echoing (among others) the work of her fellow Edinburgh student William Gear.

Michael Snow's contribution to abstract painting in Cornwall is seldom sufficiently recognised. He was an influential presence in the Penwith Society during the late 1950's and 1960's and enjoyed a significant relationship with Ben Nicholson, in the final analysis his greatest influence. In fact, Snow's dealings with Nicholson continued long after the latter's move to Switzerland, for they corresponded and Snow rented Nicholson's house 'Trezion' during the 1960's and 70's. Born in Manchester in 1930, Snow encountered Nicholson's work for the first in Manchester City Art Gallery. He also read Herbert Read's monograph of 1948. Furthermore, while a librarian in Runcorn, Snow saw an exhibition of Penwith artists, among them Nicholson, Hepworth and Barns-Graham, at Liverpool's Bluecoat Gallery. This exhibition gave 'the sensation of a particular type of landscape' they had been working in and the experience motivated him to join them. In 1951 he moved down to St. Just, where he immersed himself both in walking, to familiarise himself with the landscape, and in bold artistic experiment.

From the outset, Snow's art shared in the preoccupation with landscape and abstraction that distinguished advanced St. Ives art. In contrast to

138

Lanyon, who made constructions as open ended and incomplete experiments into structure, Snow's free standing works aimed for the self-contained and systematic expression of formal relationships that was more typical of Gabo, Nicholson and Wells. In 'Construction', Snow entered into an engagement with open form and space; thin rods of soldered brass suggests invisible planes and are closer to the constructivist strain than to Lanyon's physical and sensual expressionism. The work was a research into his surroundings but his approach therefore belonged more to what Patrick Heron described as the 'ideographic' wing of the St. Ives School. Lanyon criticised the 'sleazy research' and 'alphabet searching' of the Nicholson followers, and Snow's

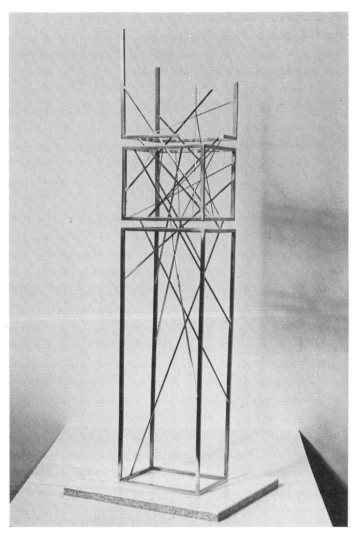

Michael Snow. Construction. *1960's.*

more cerebral approach in his expression of natural forces and rhythms would have put him in this category. Nonetheless, Snow's interest in the abstract language of proportion and symmetry was always a visual, and not just an intellectual one. He referred to 'a longstanding if generalised visual interest in the sciences, especially geology, particle physics and astronomy.'

By his own admission, Michael Snow's visual analysis of natural form, ranging from the molecular to the astronomic, 'almost requires an approach that people label 'abstract' simply because it seems to be about universality on the grand and the minute scale'. He does not express nature so much as create a separate visual language, influenced by it. He spends time observing geological patterns, wildlife, or the planets through the lens of a telescope. Again in his own words, the object for scrutiny may be 'a crystal, a tree moving in the wind, the sun moving in the sea, water pouring over a rock, or just a simple geometric shape …What it then becomes is the piece of wood or the colour on canvas.' An awareness of the separate problems involved when translating such experience into the plastic language of art made him an astute and pragmatic teacher. Snow's early 1960's pictures introduce more energetic and expressive paint handling in response to the influence of Terry Frost. Charcoal, untouched canvas and lavish paint areas make up a form of abstraction full of oblique landscape associations. John Wells's famous remark, made in the letter to Sven Berlin, concerning the need to express intangibles like the journey of a beetle, the sound of the sea, or the warmth of the sun calls for the independent language of abstraction. Snow's feeling for harmony, for the underlying cohesion behind phenomena is not so much a religious or mystic sentiment as one that shows the importance of music, an avowed influence also on the work of Nicholson and Mondrian, as well as on John Wells.

Precise, intersecting lines divide up the surfaces of some of Snow's compositions and lead, in exteme cases, to an erosion of image. These lines are not always rendered in pencil, but are frequently etched into the paint or gesso. Obsessively worked, the reading becomes one of weathered textures. Sometimes linear kite-like forms hover in a weightless reverie and recall Miro's whimsy, fantasy and graphic abandon. There are also paintings from this early period which, in the freedom of interacting colour marks, foreshadow the emotional intensity of his later work. Large canvases of the early 1990's share with the American artist Richard Pousette Dart a strange kind of celestial pointillism of optically shifting hazes. The circle dominates though is without defining edge. By the early 1960's, however, styles at the Penwith Society, where he was an active member, had generally evolved to incorporate freer, more expressive shapes, and Snow followed suit in canvases that either presented boulder-like forms compressed into the picture plane or else columns and verticals around which various localised details clustered. These formed a solo show in 1964 at the Rowan Gallery in London. While retaining an abstract language, the energy and placement of shapes in these works seemed to echo the growth, expansion or contraction of natural form. In common with Hilton, Snow sometimes used charcoal with paint, the sweeping lines or eddying rhythms of the charcoal creating an independent structure above the 'ground' colour. These works often employed the ochre or ginger grounds characteristic of the period.

Snow's earliest contribution to the Penwith came with encouragement from David Lewis. Agnes Drey sponsored his first showing at the new gallery in 1952. The following year he was elected a member, followed by his service as secretary during the mid 1950's. Difficult decisions to do with hanging of works or choosing selection committees invariably upset some. Internal politics often left him in cross-fire and Snow found Hepworth particularly difficult because her public power was greater than her private impartiality. She wanted to pull the strings and court favourites. Snow found Nicholson more objective, practical, and supportive in his approach, even though some others thought Nicholson often wanted his own way and adopted the autocratic manner that had characterised his procedures since the days of the 7&5 Society before the war. Snow's association with Hepworth extended beyond Penwith activities, and he assisted at Trewyn on an occasional basis, and also worked for Mitchell on his large elm carving 'Geevor' and other sculptures. As well as exhibiting at the Penwith, Snow showed at the Arnolfini in Bristol, at the Peterloo in his native Manchester and at London galleries like the Rowan, Gallery One, Ewan Phillips, and Angela Flowers. He also held an exhibition with the critic painter John Dalton at Exeter University in 1967. In the same year Plymouth City Art Gallery purchased two sculptures. An active role at the Penwith promoted the possibilites beyond Cornwall. He resigned from the troubled Penwith in 1965 and began teaching at Exeter College of Art. He commuted from St. Ives to Exeter, retired from teaching in 1985 and held a significant retrospective exhibition in 1993.

George Dannatt (born 1915), came to painting late. He was over forty, but his maturity enabled him to know exactly what he wanted. There was no searching around for style. He was a chartered surveyor from 1940 to 1970 (except for war service). The disciplines of running a chartered surveyor business gave him an appreciation for precision. He also spent twelve years as a music critic, and he plays the piano constantly. The abstract language of music is translated by Dannatt into both earlier 'lyrical abstract' and later 'constructivist' phases of painting. In addition to music and surveying, photography has been an abiding interest, a medium that creates its own set of visual and reproductive responses to the world.

In common with that of his friend John Wells, Dannatt's work divides into softer or more concrete forms of abstraction. The more 'romantic' compositions exploit material surface in ways that encourage association with natural texture; similarly, the precise surface divisions and intersecting geometric units are 'softened' with less predictable, undulating or curved lines that evoke, say, boat shapes. The artist grew up in Blackheath, and is aware of the nautical links between Greenwich and Cornwall. On occasions the artist exploits the play of hand in the process of paint application on wood or hardboard surfaces. A simple pair of shapes like circles on the one hand, or beer cans on the other create a playful dialogue betwen pure and associative form. In more measured, symmetrical and impersonal compositions the artist uses circles, squares, rectangles or other hard-edged components. These

141

intersect and create fluctuations and therefore rhythmical distortions between form and colour. Where one plane or segment traverses another we find a third colour area emerging in a growing harmony of musical proportions. The view of abstraction as a kind of visual music is common throughout the course

George Dannatt. White Nothe. *Mixed media, 1983.*

of modernism since Kandinsky; in unison with Kandinsky and Klee, Dannatt's abstraction represents an introspective dissatisfaction with a sad, chaotic world and a need to therefore find an inner harmony in the salutary context of art.

Dannatt wisely wrote that 'painters who strive to be original are mistaken; one should be influenced by other painters provided that the influences are sublimated ...there is little doubt that the greatest impact upon me has been the work of Ben Nicholson and of Naum Gabo.*9 Equally, he has been influenced by their followers John Wells and Denis Mitchell. Dannatt has a precise understanding of the picture as a complete object, an expressive

142

record of its own making. In 1975 he held an exhibition with John Wells and Alex Mackenzie at the Orion Gallery in Penzance, where the classical mood and clear-headedness of his work complemented theirs with fresh variations on shared themes.

George Dannatt. Three figure composition. *Oil, 1974.*

Morag Ballard is unusual in being a young artist, maturing in the 1990's, who finds mileage in a revitalised, abstract, constructive language practised by the older generation. She introduces an ongoing freshness to a mode of

143

work that one more easily associates with Gabo's closest followers, like early Lanyon, Barns-Graham and John Wells. She uses the same language of curvilinear planes, spirals and sweeping linear rhythms. She invariably composes on the surface from collaged fragments of painted board. Illusionism is a subordinate feature on concrete surfaces of interpenetrating planes, intersecting lines and rhythmic colours. She does not illustrate space, but rather constructs it in terms of an imaginative manipulation of these components. Ovals and irregular segments evoke softer organic forms like shells, pebbles or eggs. An interest in aerodynamics accounts for an expressive curvilinear energy in her work; these lines and edges travel with the exhilarating power of something moving freely through space. She enjoys the objectivity of distance and watches the way birds, kites or aircraft cut through space with a clean, decisive and supreme elegance. The works also share in the diagrammatic clarity of cartography. Lanyon's early construction 'White Track' is perhaps a prototype and certainly provides a frame of

Morag Ballard. Penzance. *Mixed media relief, 1993.*
England & Co..

144

reference for her own investigations into movement across a lateral surface.

Born in London in 1961, Ballard commenced art studies at Chelsea twenty years later. She completed her training at Bath in the mid 1980's. For her degree show she created a room-sized installation composed from plaster vessels. These were formed by pouring plaster into sheets of dangling cloths suspended from the ceiling. The objects were later unpinned and placed on the floor as giant ceramics. The interiors were filled with large plaster pellets, which assumed an enigmatic quality. A similar surreal feeling ensued in box constructions. These were significant for moving the artist away from sculptural objectivity into the realm of the pictorial, though Ballard's subsequent formal language on a flat surface continued to evoke the third dimension, either through the concrete process of collage or in terms of a full spatial illusionism. These boxes also led to an important association with England and Co., a notable London gallery specialising in box constructions. In the context of Jane England's box artists, many of whom made more representational images using found objects, Ballard comes across as a classicist, making the forms and pure shapes do the work.

After finishing at College she spent time in Venice, working as a guard at the Guggenheim Museum. This was another auspicious occasion for she met the painter Alan Kingsbury, whom she would later marry after moving to Penzance. In the meantime, she returned to Scotland, where an almost mystical interest in landscape led to works that essentially belonged to the spirit of Nash and Hitchens. Her move to Cornwall, motivated in part by the clear light and mild climate and in part by Kingsbury's awareness of art history, (he worked in the modern picture department at Bonhams), coincided with her first solo show with Jane England. Landscape, though not of a recorded topographical kind, continued to exert its presence through the distilled organic forms, evocative textures and naturalistic colours. Other compositions used the shapes of the large ceramic containers from student days. Her work is like a breath of fresh air in a depleted Cornish art scene desperately looking for a return to past glories. Ballard achieves a rare distinction among the generation of the 'nineties by reverting back to, and revitalising the language of that earlier era.

Pre-cut shapes and collage fragments give her art a constructional vitality and sense of purpose. Precision is the order of the day when hand and eye are coordinated in the processes of glueing, cutting and sandpapering down paint textures in order to create the effect of worn or weathered surfaces. Though not the first to do so, Ballard gives line the power to harmonise and traverse areas of colour. There is in fact a refreshing openness to her uncluttered compositions. She works slowly, betraying a contemplative approach. Colour is often pale or muted, though dominant whites are often offset by small areas of jewel-like colour. The choice of colour is empirical. It is guided by eye rather than head, and immediate pictorial requirements are fulfilled. It is in fact hard to find a less doctrinaire painter. One apparently abstract composition called 'Watercycle' used shapes based on a hydro-electric dam in the French Alps. The size of the dam's structure within the landscape impressed her. She took the experience further by physically exploring it. She felt the weight of water on one side counterpoised with a void on the other. The vessel-like concretion, holding vast water supplies, reminded her of the large plaster containers made at art college. The use of

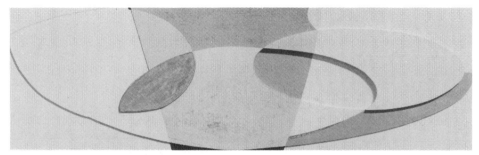

Morag Ballard. Water Cycle. *Mixed media relief, 1993.*
England & Co..

colour is naturalistic, describing the dam with beige and the sky with light blue. Intentionally or not, the work alludes to the confrontation of human and physical geography. In an ecologically conscious age the light colours perhaps convey an environmental as well as aesthetic purity in her work. The picture is architectonic yet also naturalistic, abstract yet also evocative of natural colour and texture.

Bryan Ingham (born 1936) is a visually well informed artist who takes Ben Nicholson's windowsill cubism and adds something of Juan Gris and the decorative pattern effects of other late Cubists. Ingham who generally eschews the window as a frame of reference, is more successful than his predecessor in reaching a full synthetic unity between the domestic and outdoor world. Jug handles, landscape glimpses, ocean horizon lines, profiles and silhouettes are painted in crisply delineated and flat terms. These images synthesise into a powerful composite arabesque, part abstract yet part representational, in which line, colour and texture assume more or less equal validity in the overall expressive impact. It all amounts to what the artist has explained is a desire to 'beg, borrow, consolidate and synthesize, to add, even, to the classical tradition of harmony and contained chance.'[*10] Shoreline shingles, pebbles, sands or rocky outcrops are abstracted into a rich pattern of 'pointillist' dots or larger circles. Instead of late Cubism's wallpaper or simulated wood grain we are left with the texture of the outdoors, the inevitable focus for an artist who lives in an old farmhouse on the Lizard peninsular, where he muses over the possibilities left open for a modernist artist in a pluralistic, late twentieth century world. He quotes with irony Lawrence Alloway's observation made thirty years before, that in Cornwall, artists 'combine non-figurative theory with the practice of abstraction because the landscape is so nice, nobody can quite bring themselves to leave it out of their art.'[*11] In spite of possessing a greater decorative gaiety, Ingham's work

146

bears a striking visual resemblance to Nicholson's. Assuming the independent lifestyle and position of Tunnard, Moss or Colquhoun before

Bryan Ingham. Mediterranean Head. *Oil and collage, 1992.*
Private collection.
Courtesy: Francis Graham Dixon Gallery, London.

147

him, Ingham wisely distances himself from a contemporary St. Ives art scene that is a pale reflection of its former self. 'Ingham eschews a pursuit of innovation for its own sake', wrote William Jeffett, 'and he is wise enough to understand that even the so-called innovator only remakes what is available to him. He is also wise enough to see that within the art of this century there is still much to be explored. Perhaps it is for this reason that ...he has pursued his course in relative isolation'.*12

Ingham's pictures are composed with the shallow space of Cubism in mind though a range of segmented landscape images evokes the deep space of naturalistic illusion. Although the language is planar, tied to the pictorial surface with an incisive line linking the various components, the atmosphere created is a romantic one. An array of memories, perceptions, experiences and sensations lends the work a subjectivity while never diluting the formal strength. The colour too has an enormous variety, ranging from the restrained tonal harmonies of scraped gesso grounds with their greys and off whites, to more assertive, adventurous and positive uses of hue. The frequent addition of pre-cut collage units increases tactile association. These elements enhance the range of formal and associative possibilities on offer in ambitious compositional structures and harmonies. On occasions as in the aptly named 'Mediterranean Head' (1992), the artist incorporates elements of newsprint, commercial wrapping or found paper scraps and by doing so adds richness to the imagery in a way that recalls the collages of Schwitters and the Cubists. Indeed, the works often look continental and adopt suitable titles like 'Colle Val d'Elsa'. The artist has spent much time in Germany, Spain and France. Circles in reds, blacks or blues recall the playful geometry of Miro. In spite of this, Ingham is an artist of angle, edge, plane and balanced surfaces. In common with Wells and Nicholson, he has quieter moods when creating serenely balanced rectilinear compositions of divided and sub-divided colour. The use of collage extends into the physical dimensions of bas relief. His patinated plaster reliefs, enjoying the palpable reality of the third dimension, can give forms the alternative of concrete, as opposed to illusionistic, direction. He can give line the penetration of the gouged, sliced channel. The language is again one of Cubist fragmentation, where forms are flattened and re-arranged to the requirements of a flat, or almost flat, surface. Ingham's etchings are also distinguished by bold, inter-penetrating lines that are bitten deeply into the surface of copper or zinc with conclusive incision. The etchings give him the innovative scope 'to combine the properties of sculpture gravure and paint.'*13.

Ingham's romantic Cubism, superficially reminiscent of Nicholson, Gris and others, obscures his roots in a vein of ambitious modern English art spawned in art colleges like St. Martin's or the Royal College, during the heady student days in the late 1950's and early 1960's. But unlike many of his contemporaries who, in response to either Pop, Abstract Expressionism or post painterly Abstraction, looked to America, Ingham drew what he could from a very English preoccupation with landscape, the best of continental modernism, and the sharp light of the Mediterranean world.

148

NOTES

1. Mark Glazebrook. *'John Tunnard'* p.36. Arts Council 1977.
2. Michael Canney. *'Science and the Artist'* p.519. *'Discovery'*. Sept. 1958.
3. Michael Canney. Note on Marlow Moss written for *'The St. Ives Years'*. (Wimborne) 1984.
4. Michael Canney. Letter to the author. September 1993.
5. Michael Canney. Catalogue for Belgrave Gallery exhibition. 1990.
6. Michael Canney. Notes for catalogue of exhibition at Newlyn Orion. October 1983.
7. Alex Mackenzie. Catalogue note for exhibition at Orion Gallery, Penzance. May 1975.
8. Roland Penrose and Herbert Read. Exhibition catalogue for Premio Marzetto, Rome 1963.
9. George Dannatt. Exhibition catalogue Newlyn Art Gallery. 1981.
10. Bryan Ingham. Exhibition catalogue. Francis Graham Dixon Gallery. London 1991.
11. Lawrence Alloway. *'Nine Abstract Artists'* Alec Tiranti. 1954.
12. William Jeffett. *'Painting into Sculpture'* Exhibition catalogue Francis Graham Dixon Gallery. 1991
13. Bryan Ingham. Letter to the author. 28.12.93.

CHAPTER 8

The Middle Generation

Terry Frost made his first paintings in the unlikely context of a Bavarian P.O.W. camp, where he had been encouraged to paint by a fellow prisoner, Adrian Heath. Frost's earliest works are therefore the raw but telling expressions of a naturally gifted, if as yet untrained, young painter. They do, however, show an immediate grasp of the formal as well as representational aspects of successful picture-making. Frost had to make do with whatever materials were closest to hand. A 1943 watercolour depicting the interior of a dormitory at the Staleg camp shows an awareness of how the structural components of the hut - ceiling beams, columns, walls or accessories like bunk beds - could satisfy the perspectival requirements of compositional unity in the process of fulfilling representational roles. As a rapidly maturing artist in the late 1940's and early 1950's Frost seemed to successfully integrate what for his contemporaries were the irreconcilable polarities of an abstract and constructive language on the one hand, and a more emotive and romantic style on the other. Adrian Heath later described Frost as being essentially a romantic painter, an observation based, according to Heath, 'on my belief that emotion was more important to him than reason'.[*1] When he therefore set about recreating experiences and sensations of the natural world in the independent context of painting, he embellished a constructive approach to formal composition - influenced by Jay Hambridge's ideas about proportional systems and divisions - with expressive colour and painterly exuberance. The hatched, spiralling or zigzagging brushstrokes were loaded with pigment, bodying out the flat geometric divisions and designs of the picture surface. In another early war camp picture, a still-life depicting a pair of marrows against a dark ground, Frost integrates sensuality with austerity and discipline. A residual sense of poetry such as Van Gogh also found in a forlorn and mundane subject lends the work distinction.

Frost, influenced by Heath in more ways than one, was encouraged to develop an obvious and precocious talent in the painter's colony of Cornwall, which Heath had experienced before the war with studies at Stanhope Forbes' School in Newlyn. In spite of studies at Leonard Fuller's St. Ives School of Painting, where he met and was inspired by Sven Berlin, Frost's rudimentary talents needed to develop in a more sophisticated milieu. In 1947 he did the right thing and entered Camberwell School of Arts with an ex-serviceman's grant. It turned out to be a seminal time. Frost wrote from Camberwell about 'being able to work on representational and abstract art. This I feel is much better for me, for as you will know I was always moved by things around me.' In this statement to his friend and fellow painter Yankel Feather, Frost speaks unequivocally about the dual purpose of his art. Abstraction and representation were opposite sides of the same coin. During the Camberwell period Frost lived with his young family in Albert Bridge Road, and a small painting 'Cyclists Battersea, Albert Bridge Road' shows an advanced degree of abstraction in the wake of his teacher, Victor Pasmore, making a famous move

Terry Frost. Self Portrait. *Oil, 1949.*
Belgrave Gallery, London.

over to abstract art. The battle lines between abstract and figurative art were much more marked than they are today, and this aesthetic issue was loaded with wide moral and even political meaning. Always pragmatic and empirical, Frost forged an individual style with a mixture of influences that best suited his purpose. In his social interaction too, he was evenhanded, and remained a popular figure within a highly charged and competitive art scene. He extended a magnanimity and an across-the-board conviviality, albeit one that co-existed with personal ambition.

Frost used the Camberwell period to develop an authentic mode of expression that was both personal and relevant to the contemporary development of abstraction. But it was not all plain sailing, and a sense of the struggle to find his feet is apparent in another letter to Yankel Feather, where he refers to having 'been through one of those horrible blank periods, torn between making myself paint a still-life in the representational manner or carrying on with the fight and flogging myself until I squeeze out another abstract.' In the National Portrait Gallery's 'Self Portrait' (1947) or in street scenes of Downalong in St. Ives, Frost certainly retains an empathy with subject matter, yet in the notable 1949 picture 'Madrigal', (shown in 1952 at Frost's Leicester Gallery exhibition) the artist reaches a fully non-representational style composed from rectilinear planes, lozenges or tilted squares. In spite of its formal abstraction, 'Madrigal' continues to evoke naturalistic and atmospheric associations through colour and light. Heath wrote that in 'Madrigal' the 'use of the diagonal, the dark colours and the emotive handling of the paint, created a mood and a sense of space that could only be described as poetic'.*2 At about the time this notably early picture was painted, Frost wrote of being 'Completely free to make what shapes I like and to re-invent whatever I like, not being bound to any visual image.'*3

But the key early work is 'Walk Along the Quay', owned by Heath, who found it resembled the work of Ben Nicholson on account of its 'spare strength' rather than 'suave elegance'.*4 Certainly the work, with its demonstrative paint handling, interlocking geometry of irregular planes, and associative colours, belonged more to Nicholson's earlier abstractions and reliefs rather than to the later resolutions. Frost's entire oeuvre is swashbuckling and maverick, contrasting with Nicholson's tasteful, even sanctimonious refinement. Yet Nicholson exerted considerable influence on Frost's early development, all the more so because they had adjacent Porthmeor studios in St. Ives. Nicholson could damn with faint praise, though he was seldom economical with the truth, and he once told Frost that the basic building blocks of sun-like discs, squares, rectangles, semi-circles and lines would serve him for an entire career. These shapes also described themes of equal durability - reflections of suns in flickering harbour waters, the rhythmic movements of moored boats pulling between rope and tide, or the intersection of pier or rudder with sand. Once again Heath explained the incurably associative power of Frost's most abstract shapes, particularly 'Circles which always seem anxious to play the part of a moon or sun'.*5 The vertical format of 'Walk Along the Quay' allows a stacked and sequential range of climbing forms to express the actual experience of walking along a

152

quay. The idea of the picture becoming a tilted plane that holds the experienced images in a new temporal and spatial perspective, derived from Ben Nicholson. Nicholson's Cubist compositions incorporate composite still-life and landscape motifs in a synthetic transformation of reality. Nicholson's pictorial plane reads as a tilted tabletop and the objects one associates with a tabletop - beakers, mugs, plates and so on - are re-arranged according to the dictates of overlapping Cubist construction. Surface flatness dominates over illusionistic depth. 'Walk Along the Quay' also uses a tilted format with which to express various visual fragments of experience, but the experienced imagery is re-arranged within the plastic and vertical context of the actual picture plane. By 1950, Frost was reaping benefits from the struggles at Camberwell. He later described the period that produced 'Walk Along the Quay' as being ' a lovely period of innocent discovery. I had soaked up a lot of influences'. Nicholson was an important influence, as we have seen. Another was his Camberwell teacher, Victor Pasmore.

The Camberwell period was followed by a return to St. Ives, where he worked as a part-time assistant to Barbara Hepworth until 1952. The demands of working on sculpture inhibited painting, and he stopped making pictures for nearly a year. He found that the demands of dealing with the physical shapes of sculpture undermined what he referred to as an involvement with 'the illusionistic world, of images in paint'. It toughened his sense of form, however, and he began to ease back into painting through the intermediate medium of collage and relief construction. From 1952 onwards, collage remained an inherent part of his vocabulary and, indeed, a frequent source of lyricism in his work. Pasmore, who made his first collage in 1950, influenced Frost with a range a crescent, rectangle, square or circle cut-out shapes pasted down on paper. Since colour was a pictorial component rather than a sculptural one, Frost returned to painting with a keeness to avoid the superficial colour of descriptive art. A new conceptual and functional awareness of colour led him, in the words of Tom Cross, 'To reconsider the use of colour as a structural component in painting.'*6 Frost used colour for its associative rather than naturalistic function. Colour therefore assumed a symbolic rather than descriptive role, explaining by way of analogy, emotional responses to experience of nature. Furthermore, colour could suggest itself in response to the sensual experiences of the working process.

Because Frost identifies emotionally and sensually with the medium through which his ideas are expressed, the use of collage or construction assumes considerable significance, by way of contrast, with the more usual material of paint. In 'Yellow Day' (1952) Frost uses yellow as a dominating hue. The rectangular planes of earlier paintings lose their visual sharpness and edge. The rectangles still structure the surface but lose prominence to a brisk sign language of lines and zigzagging rhythms. Movement is palpably expressed through the actual mark-making process. The movement attached to recurring motifs like moored boats, rigging, washing on clothes lines, or winds across landscape, are given abstract significance. Yellow is a favourite colour throughout all periods of Frost's work. It is used in the form of ochres in the generally drab 'ration book' and kitchen sink' post-war era, while in the artist's later work becomes bright cadmium, distinct and expressive of the sun's warm energy. Colour dominates the mood and form of the pictures to the extent that many paintings take titles from the hues. 'Mars Yellow' and 'Ochre and Yellow' are, for instance, titles of 1959 compositions. This practice indicates the high degree of abstraction from an originating natural motif. The colour themes culminate in the 'Through Yellow' series of the late 1960's; a period that also saw the artist's predilection for blue, red and black take the form of schematic tonal and chromatic variations on single hues.

Terry Frost in studio, 1950's.

A body of work bearing Yorkshire themes came about in the mid 1950s as a result of the Gregory Fellowship award. The changes that occured in his work at this time as a response to the new environment, indicate that the source of abstract imagery in the paintings remained rooted in the artist's sensory experience. The bleaker environment of Yorkshire, particularly in winter, led to a more restrained palette, dominated not by the blues, yellows or reds of the St. Ives period, but instead by snow whites, creams, browns and blacks. Similarly, the abstract patterns on the surface of the canvases - stripes, eddies, arrows, wedges - reflected the motifs, not of Cornish boats and rigging, but instead of field patterns, stone walls, toboggan tracks in winter or gusts of wind. Nowhere is the magical transformation of memories or perceptions of landscape into the plastic dimension of painting more in evidence than in Frost's famous statement recalling a walk through Yorkshire snow with Herbert Read. The artist wrote of seeing 'the white sun spinning on top of a copse ...a Naples yellow blinding circle spinning on top of black verticals'. In this instance the artist was seeing nature through the empathetic eyes and sensibility of an abstract painter. Perceptions of landscape motivated the thematic content of work, though a gestation period between visual experience and resulting work was necessary to give the artist a freshness of approach in the independent activity of constructing a picture. The Tate's well known 'Winter 1956 Yorkshire' uses scale to give expression to the largeness of the Yorkshire landscape. The experience of tobogganing down a hill is translated into the work in terms of abstracted stripe patterns. The exhilaration of fast physical movement down snow is captured on canvas with a corresponding gestural movement with the brush down the entire length of a large vertical canvas. The artist wrote that since the late 1940's he had been 'interested in the business of taking a line round what I wanted to say'.[7] By this time Frost had the confidence to chance his arm with large scale gesture, a heaped generosity of paint and strident mark-making.

The gestural correspondence between experience and plastic creation indicated a new confidence and versatility in Frost's work during the late 1950's. The work became more direct and expressive, responding to the action painting of the New York School. Brash, bold, outgoing qualities of Frost's art lent it immediate kinship with abstract expressionism. In 1960 he had a one man show at the Bertha Shaeffer Gallery, New York. He met several New York painters, among them Rothko, whom he had first met a few years before in Cornwall while the distinguished American artist was staying with the Lanyons. In 1962 he had a second show with Shaeffer, heralding an international reputation. The 1960-62 period was perhaps the high point of his entire career. He painted with an automatic overdrive, using the repertoire of shapes - zigzagging forms, arrows, wedges, eddies, stripes and spirals - that were ponderously developed in the landscape-rooted works of the 1950s. Heath explained how Frost was most moved by the 'spirit of optimistic confidence and the practice of hard work'[8] in American art. The same writer also felt that 'his debt to other painters is difficult to determine as there are no obvious links of a technical or stylistic nature to suggest a name'.[9] American art was liberating even though he never tapped its deep vein of mythic symbolism. He was also influenced by Roger Hilton, whose greater knowledge of modern French art rubbed off, particularly after Hilton took him to Paris in 1957. During this period the smaller works by Frost, Hilton and Scott are barely distinguishable from one another, with a de Stael-influenced use of abstract motifs, thick butter-like paint and restrained colour.

155

The influence of American Arts on
Trevor

During the 1960's Frost both tightened and simplified his formal language through use of large scale formats and a restricted number of pre determined collage units - painted canvas cut-outs glued down to the main canvas support. The imagery of bikinis, buttocks, breasts, boats or other forms

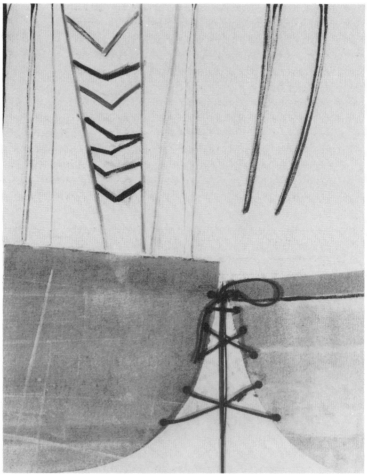

Terry Frost. Laced Grace. *Oil and collage, 1962.*
Belgrave Gallery, London.

pressing against one another were clearly evoked. By exploiting a typical St. Ives theme, that of creating sexual analogies between the landscape and figure, Frost struck a cord of hedonistic fun that marked the mood of the

1960's, and also suited the temperament of an artist who, ironically, belonged to an earlier generation. Frost also delighted in signs, emblems and traffic symbols taken from the world around him. For a time he even drew from the designs on lorries, another instance of an artist adapting to the style and spirit of the 1960's, in particular the fondness for commercially reproduced imagery. Bright colour was another feature that distinguished the new decade from the drab ochre and grey climate of the 1950's, and it showed through in Frost's work, which used greater varieties of colour in new schematic arrangements. A commentator for the magazine 'Apollo' wrote that 'During the sixties and seventies Frost has resorted to random variations on his basic vocabularly of circles, segments and stripes painted in a fierce, fully saturated colour with decorative daring, the crude assurance of his visual assault is initially stimulating but leaves little of significance after the first momentary impact'.*10 Frost's pictures also responded to minimal art when he restricted the composition to variations of white and a single dominant form. Colour of a more positive kind also became purely structural units, shorn of previous associative or symbolic functions, in the works of the late 1960's and 1970's like 'Orange Moonship'. Primaries dominate over earth colours. The autonomous colour of Matisse and Delaunay (Frost flew to New York in 1992 to see the large Matisse retrospective) and the minimal geometry of Malevich (his son studied early modern Russian art) were the dominant influences after the 1970's.

The preference for pure form and colour in the wholly abstract compositions of the 1960's and 1970's reflects the changing circumstances of an artist who had left the Cornish outdoors to teach in the 'visual laboratory' of Reading University. He commuted from Banbury to Reading, where the structural experiments made with students pushed his work further into the realm of pure abstraction. He also visited Stass Paraskoss's summer school in Cyprus, and his work identified with that of younger colour field painters like Mali Morris, Geoff Rigden and Jennifer Durrant, whom he encountered at Reading. In all probability, the structural language of the 1970's represented a renewal of plastic and imaginative faculties. The artist seemed to wipe the board clean and start afresh with an invigorated language of colour and form. It gave him the scope, during the 1980's, to re-introduce allusions to natural motifs, and re-complicate the minimal and geometric arrangements. In 1974 Frost returned to Cornwall, living on a hill high above Newlyn. The paraphernalia of Newlyn harbour - tyres, reflections, sails, rigging, buoys, quayside machinery - were roped back into the softening abstraction of his current work. Maritime association once again entered his work and the return to Cornwall enabled him to reclaim a leading position within the modern Cornish school, particularly since old colleagues like Hepworth, Hilton and Wynter all died at the time of his return.

In 1981 Frost retired from teaching and painted full-time. That same year he exhibited recent work at John Makepeace's Parnham in Dorset, while retrospectives at Reading University in 1986 and the Mayor Gallery in 1990 confirmed the enduring popularity of an artist whose later works extol the virtues of 'joie de vivre'. During the 1980's Frost threw caution to the proverbial winds with a prolific - probably too prolific - spate of strikingly colourful and decoratively exuberant work, the uncanny product of a psychologically reflective yet plastically spontaneous artist alert to practical and aesthetic problems. Frost's apparently unintellectual approach belies an inventive sensibility that feeds lived experiences into art in direct, original and unusual ways. The familiar repertoire of abstract yet landscape - evoking shapes are strung together or collaged along carefully planned axes to create strong pictorial harmonies or tensions. After a lifetime, the insistent vivacity of colour sings out loudest.

Colour also sings with a loud and consistent voice in the work of Frost's contemporary, Patrick Heron. They are fundamentally different to one another, however, for Frost is pragmatic and unintellectual in his use of an intuitive, spontaneous approach to chosen form. Heron paints with a programme in mind, one that recognises the limited range of choice available in innovative late modernist painting. A central role afforded to colour throughout Heron's oeuvre is never in doubt, though it becomes the only factor in later work, to the extent of illustrating the artist's formal and graphic limitations. Heron constructs with colour. In 1962 he wrote that 'colour is both the subject and the means; the form and the content; the image and the meaning in my painting today ...it is obvious that colour is now the only direction in which painting can travel'. Heron is nothing if not doctrinaire and his abstract colour compositions have found intellectual justification through the artist's eloquent lectures and tendentious writings. Heron's considerable understanding of modern art is based primarily on visual appreciation. This is a source of strength, though has the disadvantage of tying the artist, both practically and ideologically, to a limited formalism that misses the fuller moral meanings prescribed for subject matter by the theories of Bell, Fry, Wilenski, Hulme and later by Fuller. Do Heron's pictures have a wider content beyond purely aesthetic considerations concerning the formal, optical behaviour of colour? Do the pictures express the landscape around Eagles Nest, as the artist claims?

Heron's work is couched in a 'savoire vivre' ambience of taste, sophistication, manners and preciousness. The early paintings - representations of interiors, window views, still-lifes, cafes, nudes, harbours and churches - are homages to Matisse and particularly Braque. He uses a pronounced silhouetting of figurative form to evoke spatial ambiguity and complexity. Areas of untouched canvas vie for attention with brushed passages of positive colour. Charcoal drawing is sometimes left unpainted within a painting. In extreme cases, like the beautiful 'Harbour Window St. Ives 1951 ' - depicting a figure, table and veranda against a harbour - line is painted against a white ground as the sole pictorial agent. Heron always associates drawing with painting and synthesises the two through the practice of drawing with a tube of paint, squeezing pigment like toothpaste, and directly etching in the forms he desires to depict. This direct approach is parallelled by a palette of unmixed colour applied straight from originating tubes. Colour, in spite of being expressed in linear and figurative terms, sets up the vital mood and character of the work. Later on it submerged these linear qualities. Heron described how 'colour determines the actual shapes, or areas, which balance one another ...in my painting.'*11

In the colour field compositions of the 1960's, Heron's drawing becomes a peripheral element, a by-product of the more central issue of successful placement of colour. The floating circles or rectangles of colour, hovering over or within surrounding 'grounds' of variant hue, set up shape relationships that condition the way we actually receive colour sensations. He explained that 'the meeting lines between areas of colour are utterly crucial to our apprehension of the actual hue of those areas'. A jagged line separating two adjacent areas of complementary colour would therefore modify the sensation in a different way to a smooth line, 'The line', he explained, 'changes the colour of the colour on either side of it'. He therefore used 'increasingly sharp and precise' edges with which to divide one colour from another. Tight drawing accompanied minute inch-by-inch application of unmixed acrylic paint with a Japanese watercolour brush. The use of sharp frontiers, he went on to suggest, did not originate from an interest in boulder-like forms or tight 'jigsaw puzzle' designs per se, but rather came about because such shapes were the formal outcome of what he admitted was an 'obsession with the interaction of colours'.

Even in the earliest representational works colour begins to assume an autonomous role by way of floating free of defining outline. Patches of colour dabbed onto the canvas have only partial regard for their descriptive role in bodying out form. The function of colour as a separate entity to descriptive form certainly points the way to a later use of fully autonomous, abstract colour. In all this Heron clearly owes much to Ben Nicholson, whose Porthmeor studio was taken over by Heron in the late 1950's after the older artist moved to Switzerland. In Nicholson's still-lifes of the 1920's colour is similarly unwrapped from the confining edges of figurative contour. But Heron goes even further by integrating drawing into the process of colour construction. During the Sam Francis-influenced tachist period of the mid-1950's - represented by the vertical Garden series - Heron composes 'in order to accommodate colour as such: I had the feeling that colour determines the actual shapes, or areas, which balance one another'. Throughout all phases of Heron's work illusionistic space is reconciled with surface flatness. Colour plays a key role in integrating satisfying surface design with spatial recession. The temperature and natural space-creating dynamics of colour make it an ideal vehicle of expression. Painting for Heron 'is essentially an art of illusion ...the secret of good painting ...lies in its adjustment of an inescapable dualism; on the one hand there is the illusion of depth and on the other there is the physical reality of the flat picture surface.'*12 A pronounced feeling for the power of flat design and decorative arrangement perhaps derive from his father's Crysede silk business. It gave young Patrick an insight into use of colour, pattern and design in the applied art of fabric production. Early compositions are not merely exercises in the decorative vitality of colour and form however; rather they address themselves to the rigorous language of Cubism, with its intricate visual relationship between line, plane, colour and interval. The colour, too, is basically French and quite different to the bleached

159

tonality of Nicholson.

Heron's sumptuous paintings borrow much from Braque, with black used as a positive colour alongside more familiar brown, yellow, purple and blue. These colours enliven early still-lifes where flowers and fruit focus our attention on the surface of tables. The artist is interested in the blending of animate and inanimate, organic and architectural elements. His view of nature, far from being a first hand perception, is experienced at one remove. Heron's primary source is culture, not nature. His view of landscape is therefore a peculiarly pictorial one, seen through, and distanced by, a window frame, veranda, barbed-wire fence and the like, elements chosen as much for formal significance as for psychological effect. In his early 'Nude on an Iron Bed' Heron unleashes a poetic and visual contrast between the softness of flesh and the rigid structure of an iron bed. The best known of the early works is 'Christmas Eve', a large composite subject chosen for the Festival of Britain's, '60 Paintings for 51'. This important early work incorporates all Heron's motifs - interior, still-life, figure and window. Other interior subjects of the period were made possible by his renting a flat overlooking St. Ives harbour, which the artist used every year between 1947 and 1955. He later wrote that 'The inside-outside theme of this harbour window subject became the main feature of my paintings from 1946 onwards ...The sensation of recession was especially well accommodated by this theme'.

During the early 1950's Heron clarified ideas concerning the role of colour in his painting. In the summer of 1953 he organised the exhibition 'Space in Colour' at the Hanover Gallery, an event that fulfilled the twin purpose of promoting the work of his St. Ives colleagues and defining colour's structural role in contemporary painting. In spite of enjoying a growing critical influence, Heron was still feeling his way with uncertainty; an unconvincing flirtation with the abstracted motifs of de Stael, quickly led the artist back to more recognisable figurative form. The real spur to breaking new ground came with the move to Eagles Nest in the spring of 1956. The move elicited a series of loosely painted colour compositions based on garden themes. The garden canvases were generally vertical in format and composed with truncated marks of vibrant colour. 'Azalea Garden' (1956), painted the month after moving to Eagles Nest, reflected the artist's enduring predilection for flower motifs; its tachist markings have a speed, vitality and rhythmic energy that is matched by the brilliance of the hues. The tachist marks gradually elongated into stripes of colour that traversed the entire length of the canvas. The stripe paintings, at first horizontal but later vertical, were displayed at the Redfern Gallery's 1957 'Metavisual Tachist and Abstract' exhibition. The following year he had a solo exhibition of striped paintings at the same gallery, though their hermetic formalism, shorn of any immediate association with the natural world, made them difficult to sell.

Nevertheless, for a young artist in competition with equally, if not more gifted colleagues, these innovative canvases put his work on the international map and fulfilled a requirement to stake new ground for himself as a developing vanguard painter. A lucid understanding of recent developments on the international scene found voice in regular art critical contributions to

Colour in Contemp Painting

leading magazines like the 'New Statesman', 'New English Weekly' or 'Arts (New York)'. Though Davie and Scott were before him in directly experiencing the recent emergence of American painting, Heron was certainly one of the first of his generation to respond with intellectual clarity to New York painting and to turn away from the worn patina of European painting. Alan Bowness later referred to the stripes as 'paintings of a remarkable originality and beauty'*13, and Heron himself emphasised that their apparently advanced abstraction did not mean they had entirely broken links with nature. Indeed, Peter Fuller admired the stripe canvases precisely for their distilled associations with the natural world. They were not, to Fuller's mind, 'art shaped holes', empty of meaning as certain kinds of New York-sponsored hermetic abstraction were later deemed to be by the prominent 1980's critic. Ideologically motivated factors may, however, have played a part in Fuller's disingenous endorsement of Heron's work; the artist's famous 'Guardian' rebuke of American painting in 1974 fitted in with Fuller's simultaneous rejection of doctrinaire modernism and advancement of the traditions of British painting. In addition, Heron's stripes undoubtedly reminded Fuller of the decorative splendour of Robert Natkin's 'field paintings', which he had been avidly promoting since the 1970's.

During the 1960's and beyond, Heron developed large scale to accommodate colour and give it full spatial value. The size responded to a widespread new energy and adventurousness. During the fashion-conscious 1960's an artist who had always been aware of style kept pace with the spirit, rather than the letter, of contemporary developments and did so, moreover, by maintaining faith in a brand of abstraction that belonged to a previous decade. Heron, a supremely erudite and articulate spokesman both for his own art and for that of his contemporaries, continued to promulgate the central role of colour in the art of painting. The colours in these later compositions were uncompromisingly vibrant, creating retinal after-effects where oranges and greens, reds and blues, yellows and purples clashed. The artist also produced screenprints and gouaches, a medium that he exploited to the full, using fluid effects of stained or bled gouache paint on absorbent sheets of paper. The paintings of the late 1980's and early 1990's re-introduce drawing in the form of jazzy linear arabesques of directly squeezed tube colour. The imagery reverts back to flower or plant configurations against light untouched canvas grounds. A psychological mood of optimistic exhilaration in the face of the natural world, as well as an affirmation of the ongoing relevance of painting in a late twentieth century context, are the main moral virtues of the later art of Patrick Heron.

Trevor Bell, Alan Wood and Tony O'Malley were among a group of artists who followed in the wake of Frost and Heron. Others included Jeff Harris and Anthony Benjamin. They received not just encouragement but critical support and professional opportunities from the older artists. Like Patrick Heron, Trevor Bell was born in Leeds, though a decade later in 1930. The difference in age did not show up in the work, which adapted quickly and shared in the general abstract preoccupations of the late 1950's. Bell studied art at Leeds, where he made an impact with competently handled figurative work. Roger

Hilton, who came to view Bell as a young protegé, inspired a more adventurous use of colour and form, however, and the presence of Terry Frost in Leeds during the mid-1950's represented 'a special moment'*14 for Bell. He was compelled by these artists to simplify style, tighten language and compress the degree of figurative association. This was good advice, for Bell's industrial landscapes were still formally dependent on illusionism. Indeed, Heron wrote that when Bell arrived in Cornwall 'the acquisition of that sense of flattened planes which is inherent in all the best painting of our time …was not yet within his grasp'. Frost was advocating the need for earnest experiment and research in a quest for new discoveries. Frost encouraged him to use the studio as a visual laboratory, and in particular, told him to go to Cornwall where the modern movement of abstraction was in full swing. Through Frost, Bell met the leading young artists in Cornwall and lived in a cottage near Eagles Nest, which he helped decorate under the supervision of Keith Leonard.

Frost's more exuberant romantic temperament was complemented, in Bell's mind, by the example of Michael Snow, a contemporary who represented a calmer, constructive approach. Snow's rational formalism was echoed by John Forrester and Brian Wall, both of whom were influenced by Mondrian and by Nicholson in their structures of line and plane in space. Though Bell's

John Forrester. Space Curves. *Mixed media, 1954.*
Paisnel Gallery, London.

metier was to remain painted mark on a flat, albeit irregularly shaped, surface, these artists helped him towards a physical and conceptual appreciation of the significance of space. Peter Clough, a painter who used Frost's cottage, also became a friend. Bell met Alan Wood (with whom he later taught at Bradford) and went snorkling with Alan Davie, an artist he considered 'a good counter-influence'*15 to offset the more orthodox strains of formal abstraction. Bell followed in Davie's footsteps by exploring nature to the full. Although his

Trevor Bell. Rocks and Sea. *Gouache, 1958.*
Gordon Hepworth Gallery.

painting still used street motifs or simplified plans of aerial perspective, he gradually used paint only for expressive effect, in order to capture experiences such as a three week yachting expedition to Biarritz. Images of night sailing or of the emptiness of ocean sources have been a feature of his work ever since. In the 1980's Bell travelled to India and sought out isolated places in the Himalayas. In the classic St. Ives tradition, he absorbed exhilarating landscape experiences and translated them into painting in terms of visual simplification and abstraction.

163

In 1958 Bell was not yet thirty, but so notable was his development up to that point that he held a commercially successful show with Waddington, to whom he had been recommended by Charles Gimpel. Patrick Heron wrote that Bell was 'the best non-figurative painter under thirty in the country'. He went on to have four exhibitions with the gallery, though the final show in 1964, of shaped canvases, was not commercially succesful. Lanyon was impressed by Bell's Pennine paintings at Waddingtons, and Frost and Hilton continued to fillip his morale and maintain belief in his contribution. In 1962 he returned to Leeds for three years on a Gregory Fellowship. He exhibited in Penwith exhibitions, though resigned in response to Hepworth's perceived attempts to exert undemocratic influence on the organisation. Bell was making his way in the world beyond Cornwall, however, and after leaving Leeds in the mid-1960's had successful teaching spells at Ravensbourne, Bradford, Winchester and the Barry Summer School. He also exhibited shaped canvases in 1966 at the Demarco Gallery in Edinburgh, eliciting a typical piece of hyperbole from Heron who then considered Bell to be 'an infinitely greater painter in every way than Frank Stella'.*16 Nonetheless, the comparison with an American painter was appropriate because Bell's future lay across the Atlantic. During the 1970's he became a Professor of Painting at the Florida State University, where the colours of continuing shaped canvases, such as those that formed the nucleus of the rare London exhibition in 1990 at the Gillian Jason Gallery, have derived from the clear, translucent conditions of the Caribbean.

Alan Wood also held an exhibition with Gillian Jason in 1990. He too had moved to North America in the 1970's to take up a lucrative teaching post, in his case to British Columbia. Wood's early mentors came about not through the Leeds to St. Ives axis, but through being an art student in Liverpool. The charismatic Arthur Ballard became Wood's chief mentor at Liverpool, the tutor who introduced him to the bohemian pubs of Soho and also to the art haunts of Paris, where he met Giacometti, Cezar and Poliakoff. Wood saw his first Peter Lanyon, a picture called 'Farms Back, Zennor', in Manchester, at the Whitworth's exhibition 'New Abstract Art'. Ballard already knew Lanyon and pointed out to Wood the importance of the Cornishman's work. Ballard's fervent Liverpudlianism was matched by Lanyon's equally partisan association with Cornwall. Wood would later become better acquainted with Lanyon as a result of gaining a Dartington Trust Award, which allowed him to live and work in Cornwall. He was not shy of approaching painters of gathering fame and promise in Cornwall. The scant entree of a letter of introduction from the Liverpool-trained and Devon-based painter Clifford Fishwick was sufficient for a young artist, still little more than an enthusiast, who had been versed in the precocious, charismatic social climate of 'showy' Liverpool. Liverpool's tight knit bohemia of artists then included, in addition to Ballard, Don McKinlay, Henry Graham, Stuart Sutcliffe and Austin Davies. Wood had been a conscientious student, using traditional genre, though a predilection for landscape emerged with a series of Lake District studies, then after his move to Devon, abstractions on Dartmoor themes. His move to Cornwall in 1961, resulted in successful entry into the artistic milieu. He continued to respond to landscape. However, by the mid-1960's, ever alert to pertinent fashion, Wood introduced a more constructed language into his work using timber and other hard edge components in response to the influence of Rauschenberg. He taught at Cardiff Art College during the late 1960's and early 1970's. The art college lecturing to which he was personally so well suited proved a moveable feast, for in 1974 he emigrated to Vancouver, where he continued to teach throughout the 1980's. The availability of timber and the vast scale of the landscape in Canada led to some huge environmental timber assemblages like 'Ranch'.

Tony O'Malley in his St. Ives studio. Early 1980's.

Tony O'Malley also benefitted from the critical endorsement of Patrick Heron, who found in the Irishman a perfect apologist for his own preoccupation with colour. O'Malley's commercial success came later in his career, during the 1980's, when a buoyant market for the artist's work in his native Ireland ensured financial security after years of uncertainty living in a rented Arts Council flat behind Alfred Wallis' cottage. O'Malley returned with his Canadian wife Jane to southern Ireland, ending a 30 year exile in St. Ives. The former Dublin bank clerk first alighted on St. Ives in 1959, turning the colony into both a safe haven where he could fulfill his ambition to paint, and a spa town for a middle aged man in fragile though retrievable health. An early work like 'East Wind St. Ives', is typical of its time and place - an abundance of greys and browns expresses the desolation of winter in terms of some fishing boats on the cold foamy waters of the harbour. Cornwall is most Celtic in winter and O'Malley, the visual poet from County Clare, immediately evoked the elemental mystery common to both Cornwall and west Ireland. Yet, colour of a more positive nature distinguishes O'Malley's mature oeuvre, reaching rich sumptuous proportions in the context of the artist's Caribbean period of the 1980's. In these later years the artist spent part of each winter in the Bahamas, soaking up the extraordinary colour, investing naturalism with a new meaning, and translating it onto canvas in terms of unprecedented optical vibrancy.

The artist's Bahamas period began in 1976 and provided him with the tonic of a winter trip for the next decade. These trips highlighted a continuing Gauguinesque escape route from conventional life that had first been ushered in with his abandonment of an office job in Ireland. The trips also indicate therapeutic motives behind a desire to paint, linking him with the naive ethos of Wallis and Pearce, though painting for O'Malley assumed a still more critical role - a compulsive affirmation of his very reason for being. O'Malley came late to art; he was over thirty when he took up the brush. Moreover, he was a self-taught artist whose rejection of conventional picture-making modes, both abstract and figurative, enabled him to invest the surfaces of his art with the kind of special meaning that a cacophony of cryptic signs, symbols, image fragments and dream-like hieroglyphics provided. O'Malley bypasses the phoney war between the traditional and modern, and looks for a more timeless essence. The pictures are a repository of sensations and marks alluding to movement across a landscape. In common with his friend Bryan Wynter's 'Spoor' series, O'Malley's pictures allude to the evidence of movement and migration across a landscape. Images of birds are apt metaphors for such movement. He takes a sketchbook wherever he goes, and composite images culled from the landscape of the Scillies, Penwith, Ireland, the Bahamas, the Canaries or other regularly visited locations find their way from the sheets of a notebook onto the hardboard or canvas surfaces of paintings. He works in series, and pictures often have no individual focus of attention, with recurring features entering a number of pictures at once. The way that a wide assortment of images and signs are rearranged in a new pictorial context indicates the artist's essential skill.

O'Malley hails from a culture that is primarily literary rather than visual. While rejecting narrative genre, his paintings are built up with the kind of visual poetry that have developed over a long period of gestation and which have literary and philosophical ramifications. At the same time he adapts the St. Ives convention of landscape tactility for his own ends. Instead of scraping

166

down surfaces, O'Malley takes a razor and makes a number of rhythmic incisions to evoke the kind of drawn symbols found for instance on ancient Celtic stonework. He uses irregularly shaped boards and is alert to the object-like quality that Wallis evoked with shaped supports. An O'Malley picture is 'very much a record of its making and, by extension, his 'Body of work' is a record of a life given to this activity'.*17 If O'Malley has brought a natural ease and relaxation into painting then it is through the mysterious role of colour that the random symbols, pointillist dabs and incised lines are pulled into a coherent pictorial whole. In the mid-1970's, Heron identified the sensual luminosity of O'Malley's colour - evident in the cold greys of Cornish winters as much as in the hot melted hues of the Caribbean - as the distinguishing feature that marked off the artist from the impersonal, mechanical 'post-painterly' abstraction that still enjoyed international supremacy.

In the late 1950's Jeff Harris followed Trevor Bell from Yorkshire, and jumped on the rolling Cornish bandwagon as a result of studying under artists with St. Ives connections at Leeds College of Art. Harris's adoption of entirely non-figurative painting, and in particular his 'period' style of mosaic-like squares and rectangles of thick paint, owed something to the Basic Design principles that tutors like Thubron and Pasmore took from the Bauhaus and promulgated at this important time in art education. An interest in Klee did not lead him, at this stage, to invest the abstracted imagery of jostling boats on

Jeff Harris in St. Ives, 1960.

167

the black waters of a night harbour with any degree of symbolic or representational significance: stylistically, the influences of Scott and Stael were most apparent. Indeed, by the time he moved to St. Ives after acquiring a teaching job at a school in Hayle, Harris was painting confidently with a hot palette of red, orange, purple and brown; the gradual opening out of the multitudinous squares led to 'considerations of figure-ground, intervals, proportions'*[18] becoming important. Visually, his work resembled the contemporary mode of Hilton, Frost and Heron, as well as of Scott. Harris was entrenched in an entirely non figurative language, and he even made white reliefs, reminiscent of the Martins and Pasmore, though these were undoubtedly an ephemeral response to a contemporary spirit of wilful experimentation. Harris thought these reliefs as 'objective correlatives, to use Eliot's term, to attempt to speak in new materials and processes'. Similarly, a series of silkscreens indulged in the rich, bright and outward-going colour of the period; the images reminded one of late Wynter and Frost, with hard edged colour patterns dominating. Ironically, it was after leaving St. Ives, and indeed England, at the end of the 1960's that Harris' work came closest in its resemblance to a Cornish artist.

In the early 1970's, removed first to Tasmania then to Adelaide with his second wife, the Australian-born painter Gwen Leitch, Harris's bright paintings of colour discs and wobbling interactive colour areas, came close to the idiosyncratic English variation of colour field painting practised by the nationalistic Patrick Heron. Nevertheless, the effect of Australia eventually led to a more personal style, in the same way that Bell, Wood and Wall all broadened their work in the ex-pat situation 'after St. Ives'. Soon enough, Harris embarked on a more authentic ex-pat phase of his own, making the Heron-influenced work of the early Australian years a kind of 'withdrawal' therapy, paying homage to a twelve year St. Ives experience he later described as 'intensely rich and vital'. Moreover, he took to Australia the firm identity of a small, but internationally significant art colony experienced during that colony's heyday. As a result, he explained his bright colour fields as being 'a celebration, a joy, and a thanksgiving for safe arrival in a new land'.*[19] The teaching experience he had gained at Falmouth (under a supportive Michael Finn) was valuable prior to his move to teach in Adelaide. The psychologically liberating effect of an entirely different landscape led to a new phase of work - responding to the imagery of the landscape - that finally threw off the influence of St. Ives. Nonetheless, the influence of Ben Nicholson, long one of his revered masters, entered certain works in terms of stylised tree forms, undulating hill profiles or the use of window motifs set against a landscape. Nicholson's drawings, in particular, inspired him, and an interest in drawing generally led to his absorption of old master influences gained through studies at Oxford's Ashmolean during a six month period of paid leave from his Australian job in the mid-1970's. The Australian Landscape paintings, though coloured with the same purple, brown and ochre of earlier phases, are entirely new, and conjure something of the essential emptiness and mountainous grandeur of the continent. Furthermore, in order to describe a landscape in which 'space is palpable' Harris used a painterly approach that combined the gestural, the linear and the tactile in the evocation of a total topographic experience.

Anthony Benjamin (born 1931), was another young artist who made a significant contribution as part of the generation that followed on from Lanyon, Heron and Hilton. He studied at Fernand Léger's Studio in Paris, exhibited figurative painting at Helen Lessore's Beaux Arts Gallery and acquired a cottage near St. Ives, in order to be close to a group of artists where, much to Lessore's chagrin, he could expand his vocabulary to embrace non-figurative painting. He was inspired by the 'spatial aspects of landscape and particular moving light',[20] and as a result of these interests created large

Anthony Benjamin. Off Zennor. *Oil, 1959.*

paintings like 'Off Zennor', built up with thickly layered surfaces of pronounced tactility. The picture, with its greys and pinks, and correspondence between paint texture and landscape experience, represented a personal variation of middle generation practice. The need to earn a living made him leave Cornwall only a few years later, however, and scholarships to Italy and to Paris (he studied printmaking at Stanley Hayter's renowned Atelier 17) were steps towards a distinguished teaching career in North America. In this, he followed artists like Wall, Bell and Wood. During the 1960's his work responded to the cool geometric abstraction that followed the 'Situation' exhibitions, though a natural flair for drawing has seen him, in more recent years, return to skilfully modelled graphite compositions of still-life subjects. These are distinguished by a versatile use of line, hatching, erasing and broad tonal modelling. He works today in Norfolk, though his association with Gimpel Fils is a constant reminder of an important earlier participation in Cornish modern art.

Bryan Wynter was an inventive, if not fully innovative, painter. He was also a well liked person. His popularity was based on striking a happy balance between romanticism and modernism, between the pursuit of personal themes and adherence to general artistic imperatives, between reclusiveness and conviviality and between professional ambition and magnanimity towards the group. His closest friends were Sven Berlin and David Haughton in the earlier days, with Heron and O'Malley becoming paricularly good friends in later years. He married twice, living at Zennor Carn with his first wife Susan before moving to St. Buryan with his second wife Monica. In spite of sharing a similar early preoccupation with Braque, Wynter was a very different kind of artist to Heron. Wynter's roots lay in the cubo-surrealist 'neo-romanticism' of the 1940's. The intense identification with the British landscape, couched in an intensely linear and emotive language of spikes, cubist distortions, planes and organic geometry, never left Wynter. If not alone (Keith Vaughan and Graham Sutherland were others) Wynter was one of very few artists to have developed the illustrative pastoralism that was a hallmark of the neo-romanticism style into the realm of painterly abstraction. Wynter was alert to the question of style, a factor which governs the tempo and the marked changes in the visual nature of his work during the thirty years (1945-1975) of his intriguing development as a painter. His art lies somewhere the design conscious suaveness of Heron's art and the subjective exploratory zeal of Lanyon's. A common thread, however, links the early neo-romantic gouaches with the middle period tachist 'bead curtain' canvases and finally with the late mobiles and meandering hard edge 'river pattern' compositions. A closely observed and experienced landscape is conveyed, in the context of Wynter's art, in an elegantly delineated language.

The thematic content of early work is based on the harsh, almost lunar landscape beyond his doorstep on the Zennor moors. 'The landscape I live among is bare of houses, trees, people', he wrote, and 'is dominated by winds, by swift changes of weather, by the moods of the sea'. In particular, he was interested in the visual patterns deposited by streaks of fire or by the action of wind across water. He was fascinated by the landscape as a repository of history, seen in moulded patterns of erosion. Spoors, footprints, snake tracks and other patterns of animal movement interested him as much the action of the elements. He invested these natural forces with an emotional significance which he claimed 'enter the paintings and lend their qualities without becoming motifs.'*21 He was able to associate a rapid calligraphy with the visual and tactile experiences of an unfolding landscape. Movement was a sub plot throughout all periods, and styles, of his work. He saw hidden links and rhythmic continuities across a landscape topography. Hiking expeditions were followed, in the late 1950's, with skin-diving and finally canoeing excursions. The intrepid landscape explorer found corresponding psychological fulfilment through experiments with the mind expanding drug mescalin. Although he was never able to paint under its direct, disorientating influence there is no doubt that the hallucinogenic drug transformed his perceptions of landscape, which he experienced with a heightened awareness of topographic patterns like ribbed sands, water currents, tracks and the like.

After 1956, with paintings like 'The Interior', Wynter severed direct representational links with nature. Explosive all-over tachist canvases put his work in vogue, corresponding with international aesthetic currents while maintaining a very English preoccupation with landscape. His first, large scale 'tachist' canvases emerged during a period of several months spent away from Cornwall in Chelsea. The year was 1956, and it was indeed a watershed; his father died and the resulting sale of the family laundry business afforded a degree of financial security enabling him to work on a more ambitious scale. With new found confidence he took on an outgoing international style and submerged local references in a generalised though evocative calligraphy. The exhibition 'Modern Art in the United States' was shown in the beginning of 1956 at the Tate, and Wynter was greatly encouraged by the ambitious new abstract expressionism of the New York School. He recognised its roots in surrealist automatism, in that area of chance effect originating from the plastic working process. These issues were highly relevant to Wynter's own requirements, and there was something of the surrealist in someone who experimented with mescalin, played practical jokes on colleagues and conducted group seances and free association soirées. Furthermore, Aldous Huxley's recent book 'The Doors of Perception' gave voice to Wynter's own mystical bent, and in the new tachist phase, ushered in by 'Interior' (1956), he began to express the elusive, transient quality of visual perception in heightened states of awareness. He made apposite statements intermittently during his career, and in one he spoke about wishing to capture the eye's first innocent glances on a landscape, before the filters of conditioned response and intellectual categorisation took control. Wynter's work finds its closest equivalents in the calligraphic work of Mark Tobey and Bradley Walker Tomlin in America, and of Alfred Manessier in France. The post 1956 works continue, in spite of vastly increased scale, to employ a miniature brush language of small markings, jabs of lush paint and dry brush textures. He does not aim to increase scale of gestural mark to architectural proportions such as occured in the work of Heron, Lanyon and other contemporaries. Instead he travels inside a picture and creates a deep recessive space by use of superimposed layers of semi-transparent marks. Although the canvases are large in scale, Wynter holds their surfaces together by working in a spontaneous way, building up the picture with a maze of differentiated but self-interacting marks that cohere as a unit and as an all-over surface web. The method is a stylistic correlative of spontaneous stream-of-consciousness automatism.

By the early 1960's these all-over surfaces had become more chained to, and ordered by, a rectilinear pattern. In the Sandspoor series of the early 1960's pictorial surface was increasingly subordinated to a rigid linear design; at the same time this series lent itself to landscape interpretations with the obvious motifs of residual marks, footprints and animal tracks littering the surfaces.

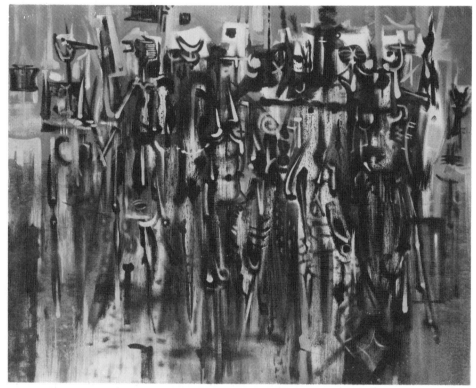

Bryan Wynter. Hostile Tribe. *Oil, 1956.*
Courtesy: British Council.

The adoption of canoeing after 1962 is significant. Moving along the smooth or disturbed surfaces of water helped familiarise him with the winding patterns of rivers. He was fascinated by the centrifugal surface ripples of disturbed water and by the reflections and repercussions beneath the stream or river. He sought out canoeing locations well beyond Cornwall, travelling to Ullapool on the north west coast of Scotland and also to Spain. The large paintings 'Saja' and 'Deva' for instance, take their titles from Spanish rivers that he explored from a rapidly moving raft. In the final decade of his career, the period from the mid-1960's to his death in 1975, Wynter created flat, hard

172

edged compositions; serene winding channels of pure colour. These river pattern pictures were accompanied by a large output of pentel pen drawings on paper that also explored in a highly schematic language of meandering lines, broken curves and undulating rhythms, the movement of water through, beneath and around topographic obstacles. Such late compositions are more lucidly designed and smoothly painted than was the case with the calligraphic frenzy of the 1950's works, which had associated themselves with the rapid flux of air bubbles, heaving water currents and windswept fire streaks. The 'Confluence' series, using a schematic range of light green, yellow or blue colour, is a highpoint of the artist's late work, preoccupied with distillations of experience. These pictorial resolutions are accompanied by the 'IMOOS' (Images Moving Out Onto Space), mobiles constructed from painted card and 'found' concave searchlight mirrors. The cards were suspended on threads and moved by air currents. The mirrors are not static neo-dada pieces of iconoclasm; rather they function in the ingenious capacity of kinetically transmitting the actual visual flux and movement that was always an important thematic element throughout his entire 'oeuvre'. In these mobiles, Wynter's obsession with movement finds literal and tangible outlet. The ever-changing imagery engages us through the vital element of time. They are 'peep' shows into Wynter's wonderful world of chance effect, metamorphosis and movement; a stage set with endlessly mutating shapes in constant process of formation, like nature itself, through sequences of time.

Unlike Wynter, Roger Hilton was not a pioneer of post-war Cornish art. Indeed, his development as a radical painter took place in the cosmopolitan centres of Paris and London. He studied at the Slade in the early 1930's, then under the French master Bissiere at the Academie Ransome. He rapidly matured as an artist of remarkable individuality in Cornwall, which he regularly visited from 1956 onwards until taking up full-time residence there in 1965. The growing association with Cornwall led to a softening of form. What had once been an uncompromising abstract language of colour and form responded once again to the figure and landscape in terms of partially retrieved figurative imagery. He had showed with the 'middle generation' in London exhibitions before the mid-1950's, though his work was very different to that of Wynter. Hilton's pictures occasionally came close, however, to the contemporary metier of Scott, Frost and Heron, though they originated in a more fluid, even anarchistic outlook. Hilton's marked individuality resulted from a restless mind that would not rest on aesthetic laurels. He resisted cosy stylism or easy commercial formulae with clumsy paint handling, irreverant gesture and willfully gauche imagery. Elements of grafitti, eroticism, and children's art characterised this imagery and betrayed Hilton's training in pre-war Paris, where first Dubuffet then later the Cobra artists sought to integrate the crude energy of such art with the more sophisticated formal content of 'high' art. Yet Hilton was, to use Wilenski's term, a more architectural artist than these emotive expressionists. His economic use of form allied him aesthetically, if not temperamentally, to the neo-plastic language of Mondrian, even though Hilton would later declare that 'Abstraction in itself is nothing. It is only a step towards a new sort of figuration, that is, one which is more true'. Nevertheless, the rigors of full abstraction gave Hilton the formal discipline he needed in order to rebel against convention and come up with his own repertoire of challenging images and gestures.

Roger Hilton. Pirate Ship. Gouache, 1974.
Graham Gallery, Tunbridge Wells.
Photo: Nicholas Turpin.

Hilton's post-war work (like Frost he was a P.O.W.) camouflaged Mondrian's purist resolutions with organic references. These works were essentially abstracted neo-romantic compositions, part geometric and part naturalistic, and came close to a contemporary like Roy Turner Durrant. He always expressed himself through the classical language of drawing and

174

painting - the painted mark and the charcoal line - which he disrupted in a way directly analogous to, and expressive of, a self destructive lifestyle. The scribbled lines and ragged forms of Hilton's art nevertheless conveyed both a salutary freshness and a sophisticated compositional mise-en-page. He was an extremely well informed modern painter, whose knowledge found more gutsy and intuitive outlet than was the case with Heron's equal, though intellectual, understanding of contemporary art. Hilton never expressed himself either through collage or surrealist textural techniques. Perhaps this is not surprising for a young artist who had learnt from his one time teacher Bissiere, the virtues of alla prima handling, the expressive value of restricted palettes, and the importance of observation of the natural world in developing an abbreviated sign language. Even Mondrian had used natural motifs - trees, the pier and ocean - as foils against which he gradually simplified, in order to fulfill neo-plastic imperatives.

Hilton held several solo exhibitions at Gimpels during the 1950's. In later years, and after his death in 1975, he was exhibited with Waddington. He supplemented income from sales by teaching at private schools, and finally at the Central School of Art in the mid-1950's. An influence on him during the period was the Dutch painter Constant, whose rationalised order and simplified structures were embodied with lush knifed pigment. These qualities found equivalence in Hilton's striking composition of whites, blacks and reds 'February 1954', owned by the Tate and displayed to good effect in the St. Ives Tate's inaugural installation. Hilton, however, introduces humour and an artful decadence into the high seriousness of Dutch art; it comes in the anatomical form of boobs and limbs extruding from the main architectural composition. The philosophical tenor of Hilton's art was existential. Tom Cross described the artist as existential hero, confronting the crisp blank canvas, an 'unknown facing him like an abyssal orifice'. Hilton gropes for imagery through a spontaneously handled mixture of descriptive and self referring marks. He viewed the general function of the artist, in the context of the second half of the century, as regaining the initiative for figurative art's associative meaning over the formal significance of abstraction. Hilton chose to title many of his compositions with the date and month of their execution. He gradually shed influences, and his work assumed an aura of originality in direct proportion to the spontaneous construction of images from his own plastic and psychological void.

Hilton, however, always retained close links with the ethos of French painting, particularly with the Lyrical Abstraction he loved. The use of figurative imagery to cut up the previously impersonal surfaces of hermetic marks and areas of abstract colour culminated in 'Oi Yoi Yoi' (1963), a dancing nude which clearly echoes the physical and emotional postures of Matisse's 'joie de vivre' figures. Charcoal lines, untouched areas and fully painted passages interplay with each other in constructing the pictorial image out of nothing. The same period saw him win the prestigious John Moores prize. By the 1960's Hilton came closest to identifying his work with a common St. Ives style in terms of introducing boat shapes, sun-like discs of hot colour, or a typical sexual association between landscape and the figure. Though expressing residual features of nature and landscape, Hilton's insouciant handling is charged with a deft freedom and masterly sense of economy. Sadly, alcohol, as much as other art, exerted a major influence on him, and his health declined sharply during the late 1960's. The final years of domestic incapacity threw him even more on himself, though it resulted in a late flowering. He produced a huge spate of drawings and gouaches, churned out from his bed as though there were no tomorrow. These are characterised with a bright decorative vitality, an irreverant humour, and a desire to emulate the innocence and directness of children's art. Hilton made a notable final statement in the most unpromising of circumstances.

Paul Feiler. Cornish Window. *Oil, 1962.*
Courtesy: Paisnel Gallery, London.

Paul Feiler was also trained at the Slade during the 1930's. Something of the precision of his Slade background resides in the work, particularly in the later 'oeuvre' of hard edged compositions. Superimposed squares of closely

176

graded tone have a quiet life and movement. Feiler came to this country as an emigré seeking shelter from growing Nazi persecution during the 1930's. Soon after the war, he began a long and distinguished teaching career in Bristol. His impastoed early work is predominated by whites, creams and greys. These thick abstracted surfaces of paint are punctuated by somble dark blues. The imagery is dense, and due to the insistent painterly surface, only unravels a visual source in nature when the pictures are seen at a distance. Feiler saw how expressionistic handling could inform and bring character to the architectonic language of post-cubist painting. He composes with concise and simple bars of knifed pigment. He is one among a number of painters who responded to the widespread influence of de Stael, though he eschewed the primaries of French art and restricted his palette to naturalistic hues, earth colours, or a tonal range of whites and greys that best express the Cornish ambiance. But Feiler's pictures gain a weight, solidity and monumentality, not only in terms of abstracted boulder-like motifs, but by virtue of a heavily larded and lush pigmentation that is the key expressive element in the image and form of painting. Then, during the 1970's Feiler suddenly made a volte face; he changed completely the whole character of his work. He began painting thin, mechanically organised surfaces. The square and circle became the central motif for meditative compositions of subtly interacting and gently changing tonal colour. Even these seemingly non-referential and rational compositions were homages to visual experience of the outside world - window views at night time being one motif.

NOTES

1. Adrian Heath. 'Recollections and Movements' p.13. 'Terry Frost painting in the 1980's', University of Reading 1986.
2. Adrian Heath. 'Recollections and Movements' p.15. 'Terry Frost painting in the 1980's', University of Reading 1986.
3. Letter to Yankel Feather.
4. Adrian Heath. p.18. Reading 1986.
5. Adrian Heath. p.16. Reading 1986.
6. Tom Cross. 'Painting the Warmth of the Sun' p.140. Alison Hodge 1984.
7. Tom Cross. 'Painting the Warmth of the Sun' p.143. Alison Hodge 1984.
8. Adrian Heath p.21. Reading 1986.
9. Adrian Heath p.21. Reading 1986.
10. 'Apollo' February 1977.
11. See Patrick Heron. Whitechapel retrospective catalogue. London 1972.
12. See Patrick Heron. Whitechapel retrospective catalogue. London 1972.
13. Introduction to Whitechapel catalogue 1972.
14. Conversation with the author. Russell Square, London 1990.
15. Conversation with the author. Russell Square, London 1990.
16. Patrick Heron. 'Studio International'. 1966.
17. Hugh Stoddart. Catalogue note for exhibition 'Cornish and Contemporary' Worcester Art Gallery. November 1985.
18. Jeff Harris. Letter to the author. 3.6.93.
19. Jeff Harris. Letter to the author. 31.5.93.
20. Conversation with the author. 12.12.93
21. Bryan Wynter. 'Notes on my painting' Catalogue for Leinhard Gallery exhibition, Zurich 1962.

CHAPTER 9

Northern Migrants

Alan Lowndes's thirty year career as a painter, spanning the period from the end of the 1940's to the late 1970's, can be divided into three distinct phases. These phases conform to incidents of the artist's biography and do not represent any significant stylistic changes. Since this peculiarly individual artist never developed his painting beyond a kind of home-brewed expressionism and honest, if naive realism, one is able to categorise his work, using only the criterion of subject matter. The artist's subjects were interesting, not for their wide use of seascape, portrait, still-life, or street scenes, but rather for pertinently expressing the life and times of a changing world. Like John Bratby, Lowndes's painting related to the bedsit realism of kitchen sink drama and his work resonates with the colloquial incidents of British working class life in the 1950's and the 1960's. Therein lay its appeal to the northern school of playwrights and actors who acquired his work. Also like Bratby, he brought a bright and colourful palette to drab subjects. Whereas Bratby later found in Venice the vehicle to fully release his innate colour sense, Lowndes did so by moving down to sub-Mediterranean Cornwall.

The artist's earlier work depicted the northern industrial scene, particularly of his native Stockport, which he continued to paint throughout his life with a feeling of poignant and evocative nostalgia. The middle phase, lasting from the late 1950's to 1970, concentrated on the Cornish scene. He lived in or near St. Ives from the time of his marriage in 1959 through to 1970, when he left with his family for a final phase in rural Gloucestershire. Thus the late work is of rural Gloucestershire subjects, with a sprinkling of late variations on the perennial theme of the Stockport of his youth, as well as a number of Cardiff dockland scenes. The three phases have no precise demarcation line, though, for it was the artist's practice to continue producing northern scenes even while living in the altogether different environment of Cornwall. Commercial pressures from his formerly Manchester, but by now London-based dealer Andreas Kalman dictated the continued production of northern 'potboilers'. But even when representing humdrum Cornish subjects, Lowndes introduced the same degree of empathy with the working man (Cornish fisherman as opposed to Mancunian mill worker) that had characterised his Stockport work.

Lowndes unwittingly revitalised a kind of genre that in St. Ives painting had not been seen since the days of Christopher Wood in the late 1920's. Although Lowndes came to live in St. Ives already well known to the existing artistic community from intermittent visits during the previous five or six years, he ploughed a lone furrow in the sense that many artists were then working to a greater or lesser degree in an abstract or constructivist way. He was not alone in being a northern artist, but unlike fellow Mancunians Bob Crossley or John Milne, remained unswayed by the abstract art prevalent in the colony. The early influence of Lowry notwithstanding, this largely self-taught painter was neither innovator or follower, though his work is relevant and slots into an important figurative strand of St. Ives art.

Lowndes's direct way of working from unassuming local subjects was ridiculed in some pseudo-sophisticated circles, but the artist was used to this. In Manchester he had been the object of envy from some artists who were jealous of his relative commercial success in selling to upwardly mobile theatre people, (principally actors and playwrights), through the prestigious Crane Gallery. One such artist was the Liverpool painter Arthur Ballard, who also made visits to Cornwall in the late 1950's, sometimes with his students from the Liverpool College of Art. (One of these, Alan Wood, was later to settle near St. Ives himself and would become friendly with Lowndes). In common with Liverpool contemporaries like Horsfield, Hart or Stuart Sutcliffe, Ballard was by then working in a more advanced avant-garde style, influenced in particular by Nicholas de Stael. Ballard's unstinting use of raw landscape motifs, (particularly apparent after acquiring a cottage in Snowdonia), paralleled the work of Peter Lanyon. In spite of de Stael's cult status among a broad group of abstract British painters at the time, the deceased French artist had developed imagery from, and retained links with, the conventional motifs of still-life or landscape. On occasions Alan Lowndes's own raw, direct, palette-knifed treatment of a compellingly simple motif was not far away from de Stael's own. If we compare Lowndes's 'Seagulls' of 1963 with de Stael's rendition of a similar theme, we see a not dissimilar painterly handling. In the hands of contemporary St. Ives abstractionists such a theme would have elicited a more cerebral approach, eschewing the buttery romanticism of de Stael and Van Gogh, and opting instead for a network of hard-edged lines with which to express the intangible rhythms of nature under the warmth of the sun.

The former Stockport artist confronted the Cornish art scene from a position of strength, having already established himself with a rising gallery in Manchester. The artist also arrived in Cornwall newly married and therefore given merciful deliverance from the uncertainties of batchelor life in an artistic bohemia then on the decline. A new sobriety set in with the decline, as artists courted galleries in London and strove to look after young families. The cheap studios and atmosphere of novelty that had characterised the decade after the war was now replaced by the cutting edge of competitiveness and career opportunism. Lowndes posed no direct threat to the abstract school, as his work was different to theirs, and socially his position had credibility due to his marriage and established London reputation with a gallery. Andreas Kalman had even been showing his paintings in the same company as the Nicholsons.

In common with his Cornish contemporaries, dubbed the 'middle generation' by the dealer Leslie Waddington, Lowndes began working on a larger scale, though a similar commitment to colour and texture did not lead him along their path of simplification. By the time he had settled down with a young family in St. Ives he was producing landscapes of the St. Ives area that showed great feeling for the colouring, movement and life of the sea. The hard, unyielding nature of the granitic landscape also brought out his talent for the scraped textures and effects of the palette knife. Following the example of his early Stockport work, Lowndes's St. Ives pictures successfully portrayed the local working class scene - in this case the industry of the seafolk, the comings and goings of vessels, the fluctuating tides and weather conditions, and the affectionate anecdotes of harbour life. He mingled with ease among the local fishing people, and Smeaton's pier became his Cornish Viaduct, while the large fishing boats that would plough the agitated seas

Alan Lowndes. Porthmeor Beach. *Oil, 1964.*
Collection: Valerie Lowndes.
Photo: Ros Lowndes.

became akin to his northcountry railway convoys. Like Kit Wood, the artist drew out the working class element in St. Ives before the picturesque harbour became ravished by popular tourism.

The artistic life of St. Ives was centred on the 'Sloop', doyen among pubs of the town. The 'Sloop' never exhibited artists in the way that Endell Mitchell's

'Castle Inn' had done in the 1940's, but the famous, old, harbour front pub was the chief rendezvous for artists. Here he met up with the poet W.S. Graham, who wrote a poem 'For Alan and Valerie'. Most of the painters frequented the bar and they took warmly to the new 'recruit' and his Yorkshire-born wife. With a little help from northern colleagues like John Milne, the Lowndes's found a temporary flat in Fore Street, but conditions were cramped and they soon moved on to better accommodation. Lowndes shared a Piazza studio with Michael Broido. He remained friendly with Milne, whom he had known from Manchester in the late 1940's. A full-length portrait that Lowndes painted of the sculptor in blue jeans and with leg up on a chair, shows how a northern 'Protestant ethic' soon relaxed into the easier mode of Cornish life. What the local writer Val Baker referred to as the 'Timeless Land' exerted a tranquillising effect on many migrants used to a more hectic urban pace.

With some help from Valerie Lowndes's Sheffield family, whose money came from the cutlery business, they were soon able to buy a small house in the Digey, a very central and strategically placed walkway linking Fore Street with Porthmeor beach at the back of the town. The problem became the constant visitors and passers by, exacerbating what was a small, tight-knit community where privacy was at a premium. At about this time, the early 1960's, Sven Berlin was writing from his exile in the New Forest that in St. Ives 'everybody knew everybody; no one could live in the town for more than a week without being gutted like a herring and spread out in the sun to dry and for all to see.' In similar vein Lowndes himself later wrote that 'everyone here seems to be primarily concerned with a sex life.' His childhood, spent in a large community-minded family where privacy in cramped conditions would have been a rare luxury, enabled him to be open and sociable even in a gossipy, seaside town.

Indeed, he enjoyed bar-room banter, and an interest in drink outstripped his appetite for food. He owned a boat, which he kept in the harbour, and he caught fish for the family. Pub room scenes form a strand in his work and telling colloquial renditions of Stockport's 'Baker's Vault', Manchester's 'Bodega' or 'St. Ives' 'Sloop' have a direct honesty, even if never emulating the sophisticated satire or academic impressionism of Ruskin Spear's Hammersmith. Lowndes and Spear exhibited together in a 1985 exhibition 'Five Very English Artists'[*1] at the Kalman gallery, though Lowndes never mixed with the other artists who were, unlike himself, R.A.s. Spear voiced some uncertainty about Lowndes's work, which he would have seen only through the Kalman outlet.[*2] Once the halcyon days of the interwar period were over, St. Ives artists had invariably shied away from R.A. involvement. Even the more conventional figurative painters like Lowndes followed the lead taken by the avant-garde Hepworth and Nicholson and avoided participation in an institution that was then perceived as conservative. As early as the 1930's St. Ives artists like Borlase Smart had been distracted from a fuller R.A. involvement because of social and geographic remove from the London hub.

Another artist who steered clear of R.A. involvement, Sven Berlin, left

St. Ives a few years before Lowndes settled in the town, and in some respects the northern artist filled the gap left by Berlin. They shared a similar antipathy towards the abstract orthodoxies of the Penwith group style. They both painted human visions, in Berlin's case extending to animals as well as to stone carving, which they relayed through an emphatically colourful palette. They painted everyday scenes and from first-hand experience of circuses and the peripatetic life of the travelling show, they produced some poetic pictures of the performing art of the gypsies. Though they never overlapped in Cornwall, the pair seem like kindred spirits and, in later years, met a couple of times. The last occasion was at the Longleat home of the Viscount Weymouth, who at the time (1978) was assembling a permanent gallery of work by Wessex artists. Berlin recalled, 'We only met twice and each time there was an immediate rapport which made me look forward to the possibility of one of those friendships that come a few times and then perhaps only with another painter. The first time we met was late at night at the Chelsea Arts Club when he introduced himself to me at the bar, and the next was at Lord Weymouth's house, where we both subsequently sold paintings for his Wessex collection.' Berlin also recalled that he was, 'a man of the people painting out of the people, with no art nonsense. He was dressed in a black corduroy jacket, a red scarf and a beret, looking exactly like an artist, and quite unaffected. As we walked through the great vaulted rooms decorated with Weymouth's murals he said looking up, 'I could live in a place like this.' They told me he came out of the railways and I thought perhaps the great interior reminded him of past stations.'*3

Lowndes moved out of Broido's studio and shared one with Lyndon Travers until eventually finding his own, in a sail loft in Norway Square, an attractive enclave between the Society's Mariner's Chapel and the St. Ives School of Painting. Later, he took on Bill Redgrave's Porthmeor studio, which had well-lit windows and excellent views onto Porthmeor beach. Redgrave, who had started the St. Peter's Loft School of Painting with Lanyon, left St. Ives and Lowndes gratefully accepted the studio. Other developments included the birth of two daughters and a son, and in 1964 the move to more secluded premises at Halsetown, a mile or so out of St. Ives on the winding road to Nancledra. He renovated the house, using skills he had acquired working for building firms in Hazel Grove after the war. Money was tight but he was on a small wage from Kalman, with whom he exhibited every few years. During the Cornish 1960's Lowndes enjoyed three exhibitions on Brompton Road, in 1961, 1965 and again in 1968. In 1964 he held a one man show in New York City, at the Osborn gallery. The American reviewer for 'Time' magazine declared that his pictures 'tell a tragic story of man and nature. His many windows speak of emptiness his street scenes of dreary sameness, and his people are dull blotches in a vivid hued environment that threatens to swallow them.' Lowndes's quest to find beauty and poetry in unlikely places clearly did not move the American, who evidently misunderstood the English artist's intentions and who represented to Kalman a squeamish or snobbish sensibility.*4 The 1960's saw the heart ripped out of many old towns, and fine buildings, were replaced by dubious new

182

developments of unsound architectural and structural quality. Trips back home during those years saddened him as the Stockport of his youth was rapidly disappearing. Like Lowry, the phenomenon of change made him paint the old streets as they lingered in the memory.

Alan Lowndes on the pier St. Ives, 1963.

He also resisted the youth culture of the swinging decade, though his dress reflected the perennial dandy, even bohemian, trait in his character. Norman Levine, the Canadian poet, echoed Berlin's descriptions of Lowndes when writing the catalogue for the Alan Lowndes memorial exhibition held at the

183

Penwith Society in 1979. In it Levine wrote that 'although he dressed in the usual painter's working class clothes - jeans and shirt or sweater - there was a touch of the dandy about him. In the black beret …the coloured cravats at his throat in the summer. And one winter he wore black leather trousers.' He clearly enjoyed the company of writers, being well read and enjoying lively social intercourse. Levine wrote, 'He liked the small social transactions, the small human rituals, as well as the talk that goes into making the hum of everyday life. And to it he brought something awkward, something stubborn, as well as humour and warmth. His paintings express clearly his won personality.' His canvases are full of the rituals that go to make the 'hum' of everyday life.

One of his later Cornish sea pictures is the predominantly viridian 'Land's End' (1970). The movement of the sea is captured by a palette knife that churns up the green paint and prevents a static, uniform surface. In other animated sea pictures, like 'The Lone Fisherman' (1966) 'Sunset Fishing' (1963) or the harbour views like 'A Rough Day' (1967) Lowndes strikes a chord that puts him in unison with Wood, Wallis and Berlin. By the end of the 1960's many of Lowndes colleagues had moved away - Frost left for a spell in Banbury, Wynter moved out to the Land's End area, and Mitchell began an exodus of artists to Newlyn. The spark of bonhomie had gone and the quiet stormy winters exagerrated the feeling of being out on a limb. It was more difficult to sell paintings in the recession-blighted 1970's and Valerie Lowndes wanted to work again after raising children. They moved to Gloucestershire in 1970. In the late summer of 1977, a year before his death, Lowndes made a final visit to Cornwall. This five week visit was significant because, during a convalescence from the first of two illnesses, he produced a spate of late pictures. The views onto the slate roofs and chimney tops of Mousehole and beyond them across Mount's Bay were magnificent, and in a number of seascapes the artist heaped on layers of dark blue paint crested with frothy whites. By the mid 1970's economic recession, ushered in by the oil crisis of 1974, had the effect of forcing Kalman to stop Lowndes's contract. But several dealers, including Christopher Hull, began buying and selling his recent work, a factor that was a big practical and moral boost. At the suggestion of Brian Bull, Alan's Bristolian mosaicist friend, Hull arranged an exhibition of recent work at the Bristol Arts Centre in the autumn of 1977. Recent Mousehole paintings were included.

The house where Lowndes stayed during this final trip to Cornwall was called 'The Old Fish Loft' and belonged to Ben John, the grandson of Augustus who, in earlier days, had often frequented Mousehole (Gus also visited the Newlyn home of the naive painter Mary Jewels and her sister Cordelia who had once been married to Frank Dobson). Lowndes was put in touch with John by Rose Hilton, and he rented the house from late July to early September, making use of the period to produce some excellent painted views of Mount's Bay in a richly coloured and impastoed palette. Gulls on rooftops, dark blue seas and the harbour front featured in these oils. Socially he spent the time quietly, though was able to drink in moderation. He used a Mousehole pub where he saw much of Jack Pender, another local painter whose renditions of harbours, boats and quaysides speak with a similarly authentic voice.

Cornwall provided Lowndes with the inspiration that was a necessary accompaniment to his ambition for success. In the final days of his life, bedridden in a Gloucestershire hospital and suffering from complications to a damaged liver, he wrote to his sister in Stockport. In it he summarised both his own humble origins and the stout will to overcome the underdog's situation. 'You remember I read a lot in my youth and adolescence', he wrote, 'George Bernard Shaw's statement 'always try to get what you like in case you end up liking what you get.' Oscar Wilde said once 'Most advice is useless good advice is fatal.' A bit cynical but not far out really. Look at me for example. Things weren't exactly promising for me becoming an artist. I know this however, had I listened to the load of advice I was generously given I'd have been a non-starter.' Cornwall was ideal for the middle and best years of Lowndes's career, for while offering a safe and sympathetic haven in a philistine world, it also provided the status that came with a large family of artists. As we can see, literature was an important influence on Lowndes; not simply for the way it provided a very necessary framework for a narrative

William Turner. St. Ives. *Oil, 1993.*

artist working in a predominantly abstract and visual painting culture, but also for the intellectual ramification it gave to a working class artist who, against all the odds of personal circumstance, sought to establish himself in a competitive, even élitist milieu.

William Turner was another figurative Manchester artist who, influenced by Lowry, came down to the south west to broaden the range of his work. Turner had lived in Polperro for two years during the 1960's and after returning to Stockport made subsequent trips to St. Ives. Here he made sketches as aide-mémoire for the production of small paintings in his Cheadle studio. Cycling was an interest which gave him a direct experience of fleeting landscape details. The blur of passing shapes corresponded with highly lyrical use of paint in which colour and mark cohere. Turner was a regular exhibitor with the Manchester Academy and held one man shows at the Tib Lane Gallery and Gibb's Bookshop. Another Lancashire artist, Wigan - born Lawrence Isherwood (1917-1989) also brought down a northern vitality to Cornwall, which he intermittently visited. Although belonging to the world of Lowry and Theodore Major, Isherwood painted the Cornish landscape with a heaped impasto and a direct, even brash use of colour. Isherwood's Cornish work, which Mervyn Levy described as 'busting with the fresh light of the nostral tickling coast',*5 sees a northerner more than compensating for the drabness of his Lancashire background.

Fred Yates was a similarly gifted painter who trod the well worn path from the industrial north to the sunshine and sands of south west Cornwall. Describing himself as a 'happy Lowry', Yates strikes at the essence of the mundane world, not by prettifying it, but by portraying everyday life on the streets with a confident impasto of rich, bright colour. The colours have the gaiety of a carnival though the subjects are essentially Lowryesque: anonymous figures going about their humdrum daily business. They complement the architectural or topographic surroundings by introducing a touch of human warmth, nostalgia or sentimentality. The figures have the crude simplicity of naive art; fat jabs of paint summarise the artist's affectionate eye for detail or quirky incident. He draws with paint, and the compositions - whether of Stockport mills, Cornish beaches, south London suburbs or French landscapes - hang together with a simple but powerful and effective feeling for structure and compositional balance. Hailing for Ardwick in Manchester, he was greatly moved by Alan Lowndes's painting, recognising in it a heightened, even theatrical realism based on the everyday, but not bound by it. For this reason, like Lowry and Lowndes before him, he painted street events, pantomines, parades or gatherings, of which a busy and crowded Cornish beach in high summer provided one instance.

Yates was born in 1922, a year after Alan Lowndes. A tall handsome man, he served in the Grenadier Guards during the war. Afterwards he lived in Bournemouth, and taught for twenty years until retiring and moving down to Cornwall. From his Cornish base this restless painter travelled to many parts of Britain, taking materials with him and setting up easel as the 'people's painter' among them on busy streets. The Cornish work has a special eye for the picturesque, poetic or unusual to the extent of divining these qualities

186

from the most ordinary or unpromising of locations. In 1990 he sold his remote west Penwith cottage and moved to France, indulging in a visual feast of bright and positive colour.

Colin Johnson, born in Blackpool in 1942, made it his business to associate with the painter's colony after discovering it as a student at Salford Art School in the late 1950's. He went on to study at Manchester School of Art, where Terry McGlynn exerted an influenece as did the older Harry Rutherford, a Sickert-influenced painter and Manchester Academy stalwart who made Cornish painting holidays (Manchester City Art Gallery own an excellent

Colin Johnson. Chalets and Sand-dunes, Hayle. *Oil, 1981.*

view of Penzance). One of Rutherford's Manchester Academy colleagues, Ian Grant, visited Cornwall and painted views of Mousehole front or St. Ives harbour. Further back, Tom Mostyn, known in Royal Academy circles as the 'Manchester painter' had spent time painting in St. Ives, and his daughter Marjorie married Leonard Fuller and set up the St. Ives School of Painting in 1938. In the summer of 1959 Johnson made his first visit and camped there for

187

three months. (Denys Val Baker's book 'Britain's Art Colony by the Sea' was published about this time, lending further support to St. Ives's growing reputation). He did not make any significant contacts until 1962, however, when he stayed with Tony Shiels and his large family near Westcott's Quay. Through Shiels, Johnson met Lanyon for the first time, (in Lanyon's local 'The Golden Lion') and also saw Alan Lowndes, though they were acquainted from earlier meetings at the Crane Gallery in Manchester.

Johnson had studied textile design among other things at Salford, and something of the stylised design and interlocking colour rhythms of textiles informed his own painting, which by now had come to focus on harbour scenes. These were composed with definite linear rhythms and animated with crisp, bright colour evocative of high summer. They capture, in absolute terms, the atmosphere of calm that characterises Paul Nash's work before the war. Such works formed the basis of one man exhibitions back in Manchester. These were popular, for Mancunians were by now coming down in their droves to St. Ives. The town was growing as a popular holiday resort, not least with Johnson himself, who made annual visits, culminating in 1965 with a six month stay at Bowling Green. He associated with former Mancunians Alan Lowndes and John Milne. Johnson felt reservations about Milne's work, however, which he felt had no 'individual strength', in the sense that it was too close to Hepworth for comfort, relying on stylisation of her forms rather than on individual content. Another Mancunian he visited was Michael Snow, then living in Ben Nicholson's house. Snow and Johnson were in differing ways influenced by the older man, the one abstractly, the other more from a representational viewpoint. Johnson also visited the Oldham-born potter Trevor Corser, whom he had met in Manchester in the 1950's. In 1981 Johnson held an exhibition at Bob Devereux's Salthouse Gallery and five years later settled in the town. He lived in St. Ives until 1991, when he moved to Teignmouth. During this time he exhibited in local galleries but also took the opportunity, whenever it arose, to exhibit throughout the country. A 1984 exhibition at the Salthouse - shared with the Falmouth-trained but Birmingham-based painter of interiors, Charlotte Moore - focussed on Cornish views seen through various windows, a typical St. Ives genre since the days of Winifred and Ben Nicholson and Kit Wood.

In contrast to Lowndes, Turner and Yates, Bob Crossley was a Manchester artist who did not resist the allure of abstraction. He attended drawing classes at the Midday Studios but was another largely self-taught artist. He struck out as an advanced painter in the Academy of the mid 1950's and his decision to move down to Cornwall in 1959 had all the hallmarks of a desire to identify with avant-garde painting. Alert and intelligent to the issues of advanced contemporary painting, matters to do with chance, gesture, design, surface, illusionism and colour dynamics, Crossley strove to develop his work independently of, if parallel to, the direction of colleagues. Economic self-sufficiency also gave him a social independence. Therefore direct influence is hard to pinpoint, though his work of the early sixties is unquestionably of its time. But business activities outside the orbit of art precluded teaching and any subsequent influence on younger artists. For entirely separate reasons to

Lowndes, Crossley therefore ploughed an individual furrow in this close-knit art colony, and he relied on a natural talent and an expert mastery of the craft in order to maintain standards. Once settled in St. Ives, he devoted over half the year to painting, for the beach shop he ran on Porthgwidden Island, opposite Sven Berlin's 'Tower', was a seasonal business, one that provided enough income for the whole year.

Crossley's artistic identity had already been formed in Manchester and if his role as shopkeeper was ridiculed in some circles, then he had by now enough confidence in his own ability to pursue his art in his own way. He had shown several times with the Manchester Academy, and had been given a one man exhibition at the Crane Gallery in 1958. Monumental and partially abstracted single figures, constructed with direct gestures of paint, characterised his work at the time, which resembled Keith Vaughan's painterly figures. With its animated paint handling and positive structural colour, Crossley's art quickly caught the eye. Terry Frost recognised the new recruit and encouraged him to join the Penwith. Brian Wall formally proposed him and, once a member, exhibited to his advantage in an active milieu. He also became more social to the extent of playing cricket in the Penwith team. His work integrated drawing into the painting process and inevitably began to respond increasingly to landscape. Moreover, the relevance of his style was complemented by his preparations for shows with both the Kalman and the Reid galleries. In 1960 the artist enjoyed his first London show at Reid, at a time when he had become one of the St. Ives artists; in 1960 a very prestigious mark of artistic pedigree.

Crossley's connection with Manchester continued to be useful, however much his work had become absorbed in the Cornish mainstream. Lowry purchased a Crossley from the London Reid exhibition, and the younger artist visited Lowry - by now a legend in all corners of British artistic life - on several occasions at Mottram. Lowry undoubtedly took to the unpretentious Crossley, liking in particular a northern blend of directness, modesty, honesty and uncomplicated belief in the craft of painting. Lowry discussed art in broad terms with the younger man, expressing the belief that artists do not improve but rather only change. This outlook matched the non-hieratic views of Anthony Blunt, whose macrocosmic view of art history led him to see, not a logical tale of progress; but rather one of cyclic change. Crossley left behind in his native Rochdale a brother, Eddie, who had bronze casting facilities. Among Penwith sculptors, Roger Leigh, Denis Mitchell and Barbara Hepworth had pieces cast in Rochdale. Indeed, Hepworth had a number of editions cast in Rochdale, and the arrangement would have continued but for one unfortunate delay, that had serious commercial consequences for a hectically busy Trewyn workshop.

Bob Crossley's work, from the self-portraits and interiors depicting Rochdale printing workshops of the late 1940's and early 1950's, always played around with patterns, linear rhythms and colour harmonies that were autonomous, formal devices imposed on conventional figurative motifs. In the late 1950's - around the time he alighted on St. Ives after accidently discovering the colony while on holiday - the artist was abstracting iconic figure and head motifs, exploiting a free range of colour and loosened gesture. He later wrote that 'my work gradually became looser, the line vanished and the masses broadened.' The purely abstract compositions that would follow in the 1960's were attendant upon precise experiments with the optical effects of fast drying acrylics and printmaking techniques. In the late 1950's the artist was developing along logical and tangibly formal lines of visual enquiry into the medium of painting itself. His pictures developed fleeting and

Bob Crossley. **Blue Headland**. *1987. Graham Gallery.*

impressionistic images of reality, a bi-product of exploiting the accidental effects of spontaneously handled paint. As a result, Crossley was able to create a high level of correspondence between paint and imagery, between the picture as a series of independent abstract marks, and a descriptive allusion to representational form. Pictures he displayed at the Reid and Kalman galleries still presented figurative form, but with a pronounced

190

feeling for both process and formal autonomy, drawing attention to the fact that the picture was foremost a piece of painterly engineering. The anonymous, monumental or generalised aspects of the imagery reflected current preoccupation with a mood of enigma or alienation.

Bob Crossley. Boats. *1962. Graham Gallery.*

By the mid 1960's Crossley's works were often fully abstract, presenting thinly painted, wedge-like shapes in vivid blue colours, offset by reds or greens. The energy resided chiefly in the vibrant, alla prima brush marks. These broad virtuoso strokes became the structural elements of the paintings. The contemporary work of Hilton, Frost and Scott was broadly recalled. In 1963 Crossley moved with his family to Wimbledon, having left the beach shop in the hands of a manager. He worked in a Pimlico studio until 1966, when he moved into a house and studio in Putney. The Contemporary Art Society were among the buyers from the artist's 1964 Reid show. In 1967 he began making silkscreen prints for Christmas cards, taking up an old St. Ives tradition that had been practised by Nicholson, Lanyon, Frost and many others. It triggered off an interest in the new silkscreen medium, and for the next few years he editioned nearly fifty prints, most of which he sold to a buoyant sixties market for brightly coloured abstract screenprints. They tapped the same market as the prints of Denny, Heron, Hoyland, Sedgeley and Riley, and Crossley sold successfully through many London galleries. The importance of printmaking was that it opened his eyes to the possibilities of glazing and the use of transparent colours superimposed over one another, creating chiaroscuro, chromatic drama and linear movement within colour itself.

In contrast to Patrick Heron, whose explorations into what he later termed the 'Colour of Colour' were systematic and theory-based, Crossley maintained a pragmatic, discover-as-you-go energy in his work. A wristy, gestural brush movement operated on an equal footing to the structural and emotional role of colour. Heron's interlocking jigsaws of colour had more of a design look about them and employed expansive areas of singular colour that interacted in a high-pitched contrast with adjacent areas of complementary hue. Space, repose, the lateral as well as push-pull dynamic of pure colour, formed the subject and content of Heron's mature 'colour field' painting. Crossley's, in contrast, presented a flickering mosaic of individuated colour strokes, one colour pushed decisively over an opposite one to set up semi-transparent veils of shimmering light. If Heron made a virtue of using unmodulated hues straight from the tubes, then Crossley's equivalent concern was to leave each brushstroke alone, once committed to the canvas or board. Any subsequent adjustments came in the form of further crisp strokes. Such habits stemmed in large part from the silkscreens. The medium's requirement for clean, clear, decisive colour statements, exploiting the transparent as well as opaque properties of the medium, led the artist to opt for water-based acrylic paints for his pictures. While promoting the effects of spontaneity and transparency that he was seeking, acrylic also mitigated the indeterminate textural and chromatic blends that had once characterised the rich quagmire of oil painting.

Crossley returned to St. Ives in 1971, and the acquisition of a large, well-lit Porthmeor studio allowed the artist to increase scale. The clear, pollution-free natural environment also seemed to reinforce the crisp, clean colour that for plastic reasons he had adopted in London. As is so often the case, artistic temperament and a desire to return full circle, led Crossley to reintroduce oils in the 1980's. Sometimes, both oil and acrylic were used in the same picture. But the later work of Crossley is committed to acrylic painting, as it is for many of the post-Situation abstract painters in London. He had two Penwith gallery retrospectives, eliciting a response from Alan Bowness that his development had been an interesting and visually intelligent one. Crossley's quiet professionalism, of great vigour and integrity, seldom sought vain limelight or prestige. He preferred letting the pictures speak for themselves, but the lesson of his career teaches us that it is possible to be both talented and professional, yet at the same time neglected in a prominent art colony that requires the politics of self promotion.

NOTES

1.   The 5 artists were Spear, Lowndes, Lowry, Weight and Fitton.
2.   Ruskin Spear in conversation with the author, Hammersmith. March 1986.
3.   Sven Berlin letter to the author, 1985.
4.   Kalman wrote these views in the catalogue notes to Alan's first Crane exhibition, in 1950.
5.   Mervyn Levy. 'Art News and Review' May 1957.

CHAPTER 10

Recent Trends

The continuing ability of St. Ives to attract artists, collectors, critics or casual 'buyers' stems as much from its seductive natural beauty - a beauty that encourages the casual buyer to reach more readily into his or her cheque book - as from its rise as a popular tourist centre. Those with a modicum of perception and taste will forget the dreadful tourist shops on the harbour front and will search for the 'real' art on the walls of the galleries and studios in the traditional artists' quarter at the back (Porthmeor) end of the town. The rise of

Carole McDowall. Madron. *Acrylic, 1993.*

the art colony occurred in the first half of the century and was helped both by the decline of traditional fishing industries and by its gradual replacement with tourism. The role of private and, since the opening of the Tate in 1993, of public galleries, in putting a front window gloss on the local art scene, has been of the utmost importance. Those newcomers who visit the St. Ives Tate Gallery can turn a corner, find a commercial gallery, and purchase a small painting by one of the modern St. Ives school artists immortalised into the annals of British art history at the new venue. The purchase of a traditional holiday memento is turned into the acquisition of a piece of high culture.

The Wills Lane, New Craftsman and Sims Galleries cater in various ways to the bluechip connoisseur as much interested in criteria of art historical importance as in the long term investment potential of fine art and craft. Bob Devereux's more contemporary-minded Salthouse Gallery, geographically closest to the new Tate, appeals to those more interested in current issues - ethnic and social, as well as purely aesthetic - that motivate art in a pluralistic post-modern culture. As such, Devereux represents a vein of contemporary art that links his enterprise back to those galleries in the 1950's and 1960's - among them Elena Gaputyte's Sail Loft, Michael Dean's Steps Gallery and Elizabeth Rainsford's Fore Street Gallery - that were more avant-garde by virtue of closer involvement with the matrix of artistic ideas and the paint-splattered shop floor of production. Further afield, galleries and collections representing St. Ives artists sprang up. The Pier Gallery in Orkney, the Kettle's Yard collection in Cambridge, for example, reflect the visionary connoisseurship and collecting acumen of Margaret Gardiner and H.S. Ede respectively. Less exalted outposts were, in their way, no less important in linking up Cornish-based artists with the mainstream of modern British art. Denis Bowen's New Vision Gallery showed many St. Ives artists during the early 1960's, giving a contemporary London location to parallel activities of the Sail Loft Gallery. Bowen showed Karl Weschke in 1958, Heinz Mack in 1960, Bill Featherston (wood constructions) in 1962, Nancy Wynne-Jones in 1963, Paul Feiler and Roger Leigh in 1964, and Dick Gilbert in 1965.

Bob Devereux (born 1940) studied graphics under Derek Hyatt at Kingston and, upon graduating in 1965, visited Cornwall, finding 'the place like a big art school'. Another criterion of genuine bohemian and avant-garde energy was the cheapness of life, and in the mid 1960's Cornwall was still able to offer inexpensive living and working conditions. He took odd jobs, including that of a deckchair attendant, an occupation that provided beachtent subject matter for many years in both oil and watercolour. Devereux excels at marine watercolour, though varying degrees of abstraction from canvas beachtent motifs are also notable achievements. He also writes and performs poetry. As if this were not enough, Devereux opened his gallery in 1979 and extended it four years later. The larger premises allowed him to give solo exhibitions to Dolf Reiser, Patrick Hayman, Tony O'Malley, Noel Betowski, Tony Giles, Yankel Feather, Steve Dove and Jane O'Malley. The gallery's commitment to the vitality of contemporary British ceramics - in the 1990's a genuine area of innovation - saw exhibitions of the pots of Jon Middlemiss, Trevor Corser, William Marshall, Martha Allen and Peter Hayes. Hayes's tall, slim vases exploit overlaps between creative ceramics and abstract sculpture. Like Hans Coper before him, Hayes is not influenced by oriental form, but instead relates his work to the sculpture of Hepworth and Brancusi.

Another casual visitor who came down to Cornwall a few years earlier,

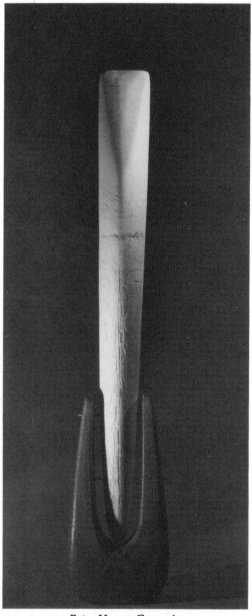

Peter Hayes. Ceramic.

Halifax-born Michael Dean, also relied on casual jobs before starting a gallery: one of these was managing a bookshop owned by Frank Godson, an experience that gave him the business confidence to start the gallery. He converted an old fish loft on Academy Steps - close to the bookshop and to the Penwith (of which he became a member) - into a studio, then a gallery. A gallery formed from an artist's studio might be expected to reflect the work of the gallery owner, but such was the variety of St. Ives art at this time of great change that this was impossible. Furthermore, Dean's work fluctuated from the impastoed and organic abstraction of the later 1950's to the ready-made sign vocabulary of the 1960's. Conroy Maddox, the distinguished surrealist, wrote how Dean's St. Ives paintings of the late 1950's were 'always in response to an experience of nature', but how, by the mid 1960's, 'He has tried to create an equivalent image through familiar symbols but no longer in direct relation to observed phenomena'.[*1] The opening show of the Steps Gallery in April 1960 included Barns-Graham, Anthony Benjamin, Jeff Harris, Gwen Leitch, Roger Leigh, Janet Leach, Roy Conn and Bob Crossley,. At the end of the year, Dean, established at both the Penwith and Newlyn, returned to London.

A Lancashire-born painter Anthony Shiels took over the gallery from the restless Dean who, by the mid 1960's, searched beyond painting for more direct means of communication, and began collecting and dealing in traditional Japanese art. Shiels, hard drinking and similarly restless, was unable to continue the enterprise for long, however, stopped painting and

Anthony Shiels. West Penwith. Oil, 1959.
Gordon Hepworth Gallery.

moved to another part of Cornwall. This was a pity because Shiels could be a talented painter as the spontaneously drawn horizontal painting 'West Penwith' indicates. Shiels made many drawings in preparation for oils like this Penwith composition. Its format contrasts with Lanyon's vertical treatment of the same theme. Shiels's aim, according to Roderick Cameron, was to reach for 'an exciting rhythmic dominance',*2 one that would reflect the values of an anarchic freedom and romantic individualism, worn on the sleeve of this colourful bohemian character. He was no slave to contemporary fashion either; in a piece of bombast to rival Shiels's own, Cameron explained that the artist's spontaneously handled paint with an unflinching motif in hand refused to make any concessions to the 'superficial modishness' and 'puerile posturings' of the contemporary cult of 'action painting'.

The Fore Street Gallery, which opened a year after the ill-fated Steps venture, fulfilled the ongoing need for a contemporary venue. It was owned by Major Wylde, who passed it on to Elizabeth Rainsford (sculptor and former wife of book dealer and part-time painter Peter Rainsford). The interior was designed by Michael Canney and John Miller; Helen Dear, a talented R.C.A.-trained painter, became curator. Like the other galleries it was independent and did not represent any one style or art society. It did, however, eschew snobbery and hidebound attitudes, giving a unique chance to young figurative painters. The gallery was centrally placed and commercially successful. As well as showing Canney and Miller, artists like Lanyon, Benjamin, Weschke, Harris, Guthrie and O'Malley were exhibited on Fore Street. The gallery did much good in promoting mixed artists, easily sidelined or ignored by the Penwith-Tate axis, at a crucial time in the art colony's history.

The Sail Loft Gallery, which operated between 1960 and 1963, was started by the talented Lithuanian sculptor, Elena Gaputyte. She had studied in Paris, and her broadly executed charcoal drawings of landscapes displayed 'admirable tautness', and were 'painful in their intensity' according to Michael Canney in 1963. One of the Sail Loft's most useful purposes was as bohemian rendezvous, entertaining in the most impromptu fashion its many visitors. With the nostalgia and hindsight of thirty years, she wrote in 1990 about St. Ives being 'like a big family, a special type of community, which functioned beautifully without planning. People dropped in almost at all hours; to argue, to rest, to eat, even to sing.'*3 Business was often good, too, and during the gallery's first couple of years many pictures were sold. While never being a major art gallery that could transform a local career into a national one, the Sail Loft nonetheless represented St. Ives arts and crafts in a most natural and unpretentious way. The gallery continued in the tradition of the Crypt, the Castle Inn and Downings Bookshop, while anticipating Marjorie Parr's Wills Lane Gallery, later taken on by Sally Hunter, then Reg Singh and finally Cyril 'Gilly' Gilbert. The Sail Loft's contribution to the local art scene between 1960 and 63 was rewarded by the town Council's invitation for it to put on a Peter Lanyon retrospective. Gaputyte later moved to London and learnt bronze casting at the Lime Grove studios of the Hammersmith College of Art. Her interest in the human form and in the columns of Brancusi resulted in pyramid-like figures. The architectural facets were created with a minimum of surface modelling. This courageous woman died after a long illness in London in 1992.

Artistic influence takes many shapes and guises. One of the most interesting cases for study is when the offspring of major artists take to the brush. Having a famous artist as a parent can be a blessing or a curse, but at least a genuine market often exists for the children, able to offer work at affordable prices. This is particularly the case when major artists like Nicholson or Lanyon become too expensive for serious collectors of limited financial means. The work of Kate Nicholson (born 1929), for example, continues the faux naif idiom of her father's Cumbria period of the late 1920's,

Kate Nicholson. St. Ives. Oil, 1949.
Collection: Clive Blackmore.

when the work of Ben, Winifred and Kit Wood seemed, for a few short years, barely indistinguishable from one another. Kate's work is a cross between that of her parents; lyrical, poetic and soulful, her painting expresses an accord with nature, particularly the landscape, through relaxed handling of paint that is simple yet deceptively artful and sophisticated. Kate visited her father and step-mother, Barbara Hepworth, in wartime Carbis Bay. She was unaffected by the advanced abstraction being practised but by 1957, after studying at Corsham and moving to St. Ives, she established herself as an independent artist and member of the Penwith. In spite of solo exhibitions at prestigious London venues like Waddingtons and later with Marjorie Parr,

199

Kate Nicholson greatly missed her father when he left the town for Switzerland, an event that came shortly after her move to St. Ives. A solo show at the Wills Lane Gallery in 1984 was enormously popular.

Unlike Kate, Rachel Nicholson (one of the triplets born to Ben Nicholson and Barbara Hepworth in 1938) was the daughter of a sculptor; this shows in her work, which with formal spareness and economy, highlights an interest in the pure shape of simple objects like domestic ceramics or silverware. She develops her father's interest in the facets and flattened shapes of cups, saucers, spoons or mugs. She also introduces venetian red highlights, and is sensitive to the decorative significance of pattern as contributing not only to the vitality of secondary pictorial imagery but also as a pleasing visual sensation in its own right. Again like her father, she gives a black rim to the

Margaret Mellis. Still Life. 1952.
Graham Gallery.

200

curves of these objects, throwing them into illusory relief. Her palette is restricted to beige, grey and blue but, as her landscape view of St. Ives Bay 'Pig 'n Fish' reveals, she can use blue with a versatility to express fully the atmosphere of a place. Her landscapes tend to focus on a distant headland or expanse of sea as viewed beyond foreground rooftop architecture. During the 1980's and beyond, this contemplative and accomplished painter has exhibited on a regular basis at the Montpelier Studio in London, proving alongside artists like Anne Rothenstein, John Hitchens, Freddie Gore, Lucien Pissarro and many others that it is possible to paint with an authentic voice even within the shadow of a giant parental tree.

Roy Conn. Abstract Composition. *Collage, 1958.*
Belgrave Gallery.

The growing number of women artists who gain prominence as a result of more serious attention is a healthy product of the new pluralism. Margaret Mellis (born 1914), has continued to produce meaningful work, without compromising values, in the contemporary context of challenging art. Collage is the common denominator thoughout her long career, which began in the 1930's with studies under Peploe at Edinburgh, then with André Lhote while on an Edinburgh Scholarship to Paris. She married Adrian Stokes, the painter and art theorist, and lived with him at Little Park Owles during the war. Although part of a special grouping during this artistically auspicious moment, marriage to Stokes was not to last long. She re-married in the late 1940's, lived in the South of France, and returned to live in Suffolk for the rest of her career. Here she uses natural materials like driftwood and found objects which are, however, assembled in visually literate combinations. These planar wall-bound reliefs are part sculptural and part pictorial, owing a debt to the flat constructed modes of Cubist assemblage. Clearly, her Scottish and French training, more even then participation in the Carbis Bay constructivism of the 1940's, was of seminal importance. Her wood constructions share with Janet Nathan both rigorous formal execution and delicacy of conception. The imagery of musical instruments is derived from the repertoire of still-life, a genre that also brings out her talent for conventional painting.

Collage has also been a feature of Roy Conn's art. Inspired by Ben Nicholson, Conn moved to St. Ives from London as the older artist was leaving Cornwall. Since that time Conn has retained faith with various kinds of hard edge abstraction through successive decades of pop, expressionism and revived figuration. He worked out visual ideas using interlocking minimal forms; the space evoked stared back, through the plastic illusion of art, towards experience of the outside world. Conn assembled with cut paper fragments, exploiting the simple yet dramatic tension created by careful placement of black shapes against a flat white surface. Pasmore, Heath and early Hilton, as well as Nicholson, were influences, though Conn possessed an intuitive ability to say something personal from the oblique corner of a restricted formal language. Furthermore, the smooth uniform surfaces favoured in his monochrome period, continued into the new decade of the sixties; the optimistic ambiance of this period found expression in bright 'colour field' painting. Frost and Heron introduced American ideas into St. Ives at this time and it was through them that Conn gained awareness of the progressive value of frontality, simplicity and interaction of bright colour. A mood was thereby created that reflected the confidence of the times. These developments culminated in Conn's contribution to the 1965 John Moores' exhibition. 'Domino (Twin Reds)' was composed with broad undulating bands of bright colour; entirely of its time, this picture gained entry into the prestigious Liverpool exhibition during the year when Clement Greenberg and Patrick Heron were jurors and when Mike Tyzack won the competition with a typical and comparable piece of cool sixties abstraction. In recent years Conn, working from a Porthmeor studio, has been a quiet presence in a St. Ives art scene that has witnessed the influx of lesser and more boisterous talents.

Since Hepworth, the Cornish art scene has reverted back to being a predominently painter's domain. The presence of Barbara Tribe and Max Barrett, who create bronze figures and crude neo-primitive wood carvings respectively, has not arrested the flow of creative energy back to painting. Indeed, Paul Mount began as a painter and not sculptor, though he later became exceptional for being an abstract sculptor, working in steel, iron and

Paul Mount. Sculpture.

other metals, who has enjoyed significant successes both with galleries and through architectural collaborations during the post-Hepworth period. Mount lives in St. Just with his wife, the painter June Miles. He studied painting at the Royal College after the war. He spent almost a decade teaching in West Africa, an experience that enriched his feeling for sculpture. Mount started an art department in Nigeria, where he made use of local woods to carve abstract pieces that inevitably showed tribal, as well as modernist influences. An interest in Benin bronzes led to experiments with casting techniques, and he made his first pieces in concrete, fibreglass and bronze. Mount's innate feeling for design spurred him to make architectural facades; the interest in bas-relief was again inspired by the best examples of the past - in particular, by seeing Romanesque work on Gothic cathedrals in wartime France. He returned to Cornwall from Africa in the mid-1950's, when he purchased a studio in St. Just. He became a Penwith member in the early 1960's. A retrospective at that same gallery in 1993 showed his versatility as both painter and sculptor. Mount was impressed by the high finish and standards of precision fostered by the Trewyn studio; he sought to emulate this quality by using stainless steel, a highly reflective material that functioned in an analogous way to the polished bronze, smoothed stone or refined wood surfaces of Hepworth. Steel also encouraged welding, a skill that he learnt from a local blacksmith; the results were intricate constructions of interlocking multiple forms. The bronze configurations were cast at foundries in St. Just or Hayle from polystyrene or plastic working models. The stainless steel pieces are slim, upright and flat surfaced; these minimal sculptures are more architectural than the cast steel or bronze pieces, which carry the figurative overtones of Moore - like madonnas or reclining warriors. Whatever the case, constructing is an essential part of Mount's process, and through this he enters into a conceptual and working engagement with space - the interaction between voids and masses that form a part of the elegant poise, balance and precision of his art. Although Mount's forms are chunky or facetted, he uses spatial direction and extension to the full, creating a versatility and breadth of expression through the uniquely sculptural manipulation of cut or carved forms.

June Miles's thinly painted canvases of landscape and still-life motifs are also alert to the tension between surface pattern and illusionist depth. Miles spent her early days in China, a factor that may in part explain a diffused pictorial language of forms dispersed across semi-transparent compositional grounds. Though trained under the formidable Schwabe at the Slade, where the discipline of measurement and placement gave her a keen sense of plastic structure, the nature of her mark and use of colour satisfies aesthetic rather than pedantically descriptive ends. She draws with paint and constructs with colour; the outline of Pyrenean villages - a 'Compact interplay of verticals and diagonals'[*4] according to Ronald Gaskell - or of perfectly rounded still-life forms are drawn with the complementary blue or orange colours she favours. She seeks out the pattern in pieces of cloth, tapestry or carpet and merges them into her pictorial scheme of colour dabs and truncated lines. The Slade manner of unerased plumb lines and measured points are, therefore, intergrated into the decorative vitality of the painting through colour. Miles does not seek to link objects through cubist overlap, but groups them in a mysterious accord through space; it is here that the Slade insistence on precise and measured relationships between objects yields fruit. These beautiful paintings are restrained, even eloquent in the classic English manner of draughtsmanship and tonal cohesion; yet her use of positive colour, though never riotous nor anarchic, together with a Cézanne-inspired love affair with the spaces of still-life and French landscape, marks her out as much more than a minor academic English painter. She shares with older contemporaries like Dunstan and Greenham (both of whom were influences on her during the Slade's wartime evacuation to Oxford) an ability to absorb the gaiety of French art into the disciplined language of the English tradition.

Clive Blackmore (born 1940), a younger painter than Miles, also breathes life into still-life painting through colour. He moved from London to Cornwall in the 1960's, worked mainly as a potter until the mid 1980's, then turned his hand to painting. No wonder, then, that a favoured motif is the ceramic plant or flower receptable on the front window. The genre, and Blackmore's handling of it, derives from Frances Hodgkins, Winifred Nicholson and Kit Wood; insistently poetic, it too, is a style that integrates the English love of nature and the landscape with a more rigorous language of architectural form. Blackmore's pictures are more loosely worked than Miles's and possess less of the authenticity of a grand tradition, redolent in her works; instead Blackmore plays homage to the formidable legacy of the Nicholsons, seen in his case in contradictory terms of composite domestic and landscape subjects, scraped and lusciously pigmented surfaces and man-made and natural forms.

A liking for the ineffable magic of illogical or disrupted juxtaposition runs

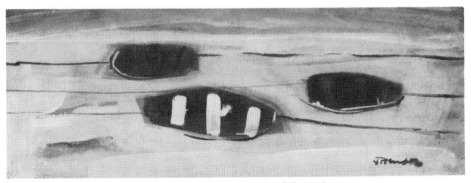

Jack Pender. Swing Boats. Oil, 1959.
Belgrave Gallery.

through the paintings of Alan Kingsbury, giving his highly conventional, even stultifying, style a captivating mystery and serenely poised poetry of sublime or ridiculous proportions. He illustrates the mood, and makes palpable the psychological and physical climate of the scene at hand. He belongs, in the words of John Russell Taylor, to 'a whole school of Post-Modernists who are unafraid of pictures that seem to tell a story.'*5 But the elusive stories that Kingsbury tells through deftly painted images are a product of the threshold of consciousness - one where reverie meets concrete experience. In the 1990's, he follows Stephen Conroy and paints with the anachronistic style of the Edwardian period, emulating the glazed atmospheres and sparkling impressionism of Degas, Sickert or Orpen. The paraphernalia of the antique shop forms his subject matter - china tea sets, the early camera, the hot air balloon, the steamboat, the shining metal telephone dial, the short-back-and-sides, or the plaited 'earphones' - and conjure up a bygone age. Kingsbury's pictures are bathed in nostalgia and melancholy, yet he is a contemporary painter conveying the confusion of alternatives, the range of possibilities that characterises the so-called Post-Modern era.

Alan Kingsbury. Seaton Bay. *Oil, 1992.*
Photo: Bob Berry.

Maurice Sumray (born 1920) also brings an almost metaphysical feeling of suspense to highly detailed and painstakingly executed figurative painting. Whereas Kingsbury's images are highly respectable, recalling a leisured middle-class world of boaters, lace collars, seaside conversation and deck top reverie, Sumray's are full of blatant sexual symbolism. His shaved women confront the spectator head-on, their full frontal postures showing off voluptuous bodies, rotund chests and sturdy thighs. Groups of bald-headed women, immaculately drawn with the fine tip of a pencil or painted with even glazes of coloured paint, look straight out of the picture plane. All eyes, boobs and vaginas, these figures are wrapped around one another in vertical piggy-back postures. These compositions possess the emphatic curvilinear rhythm and richness of evenly distributed incident that stems from Mark Gertler's famous 'Merry Go Round'. Like Gertler, Sumray brings an insistent Jewish complexion to English figurative painting; not this time the sensual impasto of Auerbach or even the fleshy obsessions of Freud, but instead an ornamental richness of decorative detail. Nothing is spared in filling the whole picture surface. Spencer's clarity and quirky fantasy of the everyday have also probably inspired Sumray, whose contribution to the landmark British Drawing exhibition at the Hayward in 1982, bore the axiomatic title 'First Draft For The Painting Apple Gatherers'.

Michael Strang is another contemporary who is unafraid of colour. He paints outdoors, glorying in the spectacle of nature which he paints with a loaded brush and broad palette that avoids grey. The golden glow of the sky against purple headlands, the blaze of colour emanating from wild flowers, or the translucent blue and turquoise of the sea enliven densely packed compositions. Strang merges the atmospheric colour of impressionism with the animated handling of Van Gogh and expressionism; his preference for working in the landscape yields pictures 'Rugged in texture and resonant in colour' according to his one-time Camberwell tutor, Anthony Eyton. These coarse and impastoed resolutions recall the work of Jack Yates or Lawrence Isherwood. The viewpoint is static and conventional; the emotional identification with nature results from 'allowing the pigment its own freedom to trap the essence',[6] according to poet Sylvia Kantaris. The same pigmented association with natural process informed Peter Lanyon's art, and Lanyon's son Martin, based at St. Agnes, follows his father into an area of painting that breathes with the rustle of leaves, the eddies of winds and movements of cloud and wave - all captured with a loaded brush in a painterly automatic overdrive.

The painterly vigour and compositional structure of Lanyon are qualities attained in the paintings of Daphne McClure who, however, introduces a gentle note of poetic symbolism closer in spirit to Hayman or Scottish painters like Gillies than to full blown abstract expressionism. McClure's work allows a mixture of fantasy and reality, and scores in terms of a broad absorption of romantic imagery and expressive handling. Her colour, too, seems an uncanny, and certainly very personal, mix of the schematic range of modern French art with the grey tones of the English School. The at times 'boisterous exuberance' of this colour does not prevent a structural strength taking hold and through this happy convergence of the drawn and the painted she is able to 'capture the flavour of particular places and make them memorable'.[7] A similar use of structural line and expressive paint distinguishes the pictures of Clifford Fishwick (born 1923), a Lancashire-born and Liverpool-trained painter long associated with Cornwall and the Penwith Gallery after becoming Principal of Exeter College of Art in 1958.

The responsibility of running an expanding art college did not prevent him from either painting regularly or exhibiting the results. Art college gave him awareness of the central issues of English painting; furthermore, even before teaching, he made visits to Paris, where the lessons of Giacometti, de Stael and Poliakoff were absorbed. The style of his classic 1950's period - when the

207

subjects of beached boats, road menders, fishermen and the like reflected both the Anglesey origins of his wife Patricia and the adoption of a West Country home - echoed the spikey romanticism of contemporary sculpture and the post-cubist pattern of painters like Keith Vaughan, Robert MacBryde and William Scott. Fishwick's gaunt stick-like figures remind one, in

Clifford Fishwick. **Family Group.** *Oil, 1954.*

particular, of Vaughan's cigarette smoking workmen, while the ochre, salmon and olive colours recall both Vaughan and the general struggle of 1950's painters out of a ration book economy of colour into a more adventurous and exuberant palette. Fishwick's work is a balance between taut linear design and imposed compositional structure on the one hand, and luscious, if coarsely applied, pigment on the other. He is not at his strongest when figures seem merely painted replicas of the contemporary bronze statues of Moore or Armitage; yet he uses the stark monumentality of sculpture's unique symbolic power to good effect in his painting of a Newlyn family, where a sitting group recalls the Family series of Moore. Patricia Fishwick's paintings seem less concerned with grinding contemporary axes; instead, she evokes the simple and soft poetry of the everyday, as her reassuring portrait of 'down home' Newlyn suggests. Since retiring from teaching in 1984, Fishwick, an avid rambler, hill climber and seaman, has focussed his work on the mountains and sea of Cornwall, Wales or the Highlands. Such pictures show an extraordinary visual memory, for these vivid and panoramic recollections of perceived landscapes could not possibly be the outcome of anything other than painstaking studio work fed from a first hand experience of nature.

If Fishwick's taut compositions use the heroic motif of fishermen and their boats, then David Haughton (1921-1991) avoids people altogether and focusses on the haunting mining town of St. Just. This Slade-trained Crypt exhibitor found a sanctuary in Cornwall during the austere post-war period. He lived in Cornwall during the late 1940's, and although he returned to London in 1951 after obtaining very necessary teaching work at the Central School of Art, continued an association with Cornwall to the end. During the length of a distinguished career he introduced successive generations of students to Cornwall, where he encouraged outdoor sketching at St. Just. The discovery of this town with Kit Barker changed the course of his professional life. 'What happened to me on that Spring day was inexplicable, but ...once one has experienced anything of that nature it is impossible to forget it. And unless one is quite unworthy of one's human dignity one must live by it for the rest of one's life. I have no idea what caused it, whether it really was the divine and transcendent visitation that it so clearly seemed to be or merely a freak of one's chemistry. But I do know that it was all important and unutterably beautiful, a trance that went beyond logic but never against it.' There is no doubting the inspirational hold that St. Just exerted on Haughton for the rest of his painting career, and he continued to draw and paint the town with an astonishing consistency thereafter. This highly subjective statement about how the spirit of a place had enraptured him and provided source material for his work belongs to a vein of St. Ives art in which the artists have often paid homage to the landscape, not only through their work but also through famous statements.

Haughton was in many ways a lonely individual and it seems likely that St. Just's haunting quality held interest as a place would that had known better days. What remained was a shell, full of a nostalgic atmosphere which gave the location the poignancy of abandonment or desolation. In spite of its poverty, the cottages of the town are built to last and this hard stone gives a permanence; furthermore, the play of light casts shadows across the buildings and throws them into relief against the dark green fields of the foreground or the grey skies of the background. The town is physically set within the landscape, with meadows and fields encroaching behind the rows of terraced cottages, such as happens at Carn Bosavern, which the artist painted on horizontal strips of board. St. Just also possessed what the artist termed 'an extraordinary variety of greys,' and therefore challenged the artist's tonal skills to the utmost. A Slade background equipped him with the highest level of draughtsmanship; a linear approach was inevitable for an artist who

David Haughton. The Road to Cape Cornwall. *Oil, 1976.*
Sims Gallery, St. Ives.

deemed that 'line is everything, without it imagination is confined to the material, without it colour becomes decoration, forms flat, and invention an impossibility.' By subjecting the entire composition to precise scrutiny, Haughton reached a dimension beyond that of the finite and defined. In striking at atmosphere Haughton inevitably attracted the support of Lanyon, who along with Nicholson admired his draughtsmanship and recognised his empathy with the spirit of place. Haughton helped form the new Penwith Society with Lanyon and exhibited at the Penwith's first group show in June 1949 at the Public Hall.

David Haughton's St. Just paintings do not depict human figures (in common with Nicholson, Barns-Graham and Wallis), yet to quote the Canadian poet Norman Levine, his 'tight row of cottages, long empty back streets, foregrounds of sprawling rubbish seem to me full of comment about human living'. His precise technique and painstaking composition create a classical quality though Haughton once remarked that 'it is perhaps inevitable that these qualities should be permeated in a northern climate by sadness, isolation and nostalgia.' His St. Just landscapes share the brooding sadness of north country artists like Lowry and Theodore Major, though his personal condition for a consistent study of the area throughout the next 35 years was the decision to retain the objectivity of the visitor. He chose to live in London, where he taught until the early 1980's. Ill health and a studio fire that destroyed much work led him to retirement. He lived until his death in 1991 in Ladbroke Grove, continuing to refine his pictures of St. Just in a well lit first floor studio. A touring exhibition in 1979, organised by Newlyn Orion, aired his work to a wider audience, and he was represented by two pictures in the large St. Ives exhibition at the London Tate in 1985.

Haughton's closest follower, Noel Betowski, was introduced to Cornwall in general and St. Just in particular, by the older man. A student at the Central, Betowski began making his own interpretations of the St. Just area while on annual student trips. He employed a similarly linear approach to the faithfully recorded subjects of terraced cottages seen from surrounding fields. Betowski's style shared the linear and tonal exactitude of his teacher, though fields of grass, flowers or plants elicited a network of thin and pretty calligraphy that is essentially illustrative rather than painterly or expressive in quality. In their less distinguished way, the pictures remind one of the earthy clarity of Andrew Wyeth. Sadly, Betowski fell from grace as an artist when he went the way of the illustrator - he moved down from London to Cornwall in 1987, starting up shop as a commercial fine artist. In his Penzance gallery he succumbed to the pressures of making a living in an economically stagnant tourist and retirement area. Haughton successfully resisted this, much to the benefit of his art, as a result of a once expanding art college support system that has sadly been denied to younger artists like Betowski. Betowski, however, retains links with London through regular participation in group exhibitions at the New Grafton Gallery.

The sub-impressionism practised by many of the more commercial, and indeed conventional Royal Academy painters has been an aspect of recent landscape painting in Cornwall. Ken Howard decided to adapt his slick language of tonal dashes, contrejour rims of light and colour dots to the depiction of Cornish beaches, cluttered with sunbathers, windbreaks and deckchairs. Eric Ward, a local St. Ives Harbour Master who started to paint in 1987, utilises the same general approach as that employed by Howard and fellow R.A.'s like Greenham and Dunstan. There is, however, something of a return to Wallis in the way that Ward, self-taught and coming late to painting, got bitten by the art bug. His interiors, still lifes and figure subjects are eminently deft and sophisticated for a self-taught artist, and in 'Interior with Red Hat', Ward constructs the image of a figure at a desk in terms of a confident placement of light and dark patches. Much the same kind of

211

handling of paint characterises the coastal landscapes of Mousehole-based
Tom Rickman, whose confident style most resembles that of Fred Cuming.

John Christopherson, who like David Haughton was a London-based
painter, made annual trips to St. Ives after discovering it on honeymoon in
1958. His wife, the Goldsmith-trained painter Anne Watson, encouraged his
pursuit of painting after he decided to leave an administrative job at the
Geological Museum in 1959. Encouraged at the outset by Dubuffet, with

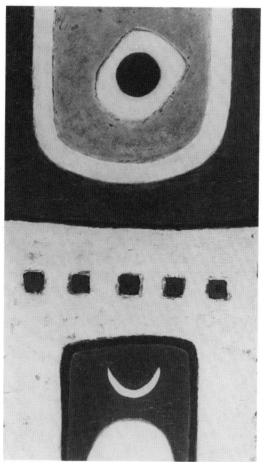

John Christopherson. Morocco. Oil, 1962.
Courtesy: England & Co..

whom he corresponded, Christopherson turned his status as a self-taught
artist to powerful advantage. An important component in the development of
Christopherson's artistic personality was his life as a collector. Not only did he

collect modern painting and sculpture, but also antiques, ceramics, tribal objects and jade. Interested since a boy in 'objects, artefacts and buildings which have been mellowed and transmuted by the hand of time', Christopherson enjoyed the aesthetic formal beauty of such objects rather than their social or anthropological significance. He was never interested in political or social history, a fact that explains the complete lack of human or figurative presence in the empty streets of his melancholic, lonely pictures. In 1989 he wrote that what inspired him most was 'the ambiguity between ancient and modern, the emphasis on texture and/or paint quality and the idea of a painting or sculpture being a thing in itself.'

What he once referred to as an interest in the 'forlorn poetry of the unregarded' seems to strike a melancholic, nostalgic and even metaphysical note of the kind prevalent in Italian art generally and in Chirico in particular. A number of Venetian subjects crop up in his work. The melancholic idea of culture being eroded by the inevitable hand of nature is evoked: Christopherson's world is a silent, stable one, impinged with sadness. The picture surface itself is subject to the process of time, in the literal sense that the artist builds up a picture slowly over the years, using many glazes of soft wet paint over time-hardened undercoats. He also uses rubbing and frottage techniques, so much a part of the Surrealist repertoire, with which to achieve granular, coarsely grained surfaces. The result is a tactility that gives the pictures a physical richness. A varnished surface adds gloss to paintings radiating with jewel-like colour embedded into dark umber grounds. The artist ingeniously parades his interest in ancient and ethnic objects, not only by alluding to them in his work, but by incorporating the hand of time in terms of the slow working process. Yet an occasional nervous scrawl indicates the more urgent energy of Dubuffet. The intimate world of pictographic zones and cryptic symbols, placed in an often small scale format, reflects the work of Klee, Alan Reynolds (an old friend) and Paolozzi.

In recent years younger artists have come to work in Cornwall, filling the gap left by significant artists of the previous generation. One aim of the new Tate is to facilitate this process; the Tate is, however, part of an expanding tourist industry that, ironically, has made life more difficult for artists by sending up the prices of living and working space. All the same, the Tate is good for business and smaller galleries, like the Porthmeor Gallery, benefit. At this venue, a frequently overlooked painter of the earlier generation, Ray Marsh, revisited St. Ives and exhibited work. The event was similar to Sven Berlin's revisit a decade earlier, when he exhibited recent work at the Wills Lane Gallery. Marsh's exhibition recalled, in the fresh language of the present, a physical confrontation with the landscape that distinguished art of the earlier period. Marsh's images are fragments abstracted and rearranged from the experience of landscape, and, as the critic Frank Ruhrmund noted, 'despite their look of the 50's, they are astonishingly fresh with a life of their own.'[8] Berlin never lost a sense of belonging to the extended family that he left in acrimonious circumstances many years before. Roger Hilton and Sven Berlin only met once, when Frost brought Hilton to Berlin's New Forest farm during the 1960's. Berlin, who referred to Hilton as 'a splendid artist', wrote to the writer Eric Quayle following the deaths of Hilton and Bryan Wynter. He wrote of the 'personal grief'*9 over the death of Wynter, his friend during the late 1940's. Old ties never fully dissolved, even though professionally there occurred a parting of ways.

Richard Ayling. Studio Model. *Oil, 1990.*

One artist who remained in Cornwall, Robert Brennan, gave up painting completely (finding the art scene elitist). Echoing the words of Elena Gaputyte in 1990, Brennan wrote that 'there was a lot of encouragement and hospitality …Later on lots of rich artists and property developers moved into St. Ives and the whole scene went down the drain.'*10 Brennan exhibited monotypes and reliefs at the Penwith in the 1950's, distinguished works with an authentic voice in spite of resembling Ben Nicholson's language of lines, squares and circles. They have a more fanciful, offbeat quality, disrupting Nicholson's order and orthogonal balance with unpredictable sequences and movements. Perhaps this has something to do with what David Lewis wrote was 'a delicacy and precision ...emphasising not a break away from nature, but attempts at construction ...sensitive to nature's proportions'*11.

Morwenna Thistlethwaite (born 1912), came down to live and paint in St. Ives late in life, even though she had long been associated with Cornish painters (she knew Borlase Smart in Scotland during the 1930's). In spite of struggling against a family hostile to art, she managed to educate herself at Birmingham School of Art, where an abiding interest in the poetry of Chardin and Matisse inspired her own calm still-life views onto a landscape. She lives near 'Ponckle' Clark, the Cat painter, whose gallery shop overlooks the artist's thoroughfare of Back Road. Bill Bolger, trained in the 1960's at Liverpool and the Royal College, also injects an unusual, even eccentric voice, into St. Ives art, painting either abstract pattern pictures based on classic Aztec design, or photorealistic monochromes of old Hollywood movie stars. Such artists continue a vein of eccentricity that runs from Wallis through to the design-conscious Patrick Hughes, the rainbow-in-a-dustbin painter who lived in St. Ives with the fun-loving writer Molly Parkin during the late 1970's.

Peter Thursby (born 1930), a west country sculptor whose abstracted forms in bronze and aluminium prove ideal for large architectural commissions, has long been associated with the artists of Cornwall. Like Cliff Fishwick, Thursby based himself in Devon and taught at Exeter, but maintained contact with Cornwall through membership of the Newlyn Society of Artists (1959-62), and the Penwith Society (1963-73). Exhibitions with the Marjorie Parr galleries were also symptomatic of Cornish links. He has undertaken numerous large scale architectural commissions, most notably a bronze fountain for Dallas, Texas, and a large bronze totem of sandwiched planes, bearing the apt title 'High Levels', at East Finchley, in north London. Thursby's preoccupation with robust, large scale outdoor commissions points to the followers of Barbara Hepworth as being fine artists immersed in an ethos of craft, without the wider ambition and facility for making commercially-motivated monuments in a public context. In a conceptual or poetic sense, Thursby is no greater a sculptor than they, yet his sheer professionalism in dealing with architects and large companies has only been matched since Barbara Hepworth's unrivalled success by the case of Paul Mount. Hepworth was also versed in the fine art tradition, in the central language of purist modern sculpture; commercial compromise would have been anathema to her. Yet, her collaboration in the 1930's with architects and artists like Gropius, Moholy-Nagy, and Mondrian - whose de Stijl colleague, Theo Van Doesburg, had helped Gropius introduce into the Bauhaus tough principles of applied design, functionalism, and mechanical production - made her realise that to achieve worldly success she needed to match private poetry with the objectives of architectural, social and urban design.

In this context, the new Tate gallery, designed to partial levels of success by Shalev and Evans, represents architecture catering to, and compromising with, the natural and man-made limitations of the geographic site and cultural location. The husband and wife team who designed this elegant and compact

215

modernist building reflect a close knit, if at times internecine local family of artists. Built on a former gas works site overlooking Porthmeor Beach, the building has some pleasing features, notably the large glass rotunda at the front, creating ample light and giving the cultural context of an art installation the appropriate background of nature, in this case Porthmeor sands. But English culture's general lack of modernist ambition, symbolised by Peter Palumbo's failure to erect a great Mies van der Rohe tower at Mansion House, in London, is echoed in the architectural small print of the new gallery by the sea. The pebbledash rendering and masonry, which adds a local note to an

St. Ives Tate Gallery. June 1993.
Photo: Nicholas Turpin.

'international style' of cubes, planes and curvilinear surfaces, the medieval turrets and the interior staircase ballustrades are all annoying, and all too typical pieces of compromise in the confused vernacular of English post modernist architecture. Like Frank Lloyd Wright's Guggenheim Museum, a supreme and far greater monument to the romantic spirit of modernism, the Shalev and Evans Tate does not seem built primarily to house the maximum number of art works, a point not lost on early visitors to the new building, who complained of sparse hanging. Interruptions to the wall space, the competition of a readily available, framed view of the magnificent sweep of St. Ives Bay, and an empty entrance room given over to an expensive stained glass window designed by Patrick Heron, are factors that restrain the scope for variety in the changing installations. It is not too difficult, in this context, to see why Mondrian saw too much nature in England, and relinquished the possibility of following his Hampstead colleagues to the pier and ocean of St. Ives by opting for the pure urban rhythms and the steel and glass environment of Manhattan.

NOTES

1. Conroy Maddox. Catalogue note for Michael Dean exhibition. New Vision Gallery. May 1965.
2. Roderick Cameron. Catalogue essay for Anthony Shiels exhibition on the theme of Warriors, Dancers and Nudes. February 1958.
3. Elena Gaputyte. Letter to author. 1990
4. Ronald Gaskell. 'June Miles' Nancherrow Studio 1988.
5. John Russell Taylor. Introduction for Alan Kingsbury exhibition 1993. Francis Kyle Gallery.
6. Sylvia Kantaris 'Catching The Image Off Guard' Peninsula Voice. February 1992.
7. Catalogue note for 'Cornwall - A Painter's Choice' Cadogan Contemporary. January 1993
8. Frank Ruhrmund. 'The St. Ives Times' June 1993.
9. Sven Berlin. Letter to Eric Quayle. 7.3.75.
10. Robert Brennan. Letter to the author. December 1993.
11. David Lewis. Catalogue note for Robert Brennan exhibition. Acton. April 1956.

Index

45
19